Semitic Residue
Signs of Early Oral Traditions in the Gospel of Matthew

Brian G. Chilton, PhD

WIPF & STOCK · Eugene, Oregon

Wipf and Stock Publishers
199 W 8th Ave, Suite 3
Eugene, OR 97401

Semitic Residue
Signs of Early Oral Traditions in the Gospel of Matthew
By Chilton, Brian G.

Softcover ISBN-13: 979-8-3852-7820-6
Hardcover ISBN-13: 979-8-3852-7821-3
eBook ISBN-13: 979-8-3852-7822-0
Publication date 3/2/2026
Previously published by IHP Academia, 2025

This edition is a scanned facsimile of the original edition published in 2025.

Praise for *Semitic Residue*

"Dr. Brian Chilton's new book is a welcome addition for those who are eager to investigate the nature and claims of the New Testament. Dr. Chilton sifts through the words in the Gospel of Matthew, collecting evidence confirming the early observations and notions about Jesus. *Semitic Residue: Signs of Early Oral Traditions in the Gospel of Matthew* will leave you convinced the story of Jesus is genuine and the details of his life, ministry, death, and Resurrection have been delivered to us accurately."

- **J. Warner Wallace**, Dateline featured Cold-Case Detective, Senior Fellow at the Colson Center for Christian Worldview, Adjunct Professor of Apologetics at Talbot School of Theology (Biola University) and Gateway Seminary, and Author of *Cold-Case Christianity* and *The Truth in True Crime*

"In *Semitic Residue*, Brian Chilton takes a fresh look at the possible presence of oral traditions in the Gospels, focusing on the Gospel of Matthew. By examining several key criteria through select portions of Matthew, Chilton argues for a high likelihood that significant portions of Matthew stem from early, oral traditions which followed "semiformal" patterns of transmission. Those interested in the history of the Gospels and early Jesus traditions will find much stimulating in this volume."

- **Dr. Chad Thornhill**, Professor of Biblical Studies and Theological Studies, Liberty University

"The best Christian theologians seek to practice the golden rule in their scholarship—treating all views the way they want theirs treated—with respect, care, and fairmindedness. I am very pleased to say that my colleague and friend Brian Chilton has exemplified these admirable qualities in his insightful book *Semitic Residue.* The book explores various models for the transmission of early oral traditions relating to the Gospel of Matthew. Working through this careful book has only served to confirm my confidence in biblical reliability and inerrancy. I hope this fine work reaches a wide audience of readers. *Tolle Lege!*"

- **Kenneth Richard Samples**, Senior Research Scholar, Reasons to Believe

"*Semitic Residue: Signs of Early Oral Traditions in the Gospel of Matthew* offers a fascinating and compelling look at the authenticity and structure of Matthew's Gospel. This book provides a depth of analysis and detail illuminating the traditions of the past authenticating the inerrancy and authenticity sought from Scripture. I commend this work for any student of God desiring a detail and depth of analysis that leads to increased faith in the canon of Scripture."

- **Dr. Virgil G. Dwyer Jr**, Senior Pastor, First Baptist Church of Stanleyville, Winston-Salem, NC

"In *Semitic Residue*, Chilton masterfully delves into an often-overlooked aspect of 1st-century Jewish culture—its Semitic characteristics—and their profound influence on the Gospel of Matthew. By focusing on Aramaic words and phrases that have been largely ignored by traditional Western scholarship, which has centered on Greek language and culture, Chilton's work brings a fresh, much-needed perspective to the study of early Jesus traditions. Through a careful exploration of the memorization and transmission practices of the time, Chilton illuminates the cultural framework that shaped the teachings and stories of Jesus. This work is an indispensable resource for scholars, students, and anyone passionate about the New Testament. A truly unique and invaluable contribution to biblical scholarship."

- **Dr. Sherene Khouri**, Assistant Professor of Arabic and Religion, Liberty University

"With a scholar's intellect and a pastor's heart, Brian Chilton takes us on a fruitful journey into the transmission of Jesus' teaching. By examining a variety of Matthean texts, he makes a compelling case for the presence of key characteristics that point to early Jesus traditions predating the written Gospel. And by suggesting a means of transmission for those traditions that safeguards their accuracy while allowing for variations found within the biblical record, he increases our confidence that the scriptures handed down to us do, indeed, give us access to the words of Christ. An excellent resource, especially for those studying the oral traditions that gave birth to the canonical gospels. I highly recommend it."

- **Rev. Alex L. Martin**, Senior Pastor, Calvary Baptist Church, Mount Airy, NC

"Brian Chilton is a first-rate New Testament scholar and a prolific writer. He is most convincing in his presentation of the evidence that Matthew did not write from his own theological presuppositions, but rather he used early historical source material that predated his finalized written Gospel. For one who desires greater confidence in the Scriptural text, reading Dr. Chilton's book will instill such confidence. A most readable book, the reader will discover abundant information which will expand one's intellect and enhance one's faith in the trustworthiness of the Gospel writers."

- **Dr. Daniel Merritt**, Director of Missions, Surry Baptist Association, Mount Airy, NC

"Building from early source material, Dr. Chilton aims to uncover the Semitic residue to reveal the book of Matthew's early dating and trustworthiness. His analyses of texts such as the Sermon on the Mount and the Son of Man bolster the reliability of this Gospel. Any student of the Bible will gain insights and confidence to develop discussions about the book of Matthew's trustworthiness."

- **Dr. Deanna Huff**, Executive Vice President of Bellator Christi Ministries, Curator for the Women of Legacy, Museum of the Bible, Oklahoma City, OK

"Brian Chilton's work has provided an in-depth and intelligent response to the question of Jesus's Jewishness as it relates to the Synoptic Gospels. He also has developed a rational Evangelical consideration of the forty-year-old Jesus Seminar that is not based on overreaction but on intellectual and scholarly considerations. As a missionary to the Jewish community for the last 25 years, I appreciate Chilton's engagement with the 2nd Temple Jewish rabbis as well as the oral teaching models of the period. Jesus and his disciples were Jewish and lived in a Jewish society. This truth is something that must be remembered as we study the Scriptures in a 21st-century world. A scholarly work that is accessible for the pastor's study."

- **Dr. Amy Downey**, Founder and President of Tzedakah Ministries

Acknowledgments

I would like to first thank my wife, Jennifer, and son, Grayson, for their loving support through the PhD program and through the numerous hours working on my dissertation, which served as the backbone of this book. The road has not always been easy, but my family has loved me endlessly through the process.

I would also like to thank my parents, Dennis and Gail Chilton, for their loving encouragement and for granting me permission to be curious and keep asking the big questions of life.

I would like to thank my dissertation committee—Dr. Leo Percer, Dr. Chad Thornhill, and Dr. Ronnie Campbell—for helping me through this journey. Their scholarship and wisdom are second to none.

Most of all, I would like to thank the Lord for his salvation and endless blessings that are too many to express. If it were not for the hand of God on my life and his sovereign direction, I would have never reached this point, and this dissertation would not have been possible.

Foreword by Leo Percer, PhD

Contemporary culture finds itself bombarded with information. That information may be virtual or textual, but we are surrounded by it. Access to this information increases with technological innovation and expertise. Nonetheless, there is an underlying feeling that we've done this before, isn't there?

Have you ever experienced a moment of déjà vu? You know, a moment when something happens that seems familiar? We all experience those moments, and some of these moments involve words or familiar sayings. We hear something said, and the words take us immediately to another event or experience where similar words were said or heard. Take, for example, the famous movie lines, "You're gonna need a bigger boat," or "We're not in Kansas anymore." These lines immediately lead people to think of the relevant movies or scenes.

Now, put yourself into a first-century AD situation. An itinerant preacher is going about proclaiming things about the kingdom of God, and many think that this man is the promised Messiah. After his death by crucifixion, his disciples claimed that he rose again. Some of them even wrote books and letters to explain the life and teachings of Jesus of Nazareth. One of the best-known and beloved of those Gospels is the Gospel according to Matthew. This book contains the story of Jesus' life, ministry, death, and resurrection from the perspective of a follower named Matthew—a former tax collector turned Messianic disciple. Matthew's Gospel contains some well-known episodes from the life of Jesus, and to some Jewish readers of the first century, some of those stories would sound vaguely familiar. But why?

Dr. Brian Chilton approaches this topic by investigating what he terms "Semitic residue" in the Gospel of Matthew. What he means is that these stories are supported by oral (and maybe even written) traditions that show a connection to Jewish perspectives. How, then, are modern readers to discover these connections? The good news is that Dr. Chilton provides a way to examine this Gospel to discover where there may exist materials underlying the story or teachings that come from a more ancient Jewish source. He outlines this process, and then applies it in this book.

I had the privilege of serving on the dissertation team from which this book originates, and I can tell you that Brian has done his homework. His offers here his solid research and sound conclusions. You will find an overview of the task at hand; a means to test for "Semitic residue"; and an explanation of how that works with specific texts from the Gospel of Matthew. The result of the research shows that much of the material Matthew relates has a firm foundation on ancient Jewish and Christian teachings.

You'll find yourself reading with Dr. Chilton and saying, "Some of this sounds familiar." That's because what you hear in this book has its foundation in the teachings and presentations in Scripture. You will discover with the rest of us that Matthew didn't write in a vacuum, but rather he interacted with the teachings of Jesus in light of other Jewish teachings. You will also learn a method that will allow you to read other sections of the New Testament and investigate their backgrounds. The method and research offered here is useful as well as erudite. I remember when I first read this book, and I am happy to introduce you to it.

I hope you walk away from this experience with new information and inspiration to read the New Testament in a fresh yet ancient manner. Seeing the life and Jesus through the lens of his Jewish background will help you to discover insights that we hope will inform and inspire you. I know this material will challenge some, but I am also convinced that it will also help many who long to understand the foundations of the New Testament better. This fresh understanding may lead you to think that you need a "bigger boat" to pursue the insights and ideas discovered. At the very least, Dr. Chilton's work will help you realize that you aren't "in Kansas anymore," as you seek to understand the background to Jesus' life and ministry. May God bless your reading of his Scripture, and may this book help you to understand God's Word better!

Foreword by Amy Downey, PhD

As a missionary to the Jewish community for the last 25 years, I often experience a longing for scholarship in the evangelical Christian community that reflects an awareness of the Jewishness of Jesus and the Hebraic nature of the Gospels. I read commentaries that superimpose Hellenistic and/or American concepts on the narratives of Jesus' life and/or the parables, and I wonder – "Do they not realize that these events happened in the first century and a Middle Eastern World?"

Let me repeat again that "Jesus Is Jewish!" And my friend Dr. Brian Chilton realizes this truth, which might be amazing to many who know that his Southern accent is strong, but his heart for conveying the Gospel truth is even stronger. This heart for presenting the truth of Jesus convincingly and engagingly is why I so appreciate Brian Chilton's engagement with the 2nd Temple Jewish rabbis as well as the oral teaching models of the period.

In fact, Brian brings the prominent rabbis of Jesus' time period, Hillel and Shammai, to the desks of evangelical pastors for whether people realize it or not Jesus quoted from them as well in the Gospels. This truth is something that must be remembered as we study the Scriptures in a 21st-century world. Yet, Brian presents to the reader a scholarly work that is still accessible for the pastor's study.

Brian Chilton's work has provided an in-depth and intelligent response to the question of Jesus's Jewishness as it relates to the Synoptic Gospels. He also has developed a rational evangelical consideration of the forty-year-old Jesus Seminar that is not based on overreaction but on intellectual and scholarly considerations.

And lest anyone believe that the false teachings of the Jesus Seminar are a thing of the past and should not be considered a danger anymore, I would only ask you to go to some of the mainline Protestant denominations and see the empty pews and the false teachings that are still rampantly being taught from the pulpit. Brian's work is even more valid today than yesterday.

Contents

CHAPTER ONE
SEMITIC RESIDUE: THE EARLY ORAL TRADITIONS UNDERGIRDING THE GOSPELS

In the mid-1800s, the biblical town of Capernaum was identified with a town then known as Tell Hum. An ancient synagogue was located within the town and became the focal point of intense scrutiny. Initial estimates dated the synagogue to the late second-century to fifth-century AD due to the white limestone used to construct the facility. While earlier explorers focused on the white limestone, a team of scholars in 1981 confirmed that the black basalt serving as the foundation for the structure was part of the very same first-century AD synagogue in which Jesus himself preached.[1] The original structure had been constructed of black basalt. Later, the facility was enhanced with white limestone.

The previous depiction of the synagogue of Capernaum serves as an illustration of the task ahead. Just like the synagogue of Capernaum, ancient texts are often built upon source material that predates the writing of the finished text. Just as the black basalt of the Capernaum synagogue indicated that the structure was much earlier than previously considered, so also do certain texts denote earlier source material upon which the ancient text is based. Using tactics in historiography among other criteria, scholars have formulated practices that identify the existence of early material that predates the texts that flowed from the writers' hands. Concerning the NT texts, this early material is called "credal material" or "confessions of the faith."[2] Early material may be found in other genres, such as hymns and the like. For simplicity's sake, early material will be deemed "credal material." Even scholars who are not conservative in their outlook toward biblical theology acknowledge the presence of credal material in certain biblical texts, particularly in 1 Cor. 15:3-7.[3]

---

[1] Paul J. Achtemeier, "Capernaum," *Harper's Bible Dictionary* (San Francisco: Harper & Row, 1985), 155.

[2] So named by Oscar Cullmann in Oscar Cullmann, *The Earliest Christian Confessions,* J. K. S. Reid, trans (Eugene, OR: Wipf & Stock, 1949, 2018), 7. For the sake of simplicity, this paper will term early texts "credal material" rather than "confessions of the faith."

[3] Bart Ehrman, who identifies as an atheist-leaning-agnostic contents that certain content of Paul's letters is identified as "a very ancient tradition that predates Paul's writings." Bart D. Ehrman, *Did Jesus Exist? The Historical Argument for Jesus of Nazareth* (New York, NY: HarperOne, 2012), 111.

The majority of the credal texts that have been identified are found in the epistles of Paul and the sermon summaries of Acts.[4] However, it must be asked whether the four canonical Gospels hold any traits that indicate early source material. Some scholars have not given much credence to the possibility that the Gospels hold early material to the degree that the epistles do. For instance, Robert Funk and the Jesus Seminar largely held that the majority of the Gospels' material originated from the Evangelists' own theological interests rather than the historical source material.[5] Because of the intensity of the debate surrounding the Gospels, Michael Licona in his investigation into the historiography of the resurrection gave the Gospels the rating of *possible* when evaluating the level of probability that the texts possessed historical material.[6] Yet if the research proposed holds, it is hopeful that the rating of confidence for the Gospels could be strengthened.

Intriguingly, the Gospels hold certain traits that resemble the credal material and sermon summaries in certain texts. These texts contain Semitic traits that do not necessarily match the Greek found in the majority of the Gospel script, denote characteristics that match what would be expected to be found in the oral source material, portray unique characteristics that are comparable to early Jewish rabbinic interpretations of the early first-century, and match what theologians have identified as primitive Christological interpretations. It is most fascinating when one realizes that the Semitisms are more likely found in the teachings of Jesus than in other parts of the Gospels. But just how many Semitisms does one find? According to NT scholar Craig Keener, as much as "80% of the Synoptic sayings material appears to fit a poetic or rhythmic form helpful for memorization."[7] If the Gospels contain Semitic material such as identifiable in the sermon summaries of Acts and the early credal material of the Epistles, could one not claim that at least certain parts of

---

[4] C. H. Dodd contends that the Aramaic nature of the Petrine sermon summaries indicate that they originate with the earliest church. C. H. Dodd, *The Apostolic Preaching and Its Developments* (New York, NY: Harper & Brothers, 1935), 20.

[5] Robert W. Funk and the Jesus Seminar, *The Acts of Jesus: What Did Jesus Really Do?* (San Francisco, CA: HarperSanFrancisco, 1997), 462.

[6] Michael R. Licona, *The Resurrection of Jesus: A New Historiographical Approach* (Downers Grove, IL; London, UK: IVP Academic; Apollos, 2010), 208.

[7] Craig S. Keener, *The Historical Jesus of the Gospels* (Grand Rapids, MI: Eerdmans, 2009), 158. See also Ben Witherington, III., *The Christology of Jesus* (Minneapolis, MN: Fortress, 1990), 16-17; and R. Reisner, *Jesus als Lehrer: Eine Untersuchung zum Ursprung der Evangelien-Uberlieferung,* WUNT 2.7 (Tubingen: J. C. B. Mohr, 1981), 507.

the Gospels could also hold early material that identified earlier source material that undergirded Gospel traditions?

The Gospel of Matthew holds more Semitic traits than necessarily the other three Gospels. Thus, if the Gospel of Matthew can be shown to hold Semitic substrata indicating early source material, then it would follow that the other Synoptic Gospels hold the same substrata, especially due to the sharing that is presupposed in form criticism. Many scholars contend that the way forward in scholarship will engage less with form criticism and more with the oral period prior to the written Gospels.[8]

Thus, our journey will examine what we will call "Semitic Residue." That is, semitic residue is evidence of early oral traditions based on the life and ministry of Jesus of Nazareth. Because of its setting and culture, these early oral traditions would largely stem from sermons first presented in Aramaic, set in the Judaism of early first-century Israel, and inundated with the early Christological and theological themes identified in the earliest church, while preserved using mnemonic devices to assist with easy memorization.

As such, Semitic residue refers to those portions of the Gospel texts that reveal previously existent source material based upon Semitic traits that portray early source material. This material may stem from sources that developed from oral tradition, written material, or a combination of both. The oral versus written nature of the source materials is of ill effect on this research. Rather, the focus will be on source material in any form as noted by the Semitic nature of the texts in question.

The material passed along from the original Aramaic messages of Jesus to the Greek manuscript of the Gospel of Matthew left behind Semitic residue that points to the early nature of the source material behind the Gospel text. Using the Gospel of Matthew as a test case due to its early and Jewish nature, the purpose of the research will be to show that Semitic residue can be traceable and will defend that the source material behind the Gospel of Matthew is early and trustworthy no matter what date is ascribed to the finished product. As an

---

[8] Richard Bauckham states more adamantly than this writer, "It is my contention that the form criticism paradigm has now been completely disproved, and it is time we adopted another paradigm for understanding how the Gospel traditions were preserved in the predominantly oral period prior to the written Gospels." Richard Bauckham, *The Christian World Around the New Testament* (Grand Rapids, MI: Baker Academic, 2017), 87.

aside, the research will show that the *informal controlled* model of oral transmission best fits the data found in the Gospel of Matthew.[9]

Challenges to Consider

The research will need to engage with five research problems pertaining to the source material behind Matthew's Gospel. While other issues are most certainly found, questions revolving around the existence of early source material, the language in which Jesus taught, how Semitisms and early source material can be detected, the trustworthiness of Jesus's message, and the means by which early traditions and materials were transmitted from oral tradition to written texts are all among the most pressing issues that must be considered.

Early Source Material

The primary problem concerning the research is whether the Gospel of Matthew contains early source material that predates the Gospel. As such, it is important to denote that even if one grants a late dating to the First Gospel, the material underlying the Gospel that does not necessarily match that of Mark's Gospel is early enough to stem from the earliest church, thereby from the mouth of Jesus himself. The means by which the research will seek to indicate the presence of said material is from Semitic traits found in the language and theological concepts documented in the teachings of Jesus.

Certain criteria are used to distinguish and illuminate early material in credal texts. The credal material does not necessarily depict all the early material in the biblical texts, but rather, it serves as a means to detect traits of earlier material used by the Christian community that did not originate from the biblical writer. If this is possible in the Epistles, then the same traits should be noted in the Gospels if early, original, and reliable source material was available—especially that of early Jesus traditions.

The first question that must be asked is whether the Gospels even claimed to use early source material. Luke most certainly claims to have used early source material to construct his Gospel. The evangelist writes,

> Many have undertaken to compile a narrative about the events that have been fulfilled among us, just as the original eyewitnesses and servants of the word handed them down to us. So it also seemed good to me, since I have carefully investigated everything from the very first, to write to you an orderly sequence, most honorable Theophilus, so

---

[9] For more information on the models at hand and the *informal controlled* model, see the "Three Models of Oral Transmission" in this chapter and a more detailed exposition in Chapter Three: The Parables of Jesus.

that you may know the certainty of the things about which you have been instructed (Luke 1:1-4).[10]

Luke's prologue has been called among the finest constructed sentences in Greek literature.[11] As was customary of other historians of the Greek and Hellenistic variety, Luke begins his work by noting the thorough reliability of the work's documentation and the veracity of its source material.[12] Liefield notes the correlation between Luke's emphasis on what had been handed down to him to that of the language used in the credal material documented by Paul in 1 Corinthians 11:23 and 15:3.[13] Thus, the evangelist notes the existence of prior material, even hinting at his knowledge of Mark's Gospel. Luke notes that his account of Jesus's life is written in an orderly fashion (Luke 1:3) which hints at the unorderly fashion that Mark recorded the events in his Gospel.[14]

Papias is quoted by Eusebius of Caesarea as saying that "Mark, having become the interpreter of Peter wrote down accurately, though not indeed in order, whatsoever he remembered of the things said or done by Christ."[15] From Papias's statement, not only can one correlate Luke's nod to the Gospel of Mark, but it can also be noted that the Second Gospel stemmed from source material that did not originate with the evangelist.

Throughout the Gospel of John, the author describes a person known as the "Beloved Disciple" (John 13:23; 19:26; 20:2; and 21:7, 20). The identity of this disciple has been hotly debated. The traditional view is that the beloved disciple is the apostle John, the son of Zebedee.[16] Eusebius notes that John

---

[10] Unless otherwise noted, all quoted Scripture comes from the *Christian Standard Bible* (Nashville, TN: Holman, 2020).

[11] Walter L. Liefeld, "Luke," *The Expositor's Bible Commentary: Matthew, Mark, Luke*, vol. 8, Frank E. Gaebelein, ed (Grand Rapids, MI: Zondervan Publishing House, 1984), 821.

[12] Ibid.

[13] Ibid.

[14] Here, "orderly" denotes the chronological fashion in which the historical events of Jesus were recorded.

[15] Eusebius of Caesaria, *Ecclesiastical History* 3.39.15, in *Eusebius: Church History, Life of Constantine the Great, and Oration in Praise of Constantine*, vol 1, A Select Library of the Nicene and Post-Nicene Fathers of the Christian Church, second series, Philip Schaff and Henry Wace, eds, Arthur Cushman McGiffert, trans (New York: Christian Literature Company, 1890), 172.

[16] This writer holds this view. However, the identity of the Gospel writers is not imperative to the book's overarching thesis.

spoke the Gospel orally before eventually recording the Gospel after the other three had been published..[17] Thus, in the traditional sense, the author recorded information that had been transmitted orally before the document was formed. But even if one does not hold to the traditional view, it is still recognized that the information in the Gospel originates from source material that precedes the Gospel text..[18] It has been recognized that John's use of γράψας in John 21:24-25 can describe authorship by transcription by a scribe..[19] Additionally, the conclusion appears to suggest that the beloved disciple may have died before the final penning of the document's conclusion. Thus, the conclusion of John's Gospel, like the prologue of the Gospel of Luke, appears to denote the source material undergirding the Gospel text..[20]

The Gospel of Matthew is unique as it does not necessarily describe the use of source material. However, the First Gospel begins with the genealogy and birth narratives of Jesus. In themselves, one would adduce that the evangelist is pulling from material that did not originate with him..[21] The clearest ascription to the First Gospel's use of early material comes from a late first century, early second-century church father by the name of Papias of Hierapolis (AD 70-163). It is from Papias that the earliest traditions are known concerning the composition of the Gospel texts. Most assuredly, Papias was in

---

[17] Eusebius, *Ecclesiastical History* 3.24.5.

[18] Ben Witherington makes a compelling case that Lazarus was the beloved disciple and that John the elder published the Fourth Gospel. See Ben Witherington, III., "Was Lazarus the Beloved Disciple?," *BenWitherington.blogspot.com* (January 29, 2007), http://benwitherington.blogspot.com/2007/01/was-lazarus-beloved-disciple.html. Richard Bauckham contends that the Gospel of John contains eyewitness testimony from a lesser-known disciple, but not John of Zebedee. Richard Bauckham, *Jesus and the Eyewitnesses: The Gospels as Eyewitness Testimony* (Grand Rapids, MI: Eerdmans, 2017), 550.

[19] Bauckham also notes that "Many ancient authors did not themselves wield the pen when they composed their writings, for writing was a craft better left to those who had been trained to do it well." Bauckham, *Jesus and the Eyewitnesses,* 359.

[20] While John of Zebedee is held to be the source behind the Fourth Gospel, this does not necessitate that other source material could not be used. For instance, the final redaction of the Gospel could easily have included the eyewitness testimony of Lazarus along with John's. Just as Paul used scribes, it is completely acceptable, at least in this writer's eyes, to accept the belief that the majority of the stories in the Fourth Gospel originated by John but were compiled and arranged by a later author or community.

[21] One such example of Matthew's use of source material stems from his use of stories found in no other place. Only Matthew records the angelic vision of Joseph of Nazareth (Matt. 1:18-25; 2:13-16) and the visitation of the Magi (Matt. 2:1-12).

a position to know the origins of the Gospel texts as he knew some of the primary and secondary witnesses. Concerning the Gospel of Matthew, Papias notes that Matthew first preached among the Hebrews. He originally recorded the oracles "in the Hebrew language, and every one interpreted them as he was able."[22]

Irenaeus interpreted Papias to say that Matthew originally penned a primitive form of his Gospel in Hebrew before writing the Gospel in Greek. Irenaeus contends that Matthew wrote the oracles of the Lord[23] in the Hebrew language, leading others to interpret them and/or translate them as best as they could.[24] Eusebius, however, seems to understand Papias's statements a bit differently. Remember, Eusebius is not a fan of Papias because of Papias's chiliastic eschatology. Nonetheless, Eusebius understand Papias to say that wrote his Gospel in the "Hebrew dialect."[25]

Evidence suggests that Irenaeus's interpretation may be closer to the truth. Jerome noted the existence of a Hebraic Gospel that he read, which many ascribe to the Hebraic form of Matthew.[26] It is at least possible that this text could have been the original form of Matthew's Gospel if one assumes Irenaeus's interpretation. Furthermore, Eusebius describes the Ebionites' exclusive use of Matthew's Gospel.[27] It is possible that the Ebionites used the Hebrew version of Matthew's Gospel. Considering Eusebius's bias against Papias and the possibility that Jerome could have viewed a primitive form of Matthew's Gospel, the former interpretation appears to make better sense of Papias's writing. Regardless of how one interprets Papias's understanding of Matthew's composition, one can still contend that the Evangelist of the First Gospel obtained his information from prior source material, either material

---

[22] Eusebius, *Ecclesiastical History* 3.39.15, in *Eusebius' Ecclesiastical History,* C. F. Cruse, trans, (Peabody, MA: Hendrickson, 1998), 105.

[23] Or teachings.

[24] Irenaeus, *Fragments of Papias* 3.7-17, 155.

[25] Eusebius, *Ecclesiastical History* 3.39.16-17, 106.

[26] Jerome wrote, "In the Gospel according to the Hebrews, which is written in the Chaldee and Syrian language, but in Hebrew characters, and is used by the Nazarenes to this day (I mean the Gospel according to the Apostles, or, as it is generally maintained, the Gospel according to Matthew, a copy of which is in the library at Caesarea)." Jerome, *Against the Pelagians* III.2, in *St. Jerome: Letters and Select Works*, A Select Library of the Nicene and Post-Nicene Fathers of the Christian Church, volume 6, 2nd series, Philip Schaff and Henry Wace, eds, W. H. Fremantle, G. Lewis, and W. G. Martley, trans (New York: Christian Literature Company, 1893), 472.

[27] Irenaeus, *Against Heresies* 3.11.7, 428.

from a Hebrew/Aramaic original or the author's own recollections, which would also serve as source material..[28]

If source material was used to formulate the Gospel of Matthew, then it can also be assumed that the source material behind Mark's Gospel is early. Additionally, if Luke used Matthew and Mark for some of his references to shape his Gospel, then the material behind the Third Gospel can be shown to be early, as well. For this query, the research must delve into the question of the language(s) of Jesus, and which language Jesus used most.

What Language Did Jesus Use to Teach?

A second difficulty revolves around the language in which Jesus spoke to the first people who heard his message. Flourishing from the sixth to third centuries BC when eastern empires dominated the Israelite region, Aramaic became the common language of the area, particularly in the course of governmental, cultural, and commercial affairs..[29] Certain areas indicate the presence of bilingualism, and sometimes trilingualism..[30] In some regions, Latin was spoken..[31] However, Aramaic was the common language of the Galilean region. If Jesus were to have spoken in the Galilean regions as depicted by the Gospels,.[32] then it would be assumed that Jesus would have spoken in Aramaic. The research would need to explore the usage of Aramaic in Jesus's region and in his time. If it can be shown that Jesus primarily taught in Aramaic,.[33] then it could be deduced that the messages preserved in the Gospels were translated

---

[28] If form criticism is correct, then it may be that Matthew recorded both his testimony and the Petrine testimony found in the Gospel of Mark to form and shape the First Gospel. But it could also be the case that Mark used some of Matthew's material in addition to the Peter's testimony to form and shape his Gospel. The former view is the majority view. Albeit, that it is the majority view does not necessitate its accuracy especially if one accepts the collection of early source materials as advocated in this research.

[29] Matthew Black, *An Aramaic Approach to the Gospels and Acts,* 3rd ed (Eugene, OR: Wipf & Stock, 1967), 15.

[30] The three languages include Aramaic for popular discourse, Hebrew for religious speech, and Greek for common business and governmental affairs. However, the former three were far more prominent. Keener, *Historical Jesus of the Gospels,* 159.

[31] Paul Barnett, *The Birth of Christianity: The First Twenty Years* (Grand Rapids, MI: Eerdmans, 2005), 113.

[32] Particularly as found in the Synoptic Gospels.

[33] Even while remaining open to the possibility that he spoke Greek and Hebrew in other areas. See Barnett, *Birth of Christianity,* 113.

from the Aramaic source material..[34] But why would the evangelists have used Greek for their texts? If Greek was the popular business language of the time, then it would make logical sense that the Evangelists would use the language which could have reached the most people for a message they wanted to share with the most people. Thus, Aramaic and/or Semitic traits found in the Greek Gospel texts can be used to detect early material as they point back to sources used to formulate the texts. However, since Jesus most likely spoke other languages in addition to Aramaic, they cannot be the exclusive means to detect early material. They are useful, however, to indicate early the presence of source material.

Detection of Semitisms and Early Materials

A third challenge that must be addressed is whether early Semitic material can be identified. Numerous scholars denote the surprising number of Semitic traits found in the Gospel texts. Keener noted that as much as 80% of the sayings of Jesus in the Synoptic Gospels portray Semitic traits, particularly mnemonic rhythmic patterns associated with the Aramaic language and the passing of received text..[35] Other scholars such as Ben Witherington.[36] and Rainer Reisner.[37] have noticed similar patterns. Even Rudolf Bultmann accepted that early material existed in the NT but delineated that the early church made no distinction between the pre-Easter sayings of Jesus from those of the post-Easter utterances of Christian prophets..[38] Contra Bultmann, Witherington sees the plausibility behind early Christians using techniques such as memorization, repetition, and notetaking to remember the teachings of Jesus but cautions that exact precision may not have been deemed necessary

---

[34] Keener argues this to be the case. Craig S. Keener, *Christobiography: Memory, History, and the Reliability of the Gospels* (Grand Rapids, MI: Eerdmans, 2019), 12. He uses the example of "Talitha koum!" in Mark 5:41 as an example. Ibid., 367. Barnett also argues this to be the case in Barnett, *Birth of Christianity,* 113; as well as Joachim Jeremias, *New Testament Theology I* (London, UK: SCM, 1971), 8-37.

[35] Keener, *Historical Jesus of the Gospels,* 158.

[36] Witherington, *Christology of Jesus*, 16-17.

[37] Rainer Reisner, *Jesus als Lehrer,* WUNT 2.7, 507.

[38] Rudolf Bultmann, *The History of the Synoptic Tradition* (Göttingen: Vanderhoeck and Ruprecht, 1931), 122-128.

especially since these sayings were transmitted from Aramaic into Greek which enjoyed more widespread use in the Greco-Roman world..[39]

The belief that Semitic material could be detected in the Gospels did not originate with the aforementioned scholars. Matthew Black led the way in the discovery of patterns in the Gospels that portray a Semitic substratum underlying the Greek texts. Black used the Aramaic Targums and the newly discovered, at least in his time, Qumran Aramaic scrolls, especially an Aramaic scroll used as a midrash on Genesis 12 and 15, to compare with the language of the Gospels..[40] While it is not feasible to discuss all the findings of his book, a few notable examples are of particular interest.

First, the structure of the sentences can illustrate a Semitic influence. Noting the work of the eminent Hellenist scholar Eduard Norden, Black contends that three aspects of word placement give rise to a Semitism. "Placing the verb first is, next to the parallelism of clauses—the two are very often combined—the surest Semitism of the New Testament, especially in those instances in which the position comes in a series of clauses.".[41] Additionally, Black argues that *casus pendens*,.[42] while not completely foreign to Greek, is found more frequently in Hebrew and Greek..[43] The *casus pendens* structure is found in at least 11 passages in the Gospel of Matthew..[44] The excessive practice of asyndeton in the Gospels and Acts is considered "highly characteristic of an Aramaic original.".[45] Black adds many more language characteristics in the Gospels and Acts that validate both the concept that Semitic residue is found in the Gospels, but also that the residue is discoverable.

Second, Black discovered patterns in the teachings of Jesus that give rise to the thought that his teachings were cast in poetic form, since the earliest of times, to aid in memorization. The poetic form of these sayings is especially viewed when the passage is translated back into Aramaic. Black claims, "When the sayings of Jesus and especially the longer connected passages are turned into simple Aramaic many examples of paronomasia, alliteration and assonance come to light. Paronomasia has been a regular feature of the style and teaching of our Lord in his native Aramaic. It has for the most part disappeared in the

---

39 Witherington, *Christology of Jesus,* 8-9.

40 Black, *Aramaic Approach to the Gospels and Acts,* 40-41.

41 Ibid., 50; Eduard Norden, *Agnostos Theos* (Berlin, DE: Verlag B. G. Teubner, 1913), 257, 365.

42 Meaning in Latin "a hanging clause."

43 Black, *Aramaic Approach to the Gospels and Acts,* 51.

44 Ibid., 53.

45 Ibid., 56.

Greek Gospels.".[46] Witherington concurs that when one takes seriously the ease by which one may translate Jesus's teaching material back into Aramaic, then one may say two things: first, that an early Aramaic form of Jesus's teachings was fixed at an early date, and second, that the material was translated into Greek early in the church's history..[47]

Joachim Jeremias is an additional scholar who has added credence to the idea of detecting early Semitic material in the Gospels. His book *Jesus and the Message of the New Testament* defends the notion that the early teachings of Jesus were preserved by the early church. Jeremias argues that the "gospel that Jesus proclaimed antedates the kerygma of the primitive community.".[48] He goes on to argue that while Paul's letters predate the Gospels,.[49] the Gospel texts contain wording that "unmistakably imply a situation prior to Easter.".[50] The way that Jeremias evaluated the early material dating back to Jesus was to reconstruct the Aramaic substratum of Jesus's sayings back to his *ipsissima vox*. Jeremias explores the substratum found in the Sermon on the Mount and, more particularly, in the Lord's Prayer.

Maurice Casey adds an additional voice to the attempt to discover early Semitic material in the Gospels. In his work *Aramaic Sources of Mark's Gospel,* Casey denotes five pieces of evidence that indicate the practice of translating Aramaic and Hebrew texts into Greek. These texts can be used to show the practice that the Evangelists and early church employed to transfer the Aramaic teachings of Jesus into Greek as found in the Gospels. The five examples include the Greek Dead Sea scrolls which are copies of Aramaic and Hebrew Scriptures; the Greek material from Masada, some of which date to AD 25-35; the Greek tomb inscriptions in Jerusalem;.[51] traditions concerning orthodox Jews from the period, most revealing are the stories concerning Gamaliel and

---

[46] Black, *Aramaic Approach to the Gospels and Acts,* 276-277.

[47] Witherington, *Christology of Jesus,* 10.

[48] Joachim Jeremias, *Jesus and the Message of the New Testament* (Minneapolis, MN: Fortress, 2002), 6.

[49] At least some of his earlier Epistles do depending on the date ascribed to the Gospel texts.

[50] Jeremias, *Jesus and the Message of the New Testament,* 7.

[51] Although most of the tomb inscriptions date after AD 70, a few of them are found around the time of Jesus.

his 500 students who learned Greek; and extra-biblical resources from the first century, particularly that of Josephus.[52]

Using the texts mentioned, Casey develops a seven-step method to show that the Gospel of Mark drew from previous Aramaic sources. His seven stages included selecting passages that exhibit signs of being translated literally (e.g., Mark 14:72); developing a possible Aramaic substratum; checking idioms in the reconstructions; interpreting the reconstructions from the perspectives of first-century Judaism; checking back through the passage from the perspective of an ancient translator; attempt to discover any deliberate editing by the evangelists; and evaluate the probability of the passage in lieu of the Jewish culture of the first-century.[53]

Casey concludes that portions of Mark's Gospel contain considerable evidence of Aramaisms which can, at times, challenge traditional understandings (e.g., that Jesus did not teach on the Eucharist as much as he was celebrating his last Passover with his disciples).[54] Casey further contends that parts of Mark's Gospel stemmed from literal translations of written Aramaic sources.[55] Because of these findings, Casey affords a high probability to the possibility that Mark's Gospel was written around AD 40.[56] and that the Aramaic material upon which the Gospel is built is even earlier still.[57] Casey continues his work by evaluating the Aramaic sources behind Q, arguably used by the Gospel of Matthew and the Gospel of Luke,[58] and uses this material to examine what can be known about Jesus of Nazareth.[59]

From the previous works examined, a strong case can be made that the Gospels do contain material, at least in part, from early Aramaic material dating back to the time of Jesus himself. It is upon the foundation constructed by these scholars that this research is built. Of particular interest is Casey's notion that the material behind Mark's Gospel is early and predates the early

---

52 Maurice Casey, *Aramaic Sources of Mark's Gospel* (Cambridge, UK: Cambridge University Press, 1999), 74-76.

53 Ibid., 107-110.

54 Ibid., 258.

55 Ibid., 254-255.

56 Ibid., 260.

57 Ibid., 259.

58 See Maurice Casey, *An Aramaic Approach to Q: Sources for the Gospels of Matthew and Mark* (Cambridge, UK: Cambridge University Press, 2002).

59 See Maurice Casey, *Jesus of Nazareth: An Independent Historian's Account of His Life and Teachings* (London, UK: T&T Clark International, 2010).

dating of the Gospel ascribed by Casey. The same could also be argued for Matthew's Gospel.

Can the Preservation of Jesus's Teachings be Trusted?

A fourth challenge, which is a hot-button theological issue in New Testament studies, concerns whether the content of Jesus's messages preserved in the Gospels links back to the authentic theological messages that the historical Jesus provided. Did the messages of Jesus in the Gospels derive from him or the evangelists' imagination? In 1985, a consortium of New Testament scholars descended upon the Estar Institute of Santa Rosa, California. The assembly would consist of over seventy scholars, half of whom graduated from Harvard, Claremont, and Vanderbilt divinity schools, who met twice a year to investigate the historicity of the teachings of Jesus in the Gospels..[60] This assembly would be known as the Jesus Seminar. Out of the 420 sayings found in the Gospel of Matthew, only 11 were deemed authentic (2.6%), 61 were viewed as most likely from Jesus (14.5%), 114 were believed to have contained some element of Jesus's teaching (27%), and a whopping 235 were held to be from the evangelist's own construction and not bearing any imprint upon the actual teachings of Jesus (55.9%)..[61] According to Robert W. Funk, the founder of the Jesus Seminar, "the narrative contexts in which the sayings of Jesus are preserved in the Gospels are the creation of the evangelists. They are fictive and secondary.".[62] The Jesus Seminar concluded that 82 percent of Jesus's words presented in the Gospels were not actually uttered by the historical Jesus..[63]

The results of the Jesus Seminar's study are not universally accepted. Many scholars take exception to their findings and not necessarily due to religious conviction alone. Norman Geisler argues that the Seminar's conclusions are based on nothing more than "unsubstantiated antisupernatural bias.".[64] William Lane Craig also substantiates Geisler's claims. Craig likens the Jesus Seminar's

---

[60] Norman L. Geisler, "Jesus Seminar," *Baker Encyclopedia of Christian Apologetics*, Baker Reference Library (Grand Rapids, MI: Baker Books, 1999), 386.

[61] The Gospel of Luke fared best with a 3.6% authenticity, followed by Matthew at 2.6%, then the extra-biblical *Gospel of Thomas* with 1.5%, Mark holding 0.6%, and then the Gospel of John bearing no authentic statements of Jesus.

[62] Robert W. Funk, "The Emerging Jesus," *Parables of Jesus: Red Letter Edition* (Sonoma, CA: Polebridge, 1988), 11.

[63] Robert W. Funk, Roy W. Hoover, and the Jesus Seminar, *The Five Gospels: What Did Jesus Really Say?* (San Francisco, CA: HarperSanFrancisco, 1993), 5.

[64] Geisler, "Jesus Seminar, *BECA,* 388.

approach to the very same bifurcation of the Jesus of history and the Christ of faith that John Robinson adopts..[65]

Furthermore, the Jesus Seminar seemingly ignored the general consensus of historical Jesus scholarship. Luke Timothy Johnson exposes at least three areas of their distance from the majority of historical Jesus scholars. First, most scholars acknowledge that Jesus was an eschatological figure, whereas the Seminar seemingly ignored Jesus's eschatological emphasis..[66] Second, the Seminar assumes too great of contrast between written and oral cultures. As will be shown in the next section, one finds good reasons to accept the overall reliability of historical transmission in Jewish first-century culture. Finally, the Seminar warns against finding a Jesus that is comfortable with the Christian faith but prefers a cultural critic instead..[67] In contrast, studies in the NT creeds demonstrate that the earliest Christology was the highest Christology..[68]

Studies into the Semitic nature of the textual content add insight to the reliability of the early source material shaping the Gospel texts because it connects back to the original settings in which Jesus of Nazareth first preached the message. Rather than holding that Jesus was a mythical figure invented by the early church,.[69] theologian/historian Rainer Riesner contends that because the presence of education was found in early Jewish synagogues—and Nazareth had a synagogue of its own; the emphasis placed on education correlated with the religious interests of the parents—and Jesus's parents were

---

[65] William Lane Craig, *Reasonable Faith: Christian Truth and Apologetics,* 3rd ed (Wheaton, IL: Crossway, 2008), 292. See also James Robinson, *A New Quest of the Historical Jesus,* Studies in Biblical Theology 25 (London, UK: SCM, 1959).

[66] In the Olivet Discourse in Matthew's Gospel, the Seminar only affords one brief parable the grade of pink (possible). The remainder of the passage is labeled as black (inauthentic) or gray (doubtful) at best. Funk, Hoover, and the Jesus Seminar, *The Five Gospels,* 247-258.

[67] Luke Timothy Johnson, *The Real Jesus: The Misguided Quest for the Historical Jesus and the Truth of the Traditional Gospels* (New York, NY: HarperOne, 1996), 24.

[68] "Thus, the earliest Christology was already *in nuce* the highlest Christology. All that remained was to work through consistently what it could mean for Jesus to belong integrally to the unique identity of the one God. Early Christian interest was primarily in soteriology and eschatology, the concerns of the gospel, and so, in the New Testament, it is primarily as sharing or implementing God's eschatological lordship that Jesus is understood to belong to the identity of God." Richard Bauckham, *Jesus and the God of Israel: God Crucified and Other Studies on the New Testament's Christology of Divine Identity* (Grand Rapids, MI: Eerdmans, 2009, x, 235.

[69] While the Jesus Myth hypothesis holds little value and merit, an absence of Semitic traits in the Gospels would provide some foothold with the movement.

quite pious (Luke 2:22-27, 42); since the Messiah was expected to be a man of great wisdom; the Synoptic tradition consisting of short words and phrases that relate to mnemonic stylistic devices; and Jesuan introductory formulas preceding mnemonic patterns; then "one can place greater trust in the reliability of the Synoptic tradition with Riesenfield and Gerhardsson than is possible from the 'formal history school.'".[70] Riesner's claims were validated and strengthened by two additional German theses: Muller's *Traditionspozess im Neuen Testament* and Zimmermann's *Urchristlichen Lehrer*..[71]

The lack of emphasis on the Aramaic and Semitic nature has led to faulty claims and unnecessary skepticism concerning the reliability of the Gospel texts while unnecessarily elevating non-biblical texts. For instance, some scholars have postulated that the *Gospel of Thomas* precedes the Gospel of Matthew and the other Synoptic Gospels..[72] However, such studies have not considered the Aramaic and Semitic traits that strengthen the case for Synoptic's validity over that of *Thomas*. One such example is found in Luke's rendering of τὰ ἐνόντα δότε ἐλεημοσύνην (Lk. 11:41) and Matthew's καθάρισον πρῶτον τὸ ἐντὸς (Matt. 23:26) which are literal interpretations of the Hebrew text..[73] The same cannot be said for the word structure in the *Gospel of Thomas*. The Semitic residue found in these passages, particularly the ease in which they relate back to the Aramaic/Hebrew language, bodes well to demonstrate the early nature of the source material found in the canonical Gospels, thereby strengthening the case that the Evangelists attempted to preserve the message

---

[70] "Da ein vorosterlicher Beginn der Jesus-Uberlieferung aus mehrenren Gruden naheliegt, darf man mit Riesenfeld und Gerhardsson ein grosseres Vertrauen in die Zuverlassigkeit der synoptischen Tradition setzen, als das vom Ansatz der 'formgeschictlichen Schule' her moglich ist." Rainer Riesner, "Judische Elementarbildung und Evangelienuberlieferung," *Gospel Perspectives: Studies of History and Tradition in the Four Gospels,* vol. 1, R. T. France and David Wenham, eds (Eugene, OR: Wipf & Stock, 1981), 218-220.

[71] Craig L. Blomberg, *The Historical Reliability of the Gospels,* 2nd ed (Nottingham, UK; Downers Grove, IL: Apollos; IVP Academic, 2007), 57.

[72] Helmut Koester argues that the *Gospel of Thomas* is more primitive than Synoptics in his 1990 work due to his close comparison of the sayings of *Thomas* 89 with Q/Luke 11:39-40. However, he only uses portions of the Q/Lukan text to compare it to the Matthean and Lukan use. Helmut Koester, *Ancient Christian Gospels: Their History and Development* (London, UK; Philadelphia, PA: Trinity Press International, 1992), 91-92.

[73] Casey, *Aramaic Approach to Q,* 38.

of Jesus as accurately as they were able.[74] As a matter of great interest, translating the texts back into Aramaic can unveil hidden puns that are not found in the Greek texts. One such case is found in Matthew 23:23-24. In the text, Jesus said of the scribes and Pharisees, "You blind guides, who strain out a gnat and swallow a camel" (Matt. 23:24, NASB)![75] In the Greek text, *κώνωπα* and *κάμηλον* respectively denote a gnat and camel. While a pun is found to some degree in the Greek text, it does not hold the punch of wordplay as found in Aramaic. The terms in Aramaic for gnat and camel are גְּמָל (*gamal*) and גַּמְלָא (*gamla*) which represent a clearer play on words.[76] That is, the hypocritical leaders spat out a *gamal* yet swallowed a *gamla.* Such word plays, often found in the Hebrew prophets, serve as evidence of a preserved earlier message which undergirds the Gospel text.

Process of Transmission

The fifth and final challenge that must be taken into consideration is the process by which the information was passed from an oral environment to the written text. Can oral traditions serve as a trustworthy means of preservation? And if so, can they accurately be transmitted over to a written text? To answer this question, one must consider the modern state of play in NT scholarship. According to the majority view among scholars, the Gospel of Mark was composed first even though the early church fathers claimed otherwise.[77] Additionally, the majority of scholarship also holds that at least two Synoptic Gospels depend on earlier source material.[78] Matthew and Luke are believed to depend on the Gospel of Mark and a theoretical Gospel named Q.[79] Yet assuming that the early church fathers are at least partially right, then it would appear that Q could represent the earliest iteration of the Gospel of Matthew. Nonetheless, two truths are still recognized regarding this research's

---

[74] Maurice Casey suggests that "Arguments of this kind cannot possibly support … [the] contention that the *Gospel of Thomas* should be dated back to the first century." Ibid.

[75] Scripture marked NASB comes from the *New American Standard Bible* (La Habra, CA: Lockman Foundation, 2020).

[76] Robert H. Stein, *The Method and Message of Jesus' Teachings,* revised ed (Louisville, KY: Westminster John Knox, 1994), 13.

[77] Keener, *Christobiography,* 14.

[78] More likely all three. Ibid.

[79] Q from the German *quelle* meaning "source."

investigation. First, Q, however one assumes it to exist,[80] which is at least one source behind the Gospel of Matthew, consists of material that predates even the Gospel of Mark and even, at times, represents teachings found in pre-Easter contexts.[81] Second, the material behind the Gospel of Matthew and the other Gospels were all, as Richard Bauckham denotes, "written within the living memory of the events they recount."[82] Additionally, the earliest traditions were remembered and established among a group that was not as spread out geographically as it would become, which helped preserve and bolster the teachings and events of Jesus.[83] It can be argued that since these traditions were eventually documented within the lifetime of the earliest eyewitnesses helped to safeguard the veracity of the message presented.

Second, one must consider the nature of oral tradition and the devices used to help memorize material (i.e., mnemonic devices).[84] Communal memory was an earmark of transmission in ancient cultures, particularly in the Middle

---

[80] No matter if Q only represents a common oral tradition, one written document, or multiple written documents; the material itself often holds traits that identify it as among the earliest of Jesus traditions.

[81] Eric Eve recognizes traces of the Jesus tradition in numerous sources as evidenced in the NT creeds found in Paul's writings, Q, and the Gospel of Mark. Eric Eve, *Behind the Gospels: Understanding the Oral Tradition* (Minneapolis, MN: Fortress, 2013), 177. One such example of a pre-Easter tradition is found in Jesus's teaching on discipleship in the Sermon on the Mount (Matt. 8:19-22; Luke 9:57-62). James D. G. Dunn, *The Oral Gospel Tradition* (Grand Rapids, MI; Cambridge, UK: Eerdmans, 2013), 91.

[82] Bauckham, *Jesus and the Eyewitnesses,* 7.

[83] Gerhardsson argues that the church was not as widespread in the first century as often thought. Thereby, historical scholars have stretched "out the chronological and geographical dimensions of the formation of the early Christian tradition in an unreasonable manner. What is needed here is a more sober approach to history." Birger Gerhardsson, *The Reliability of the Gospel Tradition* (Peabody, MS: Hendrickson, 2001), 40.

[84] Eric Eve describes six characteristics of orality and oral traditions. 1) Speech is an event and not just a thing. 2) Speech is heard and not seen. As such, oral traditions can only survive in the memory of those who witnessed or heard the event in question. 3) One can expect some variation in speeches and events as very few can remember every word spoken in a long speech. 4) Speech, outside of electronic media, always involves face-to-face interaction. Thus, some aspects of non-verbal communication are lost in transmission (i.e., the wink of an eye). 5) Speech acts occur in particular situations and are more or less formal which can restrain how and what is said. 6) Oral communication holds various cues that cannot always be duplicated. Eve, *Behind the Gospels,* 2-3.

East..[85] Although the availability of written materials was not as prevalent as they would later become, collective memories often outweigh the limitations often found in individual memory..[86] Together, people can correct and shape material according to the way an event occurred more than what one person alone could afford. Communities that employ oral traditions often employ similar tactics to help imprint certain messages and events into the minds of each individual. The Aramaic underlying the messages of Jesus often holds rhythmic patterns and figures of speech that portray the use of oral memory, thereby indicating preservation from the earliest community..[87] As such, patterns of orality that can be identified in Semitic aspects of the Gospel of Matthew can be used to point to early source material behind the Gospel text. Additionally, the distinctive style of Jesus's teaching and message can be used to denote the unique and early nature of the source material..[88]

Finally, the message of the early church's Christology can be traced to the NT creeds which predate the composition of the Gospels. Paul Barnett traces the lineage of early Christian development by showing that the movement began with Christ, then moved to the earliest Christological understandings of Jesus, which birthed the Christian religion..[89] By following Paul's chronology, it can be deemed that the earliest Christian creeds date to around AD 37..[90] Thus, if the texts holding Semitic residue can be shown to

---

[85] Keener, *Christobiography,* 414.

[86] Barry Schwartz, "Where There's Smoke, There's Fire: Memory and History," in *Memory and Identity in Ancient Judaism and Early Christianity: A Conversation with Barry Schwartz,* Tom Thatcher, ed (Atlanta, GA: SBL, 2014), 8.

[87] Keener, *Christobiography,* 490-491.

[88] Ibid., 491; Craig S. Keener, *Historical Jesus,* 187-188; Ben Witherington notes the great value he grants to a tradition that is placed within an Aramaic original or is comfortably found in the Palestinian context of the first century era. Witherington, *Christology of Jesus,* 28-29.

[89] "It was christology that gave birth to Christianity, not the reverse. Furthermore, Christ gave birth to Christology. The chronology drives us to this conclusion." Paul Barnett, *The Birth of Christianity: The First Twenty Years* (Grand Rapids, MI; Cambridge, UK: Eerdmans, 2005), 26.

[90] Ibid., 23-24.

preserve a similar Christology to what the NT creeds proclaim, then the veracity of the message is buttressed even more.

Five Models of Oral Transmission

One of the big questions facing this and any research engaging with early traditions is how much flexibility did the Jesus traditions have when being passed from the original words of Jesus to the present documented texts? Even in the present time, the notion of flexibility in the Gospel tradition has become a centerpiece of debate.

Michael Licona and Richard Burridge represent one side of the spectrum as they contend that the Gospels represent the genre of βίος, which permitted "a genre capable of flexibility, adaptation, and growth."[91] Licona notes that this flexibility offers biographers "a great deal of flexibility to rearrange material [and] invent speeches to communicate the teachings . . . of the subject."[92] Others have expressed concern that this concept, if taken too far, could lead to falsification of the early data, thus leading to erred reports.[93] Though literary devices should not be dismissed in their entirety, McGrew does bring to the surface an underlying problem if the notion of flexibility dismisses the early evangelists' focus on truth. Bauckham notes that eyewitness testimony fits well with the preface of Luke's Gospel where the evangelist claims to have spoken with "eyewitnesses from the beginning."[94]

The conversation concerning flexibility is not new, but could benefit from looking deeper into the means by which oral tradition was transmitted. At the time that this research was conducted, scholars presented three models for oral tradition. The first model comes from the German school which largely revolves around the work of Rudolf Bultmann. In his book *Jesus and the Word,* Bultmann committed himself to the *informal uncontrolled* model.[95] Bultmann argues, "I do indeed think that we can now know almost nothing concerning the life and personality of Jesus, since the early Christian sources show no interest in either, are moreover fragmentary and often legendary; and other

---

[91] Richard Burridge, *What Are the Gospels? A Comparison with Greco-Roman Biography* (Grand Rapids, MI: Eerdmans, 2004), 77.

[92] Licona, *The Resurrection of Jesus,* 593.

[93] Lydia McGrew, *The Mirror or the Mask: Liberating the Gospels from Literary Devices* (Tampa, FL: DeWard, 2019), 90–91.

[94] Richard Bauckham, *Jesus and the Eyewitnesses: The Gospels as Eyewitness Testimony,* 2nd ed (Grand Rapids, MI: Eerdmans, 2017), 9.

[95] Rudolf Bultmann, *Jesus and the Word* (New York, NY: Scribners, 1958), 8.

sources about Jesus do not exist.".[96] In Bultmann's model, almost nothing of Jesus can be known. Thus, the Gospels contain very little Semitic residue.

The second model comes from the Scandinavian school, particularly the work of Birger Gerhardsson's *Tradition and Transmission.* The Scandinavians promoted the exact opposite model to that of Bultmann's, presenting the *formal controlled* model. In this model, Gerhardsson likens the learning and communication of the NT Jesus traditions to that of the transmission of the "Oral Torah" which consisted of mnemonic techniques, condensations, use of written notes, and techniques of repetition..[97] This means of transmission was strict and took great measure to accurately convey the facts and message of those for whose life and the message they hoped to preserve. But Gerhardsson was open to accepting that some flexibility was acceptable since the gospel material was more haggadic than halakic, which permitted a "wider margin of variation in wording.".[98]

Gerhardsson's admission to the gospel material fitting haggadic material opens the door to the possibility of a third approach. To this one turns to the Bailey school, whose model he terms the *informal controlled* approach. Kenneth Bailey spent a great deal of time in the Middle East and observed the means by which they passed on information. He observed that communities could pass along large volumes of information. All the details of the story are preserved, however, there is a bit of flexibility that the storyteller has in communicating the information and reshaping it for the intended audience. However, Bailey estimates that no more than 15 percent of the information could be changed with none of that information consisting of the key, critical details of the story..[99] The system was informal in the sense that the communities preserved the information rather than a select few,.[100] but was controlled in that the core details of a narrative and message were accurately preserved.

Bailey, like Gerhardsson, is open to the possibility that the early church may have blended the *informal controlled* approach with the *formal controlled*

---

[96] Ibid.

[97] Birger Gerhardsson, *Memory and Manuscript: Oral Tradition and Written Transmission in Rabbinic Judaism and Early Christianity* (Grand Rapids, MI: Eerdmans, 122–193, 1961, 1998), 335.

[98] Ibid., 335.

[99] Kenneth Bailey, "Informal Controlled Oral Tradition and the Synoptic Gospels," *Themelios* 20, 2 (1995): 7.

[100] Albeit, Bailey argues that the system of transmission switched to *formal controlled* model around the Roman invasion of Jerusalem in AD 70. Ibid., 10.

method.[101] This research will contend that the data coincides with Bailey's model with the possibility of even meshing with Gerhardsson's. Thus, if we concede that the models of Bailey and Gerhardsson can be blended to some degree, we then establish a fourth model, one I call the *semiformal controlled* method. For the semiformal controlled method, it is maintained that Bailey's model is essentially correct. However, like Gerhardsson's view, the material was memorized and formalized a bit more than most traditions of the Middle East as it followed a rabbinic methodology. I argue that communities and the disciples selected by Jesus acted as a formal gatekeeper of the traditions. Therefore, the combined methods of Gerhardsson and Bailey's into a semiformal controlled method indicate that some formalization—more than what Bailey allows—was found in the preservation of the Jesus traditions. However, even the disciples represent a community of eyewitnesses (72 chosen in Luke 10:1–2; and 12 disciples). Thus, the preservation of the traditions by a large group rather than a smaller one represents a semiformal notion—less formal than Gerhardsson's and more formal than Bailey's.

Lastly, the conclusion of this book will evaluate the recent work of Michael Licona. His viewpoint is labeled as a fifth way to approach the oral traditions, one labeled as the formal uncontrolled method. As it will be later shown, Licona seems to suggest that the Evangelists served as the formal gatekeepers of these traditions, but that they freely used literary devices without any necessary checkpoints. As such, his view is labeled as formal—as he greatly emphasizes the importance of the individual writers of the Gospels—and uncontrolled—as he seems to permit the possibility of falsehoods in the biblical texts.[102] There may be other representatives of the formal uncontrolled viewpoint, but given the debate ensuring in the current Christian academic world involving Licona's interpretations, his methodology seemed to best

---

[101] Ibid., 10.

[102] As is noted in the conclusion of the book, Licona's work is assessed as it pertains to the transmission of oral traditions. This book does not seek to belittle, disparage, or take sides in the ongoing dispute between Michael Licona and Lydia McGrew. This author holds that both sides make compelling points. However, due to my research on oral traditions, I take a third view on the topic. Because I accept that the oral traditions behind the Gospels were transmitted accurately and preserve eyewitness testimony, I accept harmonization efforts to blend the eyewitness data. McGrew's undesigned coincidences are legitimate phenomenon that occur because of the oral traditions stemming from eyewitness testimony. However, I also acknowledge and accept the mild use of literary devices, but not to the point that blatant falsehoods are introduced to the text. In my opinion, paraphrasing, telescoping, and hyperboles are instruments of language and should not be held to the same level of introducing falsehoods into the text.

represent a formal uncontrolled method and is easily one of the most recognized.

Now that the research problem has been laid forth, it is now time to consider the research purpose and the thesis statement of the proposed research. The next section will describe the methodology used to prove the intended argument.

Methodology

Determining the probability that various Jesuan teachings in the Gospel of Matthew originated from early source material from its Semitic attributes requires a bit of explanation. Each passage will be given a color identification similar to the practice used by the Jesus Seminar but will use different color schemes. Unlike the Jesus Seminar, texts identified in the following sections were chosen because they hold some warrant to be linked to the early source material. Thus, none of the colors chosen will deny the possibility that the material could have come from early material. However, the colors do represent the probability that can be adduced to each category chosen. After the categorization is explained, the passages receiving attention in the work will be identified before describing and laying forth the seven methodological systems used to gauge the material in question.

Labeling the Text's Confidence

Detecting Semitic residue in the Gospel of Matthew requires an ability to test the probability that the text in question stems from a source that predates the written text. The research will examine nine pericopae of passages in the Gospel of Matthew divided into five categories and will use seven testable methods to analyze the level of early Semitic material found in the text. Using the colors of a stoplight—green for go, yellow for caution, and red for stop—the research will indicate what level of confidence each passage holds as it relates to Semitic material found within the passage and its relation to the message of Jesus and the earliest Christological traditions.

A new feature with this book that was not found in my dissertation upon which it is based is a new weighted grading scale. Some of these tests weigh heftier than others. Thus, with this new scale, a calculated weighted score will grade each section according to the strength of each test. Technical tests that gauge the Semitic characteristics and mnemonic patterns of the text along with their similarity with already established early Christologies will be granted heavier scores than those that look at cultural commonalities. This book will offer both tests; the one that grades the number of passed tests, and the updated weighted scale. Given the weighted scale, some Matthean texts scored higher than they did initially.

Under the old scale, if the text shows traits of 6-7 Semitic characteristics, then the text will be given the color green. The new weighted scale will label texts green that scored 20–30 points. These texts will be said to have most probably originated from early traditions stemming from Jesus of Nazareth and the earliest church. The overall green label depicts a confidence level of no less than 75 percent.

Under the old test, if the text holds 4-5 Semitic traits, then the text will be given the color yellow. The new weighted test will give the color yellow to texts that score between the range of 10–19 points. With yellow-labeled texts, one can comfortably claim that these texts most likely hold material from early traditions, but the text holds reasons to exercise caution before claiming its relation too strongly. Thus, indicating that the writer of the text likely interpreted the tradition according to his training. Thus, the yellow tag will be given to texts that hold a confidence rating from 50 to 74 percent.

Under the old scale, if the text shows 1-3 Semitic traits, then the text will be given the color red. For the new scale, texts that score 1–9 points are given the color red according to the weighted scale. These texts are warranted to hold some Semitic aspects from early material, but more work must be done before they can be comfortably held to have come from the earliest traditions. These texts likely contain traditions that were interpreted by the Gospel writer and included explanatory material. In other words, there is something within the text that indicates that it may be early, but the texts do not strongly match the criteria used to indicate as much. A confidence level of less than 50 percent must be given to texts ascribed to the red category.

Matthean Texts to Be Evaluated

Selections from Jesus's messages preserved in the Gospel of Matthew have been chosen to undergo an evaluation to see whether they derive from the early source material as evidenced by their Semitic residue..[103] Nine passages will be linked under five headings. The first section will evaluate certain texts from the Sermon on the Mount. The Beatitudes (Matt. 5:1-12), and the Lord's Prayer

[103] The texts chosen for this research were based on their affinity with Aramaisms and Jewish characteristics. These traits made them compelling for this research. Other Matthean texts are quite fascinating and deserve attention in future studies. Some texts in Matthew's Gospel, such as the Great Commission (Matt. 28:18–20), may even show signs of being an early creed. The present research seeks to assess the level of Semitic residue among the teachings in the Sermon on the Mount, a sample of the parables, the Son of Man sayings, and the interactions that Jesus had with others.

(Matthew 6:5-13).[104] both contain numerous Aramaic characteristics which make for a compelling case. Second, three Jesuan parables preserved in the Matthean Gospel will be evaluated, particularly because Jesus's parabolic didactic is unique to his teaching style. The Parable of the Harvest (Matt. 13:24–30, 36–40), the Parable of the Wise and Foolish Bridesmaids (Matt. 25:1-13), .[105] and the Parable of the Compassionate Employer (Matt. 20:1-16) will receive attention in the research. Third, the Son of Man (כְּבַר אֱנָשׁ) is of considerable interest due to their originality, Messianic overtones, and connection with the book of Daniel. The Son of Man sayings includes Jesus's teaching on exorcism and the unpardonable sin (Matt.12:22-40) and his teaching on the second coming of the Son of Man in the Olivet Discourse (Matt. 24:27, 30-44). The latter is of considerable interest as the pericope contains the greatest concentration of the Son of Man sayings among the 29 overall sayings found in Matthew. Fourth, Jesus's interactions with other individuals are of interest to the study, particularly Jesus's interaction with Peter and Peter's subsequent confession (Matt. 16:13-23) and Jesus's interaction with John the Baptist (Matt. 11:2-19). The latter is often considered to be part of Q. As such, the Semitic residue in the text will be of interest to this investigation. Thus, as a recap, the following texts will be tested with the seven prescribed methodologies and given a confidence level of green (>70% confidence of early Semitic material),.[106] yellow (50-69% confidence rating), and red (<50% confidence):

1. Sermon on the Mount
   a. The Beatitudes (Matt. 5:1-12)
   b. The Lord's Prayer (Matt. 6:5-13)
2. Parables
   a. Parable of the Harvest (13:24–30, 36–40)
   b. Parable of the Wise and Foolish Young Women (Matt. 25:1-13)
   c. Parable of the Compassionate Employer (Matt. 20:1-16)
3. Son of Man Sayings
   a. Exorcism and the Unpardonable Sin (Matt. 12:22-40)
   b. Coming of the Son of Man (Matt. 24:27, 30-44) (Of the 29 Son of Man sayings in Matthew, the greatest concentration is found in Matt. 24:27, 30, 37, 39, 44)
4. Interactions of Jesus with Others
   a. Jesus's Question and Peter's Confession (Matt. 16:13-23)

---

[104] Also known as the "Model Prayer."

[105] Otherwise known as the "Parable of the Ten Bridesmaids."

[106] Within the green categories, a confidence of 6 of 7 methods will be labeled as light green (85%) and 7 of 7 as dark green (99%).

b. Jesus and John the Baptist (Matt. 11:2-19)

Methods

If a text is to be said to hold Semitic residue that indicates early source material, the text must hold certain characteristics. A Gospel text, or pericope, denotes early Semitic material if the following aspects are found:

> 1) it uses unique rabbinic concepts that can be traced to Talmudic ideology; (2 points)
> 2) Christological concepts that have been demonstrated to derive from the earliest church; (5 points)
> 3) contains theological terminology in Greek that relate to Hebraic/Aramaic concepts found in the OT/LXX (i.e., κύριος, μαρὰν ἀθά, כְּבַר אֱנָשׁ); (4 points)
> 4) mnemonic and rhythmic patterns that relate to the transmission of oral material; (5 points)
> 5) holds overall Aramaic/Hebraic characteristics found in the translation of materials (i.e., translation from Aramaic/Hebrew into the Greek language; leftover Aramaic terms, and the ease by which the text can be translated back into Aramaic); (5 points)
> 6) retains cultural concepts that relate to the understanding of early first-century Israel; (4 points) and
> 7) similarities to the recognized structure of NT creedal material and early sermon summaries. (5 points)

Each criterium will now be further expounded. It is important to remember that this investigation compiles a cumulative approach which contends that the more traits that a text holds, the stronger the case can be made for the text's connection back to the early oral source tradition behind it.

Method One: Unique Rabbinic Concepts

The first method will be to examine the relationship of the message of the text in relation to the rabbinic teachings of the day, particularly denoting the unique nature of the interpretation espoused in the textual data. The Talmud will serve as the primary text used to compare the NT text as it is a collection of early rabbinic texts that spans 2,783 pages and consists of the Mishnah and Gemara..[107] The Mishnah, which consists of rabbinic commentary on the Scripture is comprised of an oral tradition dating from 20 BC to AD

---

[107] John C. Johnson, "Talmud," *The Lexham Bible Dictionary*, John D. Barry, et. al., eds (Bellingham, WA: Lexham Press, 2016), Logos Bible Software.

220. The term "Mishnah" means "repetition" and describes the means by which the material was learned and what it contained..[108]

The Gemara is an exposition of the Mishnah and dates from AD 220 to 900. Three levels of rabbis composed the Mishnah—the Sopherim (predating the time of Jesus), Tannaim (contemporaries of Jesus), and the Amoraim. The Sopherim and Tannaim composed the Mishnah, whereas the Gemara is a production of the Amoraim as they commented on the interpretations of their predecessors..[109] While much of the Mishnah's composition dates to the time of Jesus or after, it has been noted that both the Babylonian and the earlier Palestinian Talmuds contain oral material from an earlier period which can be useful for understanding the background and concepts of the early NT period..[110] While it may be that the Talmud postdates Jesus in his written composition, the oral traditions behind them predate their written texts..[111] As such, the Talmud's parallels can be useful in pinpointing early oral material underlying the canonical Gospels, particularly where Jesus's interpretation diverges from the rabbinic approach. It should be noted that the conviction of the rabbis was that the words of their sages were as valuable, if not more so than the prophets..[112] As such, it was believed that the Oral Law consisted of divine revelation given to the rabbis and could not be contended..[113] Interestingly, the Mishnah becomes a major sticking point between Jesus and the Pharisees..[114] Thus, Jesus's similar but unique take on

---

[108] Arnold Fruchtenbaum, *Yeshua: The Life of Messiah from a Messianic Jewish Perspective,* vol. 1 (San Antonio, TX: Ariel), 104.

[109] Ibid., 104-105.

[110] "Nevertheless, both Talmuds contain material from an earlier period and are also extremely useful for illuminating the background of the New Testament and early Christianity." Johnson, "Talmud, *LBD,* Logos Bible Software.

[111] Gary Habermas notes that much of the Mishnah was collected and organized by subject matter by Rabbi Akiba before his passing in AD 135. Gary Habermas, *The Historical Jesus: Ancient Evidence for the Life of Christ* (Joplin, MO: College Press, 1996), 202.

[112] Fruchtenbaum, *Yeshua,* vol. 1, 150.

[113] Ibid., 126; Michael S. Berger, *Rabbinic Authority* (New York, NY: Oxford University Press, 1998), 86.

[114] Fruchtenbaum and Biven hold that Jesus was similar to Hasidimic charismatic rabbis of the first century, and they note that the two versions of the Talmud "contain 'many parables and sayings that were preserved orally from his day,' thus making these documents very valuable to the understanding of first-century Israel." Fruchtenbaum, *Yeshua,* vol. 1, 108; David Bivin, *New Light on the Difficult Words of Jesus* (Holland, MI: En-Gedi, 2005), xxiii.

Talmudic theology becomes a major area of interest in the discovery of early Semitic source material and, thereby, becomes a trait one would expect to find in early Semitic source material dating back to Jesus of Nazareth and the earliest church.

With that being said, a word of caution must be given when using Talmudic sources. It is difficult to ascertain which portions of the material represent traditions that date back to the time of Jesus, if any at all. Unfortunately, the Talmud represents the best source of material one holds when seeking to understand early Jewish theology. Certainly, there are Jewish texts written in the times of Second Temple Judaism, including some texts that are pseudepigraphal. However, the Talmud, despite the late dating of its composition, provides the best way to understand Jewish beliefs. Nonetheless, one must acknowledge the difficulties connecting the Talmudic texts with early first-century Jewish thought.

Method Two: Early Christological Concepts

The second method will examine the Christological concepts presented in the text in light of the early Christology denoted by the NT creeds and early kerygma. Early Christological concepts are critical for understanding the early church's understanding of Christ. As previously noted, Christ impacted the early church's Christological understanding which, in turn, developed the Christian movement.[115] The oral proclamation dominated and formed the proclamation of the early church, the Apostolic Fathers, and became the source material for the Gospel texts.[116] Certain elementary factors relate to the NT understanding of Christ's nature: 1) Christ is God; 2) he is human; 3) he is one person; 4) he holds divine and human natures.[117] However, the earliest Christian confessions are constructed around Christological formulas in contrast to later trinitarian formulas,[118] are related to his work with creation,[119] and his overall work within the total history of revelation and salvation.[120] Cullmann notes that "Christians regarded the confession of Christ

---

[115] Barnett, *The Birth of Christianity,* 26.

[116] Aloys Grillmeier, *Christ in Christian Tradition,* Vol. 1: From the Apostolic Age to Chalcedon (451), John Bowden, trans (Atlanta, GA: John Knox, 1964), 34.

[117] Thomas C. Oden, *Classical Christianity: A Systematic Theology* (New York, NY: HarperOne, 1992), 299.

[118] Oscar Cullmann, *The Christology of the New Testament* (Waco, TX: Baylor University Press, 1959, 2018), 1.

[119] Ibid., 2.

[120] Ibid., 9.

as essential of their faith.".[121] As such, bipartite relationships between Christ and the Father.[122] and the human and spiritual nature of Jesus are among the earliest Christological understandings of the church..[123] As such, the Christological focus of the passages will need to be examined to see whether they fit within the recognized early bipartite formulation that is so prevalent in established pre-NT creedal passages.

Method Three: Theological Terminology Relating to Semitic Concepts in the LXX

Additionally, certain titles are important in relating material of early Christological concepts. Cullman lists the following titles as most important: prophet, high priest, mediator, Servant of God, Lamb of God, Messiah, Son of David, Son of Man, Judge, Holy One of God, Lord, Savior, King, Logos, Son of God, and God. .[124] Of the titles used, "Son of Man," "Lord," "Christ/Messiah," and "Son of God" are among the most important as they convey early theological titles found in the LXX and hold theological concepts centered in Second Temple Judaism..[125] For instance, the title "Son of Man," taken from the imagery found in Daniel 7:13-14, appears in several early Jewish texts of the time around and prior to Jesus's generation, including passages in *1 Enoch,* particularly the text entitled Parables or Similitudes (chaps. 37-71)..[126] The title "Lord" (Gk., κύριος) is the Greek term used in the LXX for the Hebrew term אֲדֹנָי, which was itself used in the place of the personal name of God (i.e., יהוה)..[127] As such, the use of κύριος for Jesus is considered primitive.[128] as "both *adonai* and the tetragram were equated with *kyrios* already in pre-

[121] Oscar Cullmann, *The Earliest Christian Confessions,* J. K. S. Reid, trans (Eugene, OR: Wipf & Stock, 1949), 39.

[122] Ibid., 36.

[123] Ibid., 41.

[124] Cullmann, *Christology of the New Testament,* 8.

[125] Larry W. Hurtado, *One God, One Lord: Early Christian Devotion and Ancient Jewish Monotheism,* 3rd ed (London, UK: Bloomsbury T&T Clark, 2015), 13.

[126] Ibid., 55.

[127] Martin A. Shields and Ralph K. Hawkins, "YHWH," *The Lexham Bible Dictionary,* Barry, et. al., eds, Logos Bible Software.

[128] C. H. Dodd, *The Apostolic Preaching and Its Development* (New York, NY: Harper and Brothers, 1935), 15.

Christian times."[129] The usage of these recognized early titles and concepts within the text will increase the veracity of its relationship to the early source material. Thus, the third methodology will examine any titles used for Jesus of Nazareth by either Jesus's self-understanding of himself, or the titles used by others for Jesus as preserved in the text.

Method Four: Mnemonic and Rhythmic Patterns Associated with Oral Material

The fourth methodology involves testing the text for any indications of oral material. Due to the nature of oral tradition, some elasticity can be expected.[130] Nonetheless, certain characteristics can be expected as it relates to the practice of memorizing and repeating the information.[131] While there exist overarching characteristics of oral traditions,[132] the primary task of this method will be to search for mnemonic devices and rhythmic patterns that are prevalent in oral transmission. Among the patterns that will be considered is the fourfold parallelism that C. F. Burney recognized as forms of Semitic poetry in the

---

[129] Albert Pietersma, "Kyrios or Tetagram: A Renewed Quest for the Original LXX," *De Septuaginta: Studies in Honour of John Williams Wevers on His Sixty-Fifth Birthday,* Albert Pietersma and Claude Cox, eds (Mississauga, ON: Benben, 1984), 98.

[130] Michael R. Licona, *Why Are There Differences in the Gospels?: What We Can Learn from Ancient Biography* (Oxford, UK: Oxford University Press, 2017), 2.

[131] Vernon Neufeld notes that the *homologia* of the church was closely related to the development of the *didache* of the church. Vernon H. Neufeld, *The Earliest Christian Confessions* (Leiden, NL: Brill, 1963), 144.

[132] James D. G. Dunn recognizes five major characteristics of oral traditions: 1) oral performances, 2) communal, 3) one or more individuals are responsible for performing and maintaining the community's tradition, 4) oral performances are witnesses of the original event, and 5) is both fixed and flexible. Dunn, *Oral Gospel Tradition,* 53-57.

teachings of Jesus.[133] along with the patterns of Semitic wordplay found in the text that would assist in memorizing the material..[134]

Method Five: Aramaic/Hebraic Literary Characteristics of the Text

The fifth method will consider the Aramaic and Hebraic characteristics found in the text being analyzed. In Mathew Black's treatment of Aramaisms in the Gospels and Acts, he contrived numerous tests to evaluate whether a text contained Aramaic components derived from earlier Semitic sources. While the research cannot take into account all of the tests he suggests, the fifth method will consider some of the more pronounced Aramaic tests that Black, Jeremias, and Casey employ while also leaving open the possibility of other notable Aramaic traits found in each text. Four of their tests will be used in this section.

First, Aramaic words left untranslated serve as a possible proof that early Semitic materials were used. Here, it is important to denote the admonition given by Joachim Jeremias that not every Aramaic word may be evidence of early material since Aramaic was the common tongue of the authors..[135] Nonetheless, a person, as Jeremias notes, is "drawing nearer to Jesus himself when we succeed in rediscovering the pre-Hellenistic form of the tradition.".[136] Terms such as *'Abba* and *'amen* are unique Aramaic words that help the interpreter draw closer to the *ipsissima vox* of Jesus and the "consciousness of his authority.".[137]

Second, word order is an important trait of any language. The English language uses a more established sentence structure with the subject-verb-object pattern. The Greek language is fluid in the way it constructs sentence patterns as nominative, genitive, dative, and accusative are identified by case endings rather than necessarily word order. However, Hebrew and Aramaic,

---

[133] 1) Synonymous: where some correspondence in idea is found between the two lines of a couplet, the second line reinforcing the first; 2) antithetic: contrast of the second line with the first; 3) synthetic or constructive: the thought of the second supplements or reenforces the first; and 4) climactic: where the second line adds a climax to the first. Black, *Aramaic Approach to the Gospels and Acts,* 143; C. F. Burney, *The Poetry of Our Lord: An Examination of the Formal Elements of Hebrew Poetry in the Discourses of Jesus Christ* (Eugene, OR: Wipf & Stock, 2008), 16, 20-21.

[134] Black notes that alliteration, assonance, and paronomasia are all characteristic traits of early Semitic poetry. Black, *Aramaic Approach to the Gospels and Acts,* 160.

[135] Jeremias, *Jesus and the Message of the New Testament,* 10.

[136] Ibid.

[137] Ibid.

while still somewhat fluid, settle on a more standardized word order as found in a verb-subject-object pattern. While Greek often employs the same practice, consistent V-S-O patterns in the text can potentially identify a Semitic influence.[138]

Third, Semitic phrasing can detect early Semitic material. Terms themselves can show Semitic influence. Julius Wellhausen distinguished between three levels of Aramaic terminology.[139] First-level words are unique and are not traceable to any outside influence apart from Jesus and the early church. Words in this category include but are not limited to πειράζω, βαπτίζω, Ἀναστασία, and σώζω.[140] Second-level words are those that may have originated from the early church but also hold an influence through the LXX.[141] Third-level words are natural extensions of common Greek usage. Third-level words are common terms of the time.[142] While all three levels could indicate early source material, preference is given to the first and second-level terms. Nonetheless, all three levels are important to the task ahead. Additionally, verbal usage can indicate the recording of early Semitic material. Black denotes that the use of inchoative and auxiliary usage of verbal tenses are characteristic of Aramaic,[143] as well as the impersonal plural[144] and other usages.[145]

Finally, possible mistranslations of Aramaic words are a cue to the presence of early source material. Mistranslation does not necessarily denote an error in the text. But rather, it may only denote that a term makes better sense in the Semitic languages. Casey notes that one of the challenges is to attempt to place oneself in the "perspective of an ancient translator."[146] As such, there

---

[138] "A Semitism to which Wellhausen attached much importance was the position of the verb in the sentence or clause." Black, *Aramaic Approach to the Gospels and Acts,* 50.

[139] Ibid., 132; Julius Wellhausen, *Einleitung in die drei ersten Evangelien,* 2nd ed (Berlin, DE: Druck und Verlag Von Georg Reimer, 1905), 33.

[140] Ibid.

[141] Ibid.

[142] Ibid.

[143] Black, *Aramaic Approach to the Gospels and Acts,* 125.

[144] The impersonal plural is uniquely found in the teachings of Jesus more than any other portion of the Gospel texts. Ibid.; Wellhausen, *Einl.,* 18.

[145] He also includes generalizing plural and certain tenses including the aorist for the Semitic perfect, periphrastic tenses—participial present or imperfect. Black, *Aramaic Approach to the Gospels and Acts,* 128-132.

[146] Casey, *Aramaic Approach to Q,* 62.

exists the possibility that some words may not translate accurately into another language. When terms make better sense in Aramaic and Hebrew.[147] than in the recorded Greek, then it can be argued that the passage stems from early Semitic material. One such example is found in Luke 13:31. In the passage, Jesus is noted as saying, "Go and tell that fox, 'Behold, I am casting out demons and performing healings today and tomorrow, and on the third day I reach My goal'" (Luke 13:31, NASB). The word for fox in Greek is ἀλώπηξ which has led some to believe that Jesus references Herod's cunningness..[148] Casey points out that the Aramaic word תעלא (*ta'ala*).[149] better suits the context than ἀλώπηξ. The Aramaic שׁוּעָל is defined as a jackal which was more numerous in the region than foxes..[150] The jackal was known as a "noisy, unclean nuisance of an animal, a predator which hunted in packs.".[151] While either interpretation is possible, it does appear that the Aramaic version better suits the context than the traditional understanding of the fox. As such, the text could serve as an indicator of an earlier source due to the potential better interpretation in the Aramaic context.

Other Aramaic characteristics are noted in the works of Casey, Black, and Jeremias. However, the four aforementioned traits are among the most notable. Weight will be ascribed to those texts that hold Semitic literary characteristics that strengthen their connection to the original source material.

---

[147] Some overlap from Aramaic to Hebrew is to be expected since some interference occurred after a long period of diglossia. Ibid., 52.

[148] Edwards contends that fox could represent a sly person. Yet in Jewish circles, the metaphor could also refer to a person who believed himself to be a lion but, in reality, was much smaller game. James R. Edwards, *The Gospel According to Luke*, The Pillar New Testament Commentary, D. A. Carson, ed (Grand Rapids, MI; Cambridge, U.K.; Nottingham, England: Eerdmans; Apollos, 2015), 405.

[149] Not to be confused with the Arabic *ta'ala* which is a simple word for God, Divine, Supreme, or Almighty.

[150] Maurice Casey, *Jesus of Nazareth: An Independent Historian's Account of His Life and Teaching* (New York, NY: T&T Clark, 2010), 114.

[151] Ibid.

The more traits that can be found, the greater the possibility of its Semitic nature.

Method Six: Retains Semitic Cultural Concepts of First Century Israel

The sixth method will consider cultural concepts exclusive to the Semitic region in first-century Israel in addition to the rhetoric of the time.[152] Hellenistic interpretations can somewhat differ from Semitic ones.[153] For instance, when examining Luke 5:1-11, Bailey distinguishes between the segmentation of spirit and matter in the Greek world, as opposed to the Semitic concept of the good and bad nature of the spirit world and material goods being seen as blessings or curses.[154] A similar practice will prove useful when engaging possible early source material. Even if a text holds Aramaic traits, it does not bode well for its association with early data if the content of the material does not match the setting and beliefs of first-century Israel. The Evangelists most assuredly wrote their Gospels for their respective communities.[155] Nonetheless, they still maintained a great concern for preserving the traditions[156] of Jesus's messages and his story[157] as they also recognized that their movement had a worldwide mission.[158] Thus, cultural assimilation with the culture and times of first-century Israel will prove extremely beneficial.

Method Seven: Similarities to Early NT Creeds,
Sermon Summaries, & Early Literature

The seventh and final method will compare the content of each text with recognized early creeds in the NT Epistles, the sermon summaries of Acts,

---

[152] Kenneth E. Bailey, *Jesus Through Middle Eastern Eyes: Cultural Studies in the Gospels* (Downers Grove, IL: IVP Academic, 2008), 13.

[153] James Charlesworth, "Can One Recover Aramaic Sources Behind Mark's Gospel?," *The Review of Rabbinic Judaism* 5,2 (June 2002): 250.

[154] Ibid., 135.

[155] Bauckham, *The Christian World Around the New Testament,*12-13.

[156] Bauckham notes that books could preserve information more efficiently than oral traditions could. Hence, this must have been a factor behind the move from a focus on oral tradition to written texts. Ibid., 24.

[157] Dunn denotes two important motifs in the NT that confirm this emphasis: 1) *bearing witness* in Acts and John, and 2) *remembering* in the Pauline epistles. James D. G. Dunn, *Jesus Remembered,* Christianity in the Making, vol. 1 (Grand Rapids, MI; Cambridge, UK: Eerdmans, 2003), 177-179.

[158] Bauckham, *Christian World Around the NT,* 27.

and early NT literature. Scholars recognize certain passages in the NT creeds as predating the finished written text. While the NT creeds are structured more stringently and precisely than the passages in the NT, the creeds are based on five themes: 1) Baptism and catechumenisms, 2) worship, 3) exorcism, 4) encouragement against persecution, and 5) polemics against heresies..[159] The creeds are structured around three types of materials: 1) single-statement declarations, 2) formulaic prose, or *homologiai,* and 3) hymns and poetry..[160] Numerous creeds are found throughout the NT Epistles including 1 Corinthians 15:3-9, the Philippian hymn in Philippians 2:5-11, Colossians 1:15-20,.[161] and numerous other texts..[162]

Like the creeds, the sermon summaries of Acts have been recognized as presenting early material that has been condensed into easily memorized form. Due to financial restraints, the early church had to limit the length of the Gospels and Acts to what would have been considered within the parameters of what one scroll would have held..[163] Thus, the messages would need to be condensed so that both the messages and the narrative could be recorded. Additionally, observing the structure and Semitic nature of the sermon summaries of Stephen, Peter, and Paul; the sermon summaries most probably represent source material that was in an established form..[164] Even if the summaries were memorized in Greek, they still contain an underlying Semitic form which indicates their early nature.

The methodology employed in this research will use a cumulative approach. As was noted in the first portion of this section, the more traits a text holds with the methodology employed, the higher the likelihood that one could correlate the text with the early source material. That is to say, one should not anticipate a 100 percent correlation between a text and early source

---

159 Cullmann, *Earliest Christian Confessions,* 18.

160 Richard N. Longenecker, *New Wine into Fresh Wineskins: Contextualizing the Early Christian Confessions* (Peabody, MA: Hendrickson, 1999), 7.

161 A word needs to be said about the creed in Colossians. Colossians is often held to be deuteron-Pauline. If so, the document itself would be much later than those held to be authentically Pauline. While the creed may still be early as it could have been used by one of Paul's disciples, one must also consider that the epistle may not hold the same evidential quality that authentic Pauline epistles do.

162 Bart Ehrman concurs that the NT creeds represent a "very ancient tradition that predates Paul's writings." Bart D. Ehrman, *Did Jesus Exist?: The Historical Argument for Jesus of Nazareth* (New York, NY: HarperOne, 2012), 111.

163 Martin Hengel, *Acts and the History of Earliest Christianity* (Eugene, OR: Wipf & Stock, 1979), 8.

164 Max Wilcox, *The Semitisms of Acts* (Oxford, UK: Clarendon, 1965), 54-55.

material. At best, one could say that certain texts are highly probable in their correlation with pre-Gospel data.

Delimitations of the Research

As the research progresses, certain delimitations and caveats must be given before moving forward. The scope of research is primarily concerned with Semitic aspects of early material which provides clues to the source material behind the Gospel of Matthew. As such, seven considerations must be afforded.

First, the research will not necessarily focus attention on whether the material behind the Gospel of Matthew was written or oral in nature. The importance of oral material has already been noted. Thus, there is no need to rehash the material here. Nonetheless, it is possible that some of the source material could have been preserved early in the church's history, even possibly dating back to the earliest apostles as notetaking was possible with some of the men in the group.[165] However, the research is not set up to make a conclusive decision on the matter. Even when using the term Q, it is neither assumed that Q represents a written source, an oral one, nor a combination of both.[166] Q merely references the material used by Matthew and Luke that is independent of the Gospel of Mark.

Second, while this writer holds to the traditional view of the Gospels' authorship,[167] the text will not attempt to prove or disprove who wrote the Gospel of Matthew. Because the First Gospel is traditionally ascribed to Matthew, the text will be called the Gospel of Matthew without making a definitive statement either way. The focus of research will be primarily on the

[165] Considering that Matthew was a tax-collector, he would have been skilled in the art of shorthand note-taking which holds him as a prime candidate as a collector of Jesus's sayings material. Increasing evidence suggests that wax tablets could have been used for such notetaking. The more literate members of Jesus's group could most assuredly have used these means to record his teachings. Barnett, *The Birth of Christianity,*114; Alan Millard, *Reading and Writing in the Time of Jesus* (Sheffield: Sheffield Academic, 2000), 26-27, 28, 63, 67.

[166] J. Ed Komoszewski, M. James Sawyer, and Daniel B. Wallace, *Reinventing Jesus: How Contemporary Skeptics Miss the Real Jesus and Mislead Popular Culture* (Grand Rapids, MI: Kregel, 2006), 23.

[167] That is, that the apostle Matthew wrote the First Gospel, John Mark was the collector of Peter's teachings and penned the Second Gospel, Luke—the physician and colleague of the apostle Paul—wrote the Third Gospel and the book of Acts, and John the apostle wrote, or at least dictated, the contents of the Fourth Gospel.

source material behind Matthew's Gospel and its early nature more than the evangelist responsible for compiling the Gospel.

Third, while the research will be directed toward the Semitic nature of sources in Matthew's Gospel, the possibility of early non-Semitic texts will not be dismissed. In various places, Jesus engages Gentiles (i.e., the Syro-Phoenician woman in Matthew 15:22ff). More likely, Jesus used Greek to interact with these individuals. Additionally, one cannot dismiss the Hellenist community of early Christianity which included Stephen the first Christian martyr..[168] Most assuredly, the Hellenist passed along early Semitic sayings of Jesus cast into their own Greek language. As such, the possibility exists that some non-Semitic material could be deemed early alongside its Semitic counterpart.

Fourth, as noted previously, 80 percent of Jesus's sayings in the Gospels find an Aramaic pattern to them that indicates its early nature..[169] Because of the frequency found in Jesus's teachings, the research will not examine all possible Semitisms in all parts of Matthew's Gospel. Rather, attention will be given to those passages that exhibit the most compelling cases.

Fifth, the research will only focus on the Semitism found in the Gospel of Matthew and not the other three Gospel texts. Surprisingly, the *Logos* title in John's prologue, the structure in portions of Mark, in addition to the parables in Luke's Gospel provide ample fruit for further investigations. However, to limit the scope of research, the focus will only be on Matthew's Gospel, the most Semitic of the four.

Sixth, it must be admitted that this investigator is not fluent in all the biblical languages referenced in this research, particularly Aramaic. Having received training in both Greek and Hebrew, he comes to the investigation with some knowledge of the biblical languages. Because of this limitation, attention is given to those who are fluent in the language, particularly Casey and Black..[170] However, the research does not exclusively examine those traits of the Aramaic language, but it also peers into the theological underpinnings so prevalent in the earliest resources of the church (i.e., creeds, hymns, confessions, etc.).

Seventh and considering the last delimitation, a cumulative approach will be afforded in the research. As is the case with historical studies, the best one can offer is a strong probability that x or y was true. The same is the case for this research. However, the more a text shows signs of early Semitic

---

[168] Barnett, *The Birth of Christianity,* 31.

[169] Keener, *The Historical Jesus of the Gospels*, 158; Witherington, III., *The Christology of Jesus*, 16-17; R. Reisner, *Jesus als Lehrer*, 507; and Barnett, *The Birth of Christianity,* 114.

[170] Bruce Chilton is also an expert in Aramaic.

material, the greater the probability that can be given to the text as arising from earlier sources that predate the Gospel texts.

State of Current Research/Precedent Literature

Several books have paved the way for this research. While numerous other resources will prove beneficial to the task ahead, the books found in this section are among the most prevalent and important for the research that is to be conducted. They also portray the foundation upon which this study is built. The methods for this work have been extracted largely through the criteria established in these sources and others like them. It will seek to collaborate and compile the Christology, Aramaic traits, and terminology so predominant in the early church.

Black, Matthew. *An Aramaic Approach to the Gospels and Acts.* Third Edition. Eugene, OR: Wipf & Stock, 1967.

Matthew Black was a biblical scholar of Scottish descent. He served as the first editor of *New Testament Studies* and, in addition to Kurt Aland and Bruce Metzger among others, served on the committee that established the Greek text used by the *Novum Testamentum Graece.* In his book *An Aramaic Approach to the Gospel and Acts,* Black uses his expertise in Aramaic and other biblical languages to investigate the Aramaic nature of the Gospels and Acts. His work is divided into four parts with individual chapters within each part. The first part lays out the approach used for his study, particularly focusing on the linguistic and textual approaches, while also noting the importance of the Aramaic Targums. The second part discusses the syntax, grammar, and vocabulary of the Aramaic language. It is here that Black's work excels. He describes the structure used primarily by the Aramaic of Jesus's day along with distinguishing marks that set it apart from other biblical languages. The third part delves into the poetic form of Aramaic and how it can serve as a factor in distinguishing Semitisms. The fourth part denotes the variants that can result from translating an Aramaic source into Greek. While Black's work may hold a few problem areas, by far it stands out as the face of Aramaic studies. Black's work is invaluable to this research as he denotes the characteristics and traits of the Aramaic language which serve as one of the bases to test early Semitisms.

Keener, Craig S. *The Historical Jesus of the Gospels.* Grand Rapids, MI: Eerdmans, 2009.

Craig Keener is no stranger to academics involved in theological and NT studies. A voluminous writer who is extremely important to NT studies, Keener is a professor of New Testament at Asbury Theological Seminary in Willmore, Kentucky. He has written other such works such as *The Gospel of*

Matthew: A Socio-Rhetorical Commentary, The Gospel of John: A Commentary, and a multi-volume series on the book of Acts.

In his work *The Historical Jesus of the Gospels,* Keener conducts a historical examination of the life of Jesus of Nazareth in the canonical Gospels and contends that they are historically reliable..[171] Due to the nature of his research, his work becomes useful for this project. But additionally, Keener's preference for the Jewish context of Jesus's life proves extremely useful..[172] Keener's work first examines the views of Jesus that have not proven useful or beneficial. This includes the view that Jesus was only a sage and/or a cynic. The second part of the work peers into the character of the Gospels themselves and contends that they meet the criteria of historical *bioi.* Here, he also explores the sources behind the Gospels, the process and flow of oral traditions, and notetaking in antiquity. The third section of the work, by far the largest, explores what can be known about Jesus of Nazareth from the canonical Gospels. *The Historical Jesus of the Gospels* proves an invaluable resource for this project.

Casey, Maurice. *Jesus of Nazareth: An Independent Historian's Account of His Life and Teaching.* New York, NY: T&T Clark, 2010.

Maurice Casey is the Emeritus Professor of New Testament Languages and Literature at the University of Nottingham in the United Kingdom. He is fluent in the Aramaic language which makes him a formidable force in NT studies. In a private correspondence with Craig Keener and Ben Witherington, both suggested referencing Maurice Casey's works in any work engaging Semitic studies. In his work *Jesus of Nazareth,* Casey approaches historical Jesus studies from what he terms a "perspective of an independent historian".[173] because he does not belong to a particular religious system. He uses his expertise in Aramaic and other biblical languages to construct his depiction of

---

171 Keener, *Historical Jesus of the Gospels,* xxxii.

172 Ibid., xxxv.

173 Casey, *Jesus of Nazareth,* 2.

Jesus of Nazareth. His work largely matches the evangelical interpretation with a few exceptions, especially his view of the resurrection..[174]

Casey, Maurice. *An Aramaic Approach to Q: Sources for the Gospels of Matthew and Luke.* Cambridge, UK: Cambridge University Press, 2002.

As previously noted, Casey is the Emeritus Professor of New Testament Languages and Literature at the University of Nottingham in the United Kingdom. He is fluent in all the biblical languages (i.e., Aramaic, Greek, and Hebrew). In *An Aramaic Approach to Q,* Casey uses the same focus on the Aramaic literary sources behind Q that he did for the Gospel of Mark in *Aramaic Sources of Mark's Gospel.* The only drawback to his work is that he does not consider the theological Semitic aspects of Matthew's Gospel and only examines three areas: Scribes and Pharisees (Matt. 23:23-36), John the Baptist (Matt. 11:2-19), and Jesus's exorcisms (Matt. 12:22-32). Nonetheless, Casey's methodology and his approach to these texts have helped shape the methodology of this work. Additionally, his insights into the texts he covers will serve extremely useful when this work approaches them.

Bauckham, Richard. *Jesus and the Eyewitnesses: The Gospels as Eyewitness Testimony.* Second Edition. Grand Rapids, MI: Eerdmans, 2017.

Richard Bauckham is the Professor Emeritus of New Testament Studies at the University of St. Andrews in Scotland. Additionally, he serves as a senior scholar at Ridley Hall at Cambridge and a fellow of both the British Academy and the Royal Society of Edinburgh. He has written voluminously including such works as *Jesus and the God of Israel, Gospel Women,* and *Jesus: A Very Short Introduction.* His book *Jesus and the Eyewitnesses* argues that the period between the historical Jesus and the finished product of the canonical Gospels was spanned by the "continuing presence and testimony of the eyewitnesses, who remained the authoritative sources of their traditions until their deaths, then the usual ways of thinking of oral tradition are not appropriate at all.".[175] Bauckham, in traditional style, pens a masterful work that affords a variety of reasons to hold to the historical validity behind the Gospels' preserved message. The book provides extensive coverage of Semitic eyewitness testimony and their impact on the finished written Gospels. While this writer

[174] Casey holds that Jesus's resurrection was a spiritual event rather than a physical one. He believes that the disciples experienced real visions of Jesus, but that Jesus's body remained in a criminal's grave likened to John Dominick Crossan's approach. Ibid., 497.

[175] Bauckham, *Jesus and the Eyewitnesses,* 8.

differs from Bauckham on a few issues,[176] his work will serve extremely useful when dealing with the texts, especially concerning oral tradition, early written texts, and the history between Jesus and the Gospels.

Witherington, III, Ben. *The Christology of Jesus.* Minneapolis, MN: Fortress, 1990.

Ben Witherington, III is a world-renown scholar who is the Amos Professor of New Testament at Asbury Theological Seminary in Wilmore, Kentucky. He has also taught at Ashland Theological Seminary, Vanderbilt University, Duke Divinity School, and Gordon-Conwell. He has written over 50 books including the *Indelible Image, The Jesus Quest,* and *The Paul Quest.* Witherington has been interviewed on numerous radio stations and has been seen on the History Channel, NBC, ABC, CBS, CNN, the Discovery Channel, A&E, and the PAX Network.

In *Christology of Jesus,* Witherington uses historical and theological data to describe how Jesus most likely interpreted himself and how the earliest church understood Christology.[177] Jesus's own Christology is exposed by his relationships with John the Baptist, the Pharisees, the Romans, and his own disciples. The deeds and messages of Jesus are also shown to express the self-understanding of Jesus. As Semitic Christology is a major focus of this work, Witherington's book will serve as a useful tool of engagement.

Barnett, Paul. *The Birth of Christianity: The First Twenty Years.* Grand Rapids, MI; Cambridge, UK: Eerdmans, 2005.

Paul Barnett is a Visiting Professor in Ancient History at Macquarie University. He teaches at Moore College in Sydney, Australia, and at Regent College in Vancouver, British Columbia. He has written other works including *Paul: Missionary of Jesus* and *Finding the Historical Christ.* In his book *The Birth of Christianity,* Barnett argues that the origin of Christianity is intricately linked with early Christology.[178] As Richard Bauckham has noted in his works,[179] Barnett also concurs that the earliest Christology was the highest Christology. In fact, he shows throughout his work that a high Christology came about in the "immediate aftermath of Jesus."[180] *The Birth of Christianity* traces early Christology's impact on the most primitive teachings of the church. Special

176 Primarily his view of the authorship of the Gospel of John.

177 Witherington, *Christology of Jesus,* 2.

178 Barnett, *The Birth of Christianity,* 8.

179 Bauckham, *Jesus and the God of Israel,* x, 235.

180 Barnett, *The Birth of Christianity,* 8.

attention is given to Christology's impact on Q.[181] Because of his focus on early Christology and source material, Barnett's work will prove beneficial for this research.

Wilcox, Max. *The Semitisms of Acts.* Oxford, UK: Oxford University Press, 1965.

Max Wilcox's book *Semitisms of Acts* is a classic exposition examining the Semitisms found in the book of Acts, as the name implies. His work was originally presented as a thesis for his Ph.D. degree at the University of Edinburgh in 1955. Wilcox denotes the presence of the OT in the book of Acts, compares the LXX and the diction in Acts—granting special attention to Septuagintalisms in Acts and liturgical/apologetic factors, notes the Semitic vocabulary in Acts[182] and exposes other Semitic characteristics,[183] before exploring the source material, creedal elements, and Semitisms in the composition of Acts. While Wilcox examines the sermon summaries of Acts, numerous parallels can be found between the sayings of Jesus in Matthew's Gospel and the findings of Wilcox. Wilcox's methodology is especially beneficial to this work.

Keener, Craig S. *Christobiography: Memory, History, and the Reliability of the Gospels.* Grand Rapids, MI: Eerdmans, 2019.

As previously noted, Keener has written voluminous works on the history of Jesus and the early church. He writes another masterpiece with his book *Christobiography.* In this work, Keener draws attention to the genre of the Gospel texts and links them with ancient biographies, also known as *bioi.*[184] *Christobiography* is divided into five sections. The first part describes the nature of ancient biographies, and what writers and readers expected from the literature. The second part links the historical veracity of the genre, even though some shaping of the texts was permitted. The third part labels the range and deviation that were allowable for ancient *bioi.* The fourth part answers the objections often posed for the Gospels being ancient biographies. Finally, the fifth and final part is the most pertinent to the research at hand. In this section, Keener articulates how the memories of Jesus were preserved and how oral traditions became oral history. His research on oral traditions and how they

181 Ibid., 138-149.

182 He also calls this "Semitic residue." Wilcox, *Semitisms of Acts,* 87.

183 Such as word order, verbs, pronouns, idioms, mistranslations, and other traits also noted by Black in *Aramaic Approach to the Gospels and Acts.*

184 Keener, *Christobiography,* 1.

were eventually preserved by the written text provides ample bounty for the task at hand.

Cullmann, Oscar. *Christology of the New Testament.* Translated by Shirley C. Guthrie and Charles A. M. Hall. Waco, TX: Baylor University Press, 1959, 2018.

Oscar Cullmann was a professor of Greek, New Testament, and Early Christianity at the University of Strasbourg, the University of Basel, and the Sorbonne in Paris, France. Around the time of his death at the tender age of 96, Cullmann was awarded for his ecumenical work by the World Council of Churches. Cullmann argues that the oldest formulas are expressed in Christological terms..[185] Thus, the earliest theology of the Christian movement was exclusively focused on Christology..[186] Throughout his work, he examines the Christological titles of Christ and how they relate to the work of Christ now, in the future, and while he was on Earth. Furthermore, he notes how the titles relate to the pre-existent nature of Christ. Cullmann's work proves beneficial to show how the early Christological titles can be used to detect early material that precedes the written Gospel texts.

Dunn, James D. G. *Jesus Remembered: Christianity in the Making.* Volume One. Grand Rapids, MI; Cambridge, UK: Eerdmans, 2003.

The late James D. G. Dunn was the Lightfoot Professor of Divinity at the University of Durham, United Kingdom. He is also known as one of the foremost thinkers in biblical scholarship. Dunn also penned such works as *The Theology of Paul the Apostle, Christology in the Making,* and *Jesus and the Spirit.* In *Jesus Remembered,* Dunn explores how the early traditions can help one understand more about the historical Jesus. He assesses five areas of early traditions and the historical Jesus: 1) faith and the historical Jesus, 2) the sources and traditions behind the Gospels, 3) the mission of Jesus, 4) Jesus's self-understanding, and 5) the climactic conclusion to Jesus's life and ministry. The socio-scientific methods used by Dunn in addition to his historical-critical methodology and engagement with the Dead Sea Scrolls and other early materials make Dunn's work an essential resource for this work.

Summary of the Design

Before concluding the proposal, a brief summary of the research's design should be noted before moving forward. In each subsequent chapter, a large pericope of Matthew's Gospel will be investigated. The Sermon of the Mount will be the focus of the second chapter. The Beatitudes and the Lord's

---

[185] Cullmann, *Christology of the New Testament,* 1.

[186] Ibid., 2-3.

Prayer will serve as subsections within the chapter as each will be examined according to the methodology previously given. After the texts have been properly evaluated, a color assignment will be assigned to each Scripture. Then, the overall weight of the Sermon on the Mount's relationship with early Semitic material will be measured.

The same will hold true for succeeding chapters. The third chapter will investigate three parables of Jesus in Matthew's Gospel. The Parable of the Harvest, Parable of the Wise and Foolish Young Bridesmaids, and the Parable of the Compassionate Employer will be assigned a color before the parables are reviewed. Like the previous chapter, a final assessment of the parables' relationship with early material will be gauged. The fourth chapter will consider the Son of Man sayings found in Matthew's Gospel. While numerous Son of Man sayings is found in the First Gospel, special attention will be given to Jesus's teaching of exorcism and the unpardonable sin in Matthew 12:22-40 and the coming of the Son of Man given in the Olivet Discourse in Matthew 24:27-44.

The last two passages of Scripture will stand alone as they are not linked with an overarching message or segment of Scripture. The fifth chapter will examine Peter's confession in Matthew 16:13-23 using the same criteria used for previous passages in the research. A color will be assigned to the text before examining Jesus's interaction with John the Baptist in Matthew 11:2-19 in the same chapter. A brief conclusion will follow the five major chapters which will provide any definitive assessments, conclusions, and deductions acquired. The final chapter will also examine future areas of research. It will also note how this research affects one's understanding of early source material and how this could benefit modern apologists and theologians seeking to defend the inspiration and authority of the Gospel texts along with defending the validity of Jesus's life and ministry

CHAPTER TWO THE SERMON ON THE MOUNT

The Sermon on the Mount has been recognized as one of the greatest messages ever given. The *Atlantic* asked Robert Schlesinger of *US News* and 19 other individuals to rank the greatest speeches ever given. Without debate, all 20 individuals selected the Sermon on the Mount as the greatest of all time. Even though an agnostic, Schlesinger confesses, "For sheer reach and influence, it's hard to argue against Jesus' Sermon on the Mount. It's perhaps the central teaching of one of the world's great religions, still studied and recounted not just in academia and religious institutions but by lay people all around the world.".[187] Charles Quarles would agree, noting that "No sermon ever preached has been more significant to the Christian church than the Sermon on the Mount.".[188] Thus, the significance of the Sermon on the Mount cannot be overstated as individuals from Christian and other worldviews have been influenced by its message.

While the Sermon on the Mount has had significant influence, a couple of questions must be considered concerning its structure before exploring the antiquity of its material. The latter weighs more in importance to the cause of this study more so than the former. First, one of the bigger questions concerning the Sermon on the Mount is whether the teachings found in the sermon are part of one long message or a collection of sayings highlighting various messages given by Jesus.

From the structure of Matthew's version of the Sermon on the Mount and that of Luke's Sermon on the Plain, it appears that the entire message comprises small chunks.[189] of material collected in a larger body. D. A. Carson holds that scholars from the schools of form and redaction criticism have held that the material is a composite product..[190] However, a problem comes with

---

[187] Robert Schlesinger, "Greatest Speech Ever?," *USNews.com* (Sept. 20, 2013), https://www.usnews.com/opinion/blogs/robert-schlesinger/2013/09/20/greatest-speech-ever-jesus-christ-pericles-abraham-lincoln-or-bluto.

[188] Charles Quarles, "Sermon on the Mount," in *Holman Christian Standard Bible: Harmony of the Gospels* (Nashville, TN: Holman Bible Publishers, 2007), 299.

[189] These small chunks could possibly represent summaries of individual messages.

[190] "Form and redaction criticism have regularly viewed this arrangement of material, like that of the other four major discourses of Jesus in Matthew, as a composite product, a collection of shorter sayings of Jesus from various original contexts." Craig Blomberg, *Matthew*, The New American Commentary, vol. 22 (Nashville: Broadman & Holman Publishers, 1992), 96.

Matthew 7:28 which appears to claim that the message was given in one sitting, saying, "When Jesus had finished saying these things, the crowds were astonished at his teaching" (Matt. 7:28). But is such an interpretation necessary? Not necessarily. If Jesus were to have preached a number of sermons in the same location, then the people would have heard the messages that comprised the Sermon on the Mount. This is comparable to a preacher preaching a series of messages in one's church. The main thrust of the individual messages could be collected to make a composite sketch of the series. This also holds support with the writing practices of the time.

Ancient authors of *bioi* may also hold a clue to the conundrum. It was the practice of ancient biographical writers to condense material due to numerous factors—most prevalent, perhaps, was the cost of writing material which could range from around $1,000 to $2,000 for a work the size of the Gospel of Mark..[191] Condensing material would have been natural for the time since even the Targums used the same practice..[192] The practice of condensing materials is often called *compression* which is a tactic that was also used by the ancient historian Plutarch (AD 46-119)..[193] Thus, the condensing of Jesus's messages in a composite collection is not something that would have been out of the ordinary in the creation of a first-century *bios* of the life of Jesus of Nazareth.

Second, if the message comprises various summaries of circuit messages presented in the area, then one must ask why Luke's Sermon on the Plain differs from Matthew's Sermon on the Mount. If there was a body of ancient literature that derived from the lips of the historical Jesus, then why are there differences between the two presentations in the Gospels of Luke and Matthew? The differences in the two presentations will be given further consideration throughout the investigation. However, for the time being, it is important to note that the teachings of Jesus as found in Matthew's Sermon on the Mount are found scattered throughout the Gospel of Luke. Some have proposed that since only four of Matthew's beatitudes are paralleled in Luke (Luke 6:20b-33), then he must have used another source that was independent

---

[191] John H. Walton and Craig S. Keener, "Introduction to the Gospels and Acts," *NIV Cultural Backgrounds Study Bible* (Grand Rapids, IL: Zondervan, 2016), 1603.

[192] Craig L. Blomberg, *The Historical Reliability of the Gospels,* 2nd ed (Nottingham, UK; Downers Grove, IL: Apollos; IVP Academic, 2007), 182.

[193] Michael Licona defines *compression* as the practice of "[portraying] events over a shorter period of time than the actual time it took for those events to occur, the author has compressed the story." Michael R. Licona, *Why are There Differences in the Gospels?: What We Can Learn from Ancient Biography* (Oxford, UK: Oxford University Press, 2017), 20.

of Matthew's..[194] However, it is just as likely that the two evangelists drew from different parts of the same previously existing material, especially if Hagner is correct in that the early Christian community committed the entire material to memory..[195]

A solution to this problem is found in the writing style of Matthew. Matthew appears to be more topically inclined as compared to the chronological methodology of Luke..[196] For instance, Luke notes that the Twelve disciples had already been called and established prior to the Sermon (Luke 5:1-11, 27-32; 6:12-19), whereas Matthew does not mention the calling of the Twelve disciples until much later in his book (Matt. 9:9-13; 10:1-15). However, Matthew does mention the calling of the first disciples—i.e., Peter, James, John, and Andrew—prior to the Sermon on the Mount (Matt. 4:18-22). Thus, Matthew presents an early Christian didactic composed of the essentials of Jesus's theological and ethical standards..[197] Hagner notes that while questions exist about the compositional structure and flow of the sermon, the "essential structure of the beatitudes can indeed go back to Jesus himself.".[198] This is not to say that Jesus did not present the material that he did when he spoke on the hillside that day. It is highly likely that Jesus preached his sermons on more than one occasion. Tatian composed his harmony of the Gospels, called the *Diatessaron.* According to Tatian, Jesus began preaching his message

---

[194] Hagner argues, "It may be well be that each evangelist follows an independent, though overlapping, oral tradition. This material, as it is found in both of the Gospels, exhibits content and form that the early Church very likely would have committed to memory." Donald A. Hagner, *Matthew 1–13*, Word Biblical Commentary, vol. 33A (Dallas: Word, Incorporated, 1993), 89.

[195] Ibid.

[196] While Luke occasionally presents his material in topical form, he is committed to a more orderly account of the life of Jesus from the first words of his Gospel. Luke states, "So it also seemed good to me, since I have carefully investigated everything from the very first, to write to you in an orderly sequence, most honorable Theophilus, so that you may know the certainty of the things about which you have been instructed" (Luke 1:3-4). See also James D. G. Dunn, *The Oral Gospel Tradition* (Grand Rapids, MI; Cambridge, UK: Eerdmans, 2013), 321.

[197] Dunn holds that due to the Sermon on the Mount material being scattered throughout the Gospel of Luke, that it speaks to Matthew's gathering of Jesus's teaching material to place it in one location "from the remembered teachings of Jesus, and to frame it in a way that made it more easily rememberable by those who taught in turn." Dunn, *Oral Gospel Tradition,* 321.

[198] Hagner, *Matthew 1-13,* WBC, 90.

in the mountains, as indicated by Luke (Luke 6:12-13),[199] but then later came down to a plain lower on the mountain to accommodate the crowds. Tatian could possibly be correct in his assessment, but it not essential that he was. An evidentialist attempting to show the historical grounds for a teaching is not required to be contained within one apologetic parameter but can adopt multiple varieties in demonstrating one's case.[200] The best answer is that Jesus preached a variety of messages in the region which were summarized and compiled in the modern form. It is not beyond the scope of possibility that Jesus preached messages that included both the material found in Luke's Gospel and Matthew's Gospel. These messages were summarized[201] and compiled into the current sermons preserved in Matthew and Luke, with Matthew and Luke focusing on different messages and/or concepts within the overall series. Certainly, one must not be committed to that perspective. It could have easily been just as acceptable for Matthew and Luke to compile the messages from various stages in Jesus's ministry. However, this model holds to Matthew 7:28 which states, "When Jesus had finished saying these things, the crowds were amazed at his teaching, because he taught as one who had authority, and not as their teachers of the law" (Matt. 7:28, NIV).[202]

The Jesus Seminar grants a mixed depiction of the Matthean beatitudes. On the one hand, they grade verses 3–4 and verse 6 in the pink, the second highest rating.[203] Verses 10–12 are listed in gray. Oddly, verses 5 and 7–9 are listed in black.[204] The Seminar states that they nearly rated the first few verses in red but thought that Matthew incorporated his own virtues rather

---

[199] Luke's presentation is interesting in that he places the calling of the disciples around this period (Luke 6:13-16).

[200] Craig Blomberg asserts, "As the 'evidentialist' approach to Christian apologetics stresses, one can apply widely accepted historical criteria to demonstrate the general trustworthiness of the Gospels." He later states that room exists for both the evidentialist and presuppositionalist approaches when defending the message of the NT. Blomberg, *The Historical Reliability of the Gospels,* 35.

[201] Possibly even at times being simply a one sentence summary of the message.

[202] Scriptures noted as NIV come from the *New International Version* (Grand Rapids, MI: Biblica, 2011).

[203] Robert W. Funk, Roy W. Hoover, and the Jesus Seminar, *The Five Gospels: What Did Jesus Really Say?* (New York, NY: Harper Collins, 1983), 138.

[204] Ibid.

than socioeconomic reasons.[205] The Seminar's logic seems a bit questionable. Since Jesus most assuredly focused on religious virtues, one cannot rightly dismiss his emphasis on religious and ethical matters. While Jesus concerned himself with the plight of the poor, his primary focus was on the kingdom of God and the divine eschatological activities that were prominent in his teachings.[206] Their dismissal of Jesus's emphasis on social concerns makes it even more bizarre that they would completely reject the authenticity of verses 5, 7–9 since those verses speak of the importance of gentleness, mercy, and working for peace. However, it should be noted that Jesus taught that the kingdom had come to earth. Therefore, the teachings of Jesus may have emphasized both the spiritual dynamics of theology and ethics while also incorporating socioeconomic insights as well. Thus, to say that the teachings of Jesus were only interested in one area over the other is a bit myopic, especially considering the exquisite complexities of Jesus's theological perspective.

But the main question of this chapter is whether the Sermon on the Mount shows signs of ancient, pre-existing material that predates the Gospel text. As noted in the previous chapter, seven methodologies will be used to test the early nature of the Sermon on the Mount. Two areas of the Sermon on the Mount will be analyzed for their early Semitic residue: The Beatitudes in Matthew 5:1-12 and the Lord's Prayer in Matthew 6:5-13. After each segment is analyzed, a color assignment will be given to the pericope as determined by the strength of its connection with early material.

The Beatitudes (Matt. 5:1-12)

The first passage of Scripture to be examined in the Sermon on the Mount is the Beatitudes, so named after an OT literary style that describes the blessings or happiness that comes from following God's ethical commands in anticipation of his future eschatological reign.[207] Jesus indicates that the most unlikely of individuals are blessed, including the "poor in spirit" (5:3), "those who mourn" (5:4), "the humble" (5:5), "those who hunger and thirst for righteousness" (5:6), "the merciful" (5:7), "pure in heart" (5:8), "the peacemakers" (5:9), "the persecuted" (5:10), and those who are insulted (5:11).

---

[205] Ibid., 139.

[206] This will become more evident in Chapter 5.

[207] Craig S. Keener, *IVP Bible Background Commentary: New Testament* (Downers Grove, IL: IVP Academic, 1993), 55-56.

In a time where zealots called for revolution,[208] the words of Jesus must have seemed radical in a different sense. But do the classic Beatitudes hold any Semitic residue that points to its pre-Gospel tradition, or is this merely the creation of the evangelist? Applying the methodologies previously set forth, it is now time to test the early Semitic nature of the Beatitudes.

Unique Rabbinic Concepts

K. C. Hanson argues that "a good deal of what is found in the Sermon on the Mount can also be found in the Talmud, not merely the Golden Rule."[209] Hanson makes this case for good reason. Clearly, Jesus had a great deal of knowledge of the Talmud and rabbinic practices.[210] Matthew points out that Jesus assumed the role of a rabbinic teacher by sitting, even noting that the disciples came to him after assuming the seated position.[211] Matthew writes, "When he saw the crowds, he went up on the mountain, and after he sat down, his disciples came to him" (Matt. 5:1).

The similarities of the Sermon on the Mount are not only found with the teaching posture of Jesus. When one examines the content of the message, the commonalities of Jesus's message with the Talmud becomes expressly clear. Later, the Greek term μακάριος will be given attention. But for the time being, it should be noted that the term μακάριος and Jesus's expressions of hope are connected back to the Jewish understanding of the blessed hope found in Isaiah

---

[208] Josephus indicates that the Zealots were a band of radical Jewish revolutionaries who called for the expulsion of the Roman Empire from Israel by force. Josephus writes, "At the first this quarrelsome temper caught hold of private families, who could not agree among themselves; after which those people that were the dearest to one another, brake through all restraints with regard to each other, and everyone associated with those of his own opinion, and already began to stand in opposition to another, so that seditions arose everywhere…" Josephus, *Wars of the Jews* 4.132-133a, in *The Works of Josephus,* updated ed, William Whiston, trans (Peabody, MA: Hendrickson, 1987), 670.; See also Mark Allan Powell, "Zealots," *HarperCollins Bible Dictionary,* revised ed (New York, NY: HarperCollins, 2011), 1123.

[209] K. C. Hanson, *Jesus and the Message of the New Testament,* Fortress Classics in Biblical Studies, (Minneapolis, MN: Fortress Press, 2002), 20.

[210] To be fair, the emphasis on the OT by both Jesus and the rabbinic teachers provides another dimension to their similarity. The Beatitudes contains many OT references.

[211] Arnold G. Fruchtenbaum, *Yeshua: The Life of Messiah from a Messianic Jewish Perspective,* vol. 2 (San Antonio, TX: Ariel, 2018), 277.

61.[212] Similar expressions of this Jewish interpretation are found in 11QMelch 2.4, 6, 9, 13, 17, 20; *Targum Pseudo-Jonathan*; and *Midrash Ekhah* on Lamentations 3:5.

Another intriguing similarity to the Talmud is found in Matthew 5:7. In that passage, Jesus says, "Blessed are the merciful, for they will be shown mercy" (Matt. 5:7). Rabbi Gamaliel expressed a similar sentiment, saying, "He who is merciful to others, mercy is shown to him by heaven."[213] Furthermore, the Mishnah says, "So long as you are merciful, He will have mercy on you … When you are not merciful, the Omnipresent will not have mercy on you."[214] It is interesting to note that Gamaliel uses the term heaven rather than God which is also found in Jesus's teachings. Furthermore, other aspects of Jesus's message are found in the Talmud. Parallels can be found between Jesus's teaching on persecution, where he says, "Blessed are those who are persecuted because of righteousness, for the king of heaven is theirs" (Matt. 5:10), with the teaching of Rabbi Abbahu, who said, "A man should always strive to be rather of the persecuted than of the persecutors."[215] Even Jesus's form of argumentation found in Matthew 5-7 fits within a rabbinic halakhic didactic of the early rabbis.[216] Some scholars have even argued that Jesus's Beatitudes show how one can remain within the limits of Judaism itself.[217] While the latter is debatable, it is beyond a reasonable doubt that Jesus's Beatitudes find a home within the early rabbinic community.

While similarities can be found in Jesus's message in the Sermon on the Mount with the Talmud, particular differences arise in Jesus's blessing of the poor, his take on divorce, turning the other cheek, and the call for loving one's enemies.[218] D. A. Carson adds that if one were to "Read any fifty pages

---

[212] Darrell L. Bock and Benjamin I. Simpson, *Jesus According to Scripture: Restoring the Portrait from the Gospels,* 2nd ed (Grand Rapids, MI: Baker Academic, 2017), 128.

[213] *b. Shabbat* 151b.

[214] *y. Baba Qamma* 8.7.

[215] *b. Baba Kamma* 93a. While Rabbi Abbahu came far after Jesus, his rabbinical teaching still illustrates the accepted rabbinical teaching of the day with that of Jesus's.

[216] Carson, *EBC,* 126; Gary A. Tuttle, "The Sermon on the Mount: Its Wisdom Affinities and Their Relation to Its Structure," *JETS* 20 (1977): 213-230.

[217] Maurice Casey, *Jesus of Nazareth: An Independent Historian's Account of His Life and Teaching* (New York, NY: T&T Clark, 2010), 40.

[218] Hanson, *Jesus and the Message of the New Testament,* 20; Joachim Jeremias, *Jesus and the Message of the New Testament* (Minneapolis, MN: Fortress, 2002), 20.

of the Babylonian Talmud and compare them with Matthew 5–7 ... [then] it becomes obvious that they are not saying the same things."[219] Furthermore, as will be discussed in further detail in the next section, Jesus makes a connection with the apocalyptic portion of Isaiah.[220] In Isaiah 61 and following, the prophet depicts a time when an anointed one spoke for God.[221] Recognizing this connection was not necessarily unique. However, Jesus's identification with the Anointed One in Isaiah 61 (Luke 4:16-20) makes his interpretation unique.[222]

Noting the similarities found in the Beatitudes and Talmud, one can safely hold that the material finds a connection with early interpretations of Jesus's day. However, there are numerous areas where Jesus diverges from the rabbinical teaching. It is clear that Jesus is not merely accepting rabbinic interpretations at face value. While not in the section of the Beatitudes, Jesus's teaching on divorce and his association with the less favored Rabbi Shammai over the more popular Rabbi Hillel is one such example (Matt. 5:31-32). Thus, with this in mind, one can give a green light to the Beatitudes' connection with a unique take on rabbinic concepts and add 2 points to the new weighted scale.

Early Christological Concepts

At first glance, the Beatitudes may not appear to hold many early Christological concepts, if any at all. However, when mining the depths of the text, then one finds an underlying Christological underpinning. Two areas are of special interest: Jesus's eschatological focus in the Beatitudes and his bipartite connection with the Father. As previously noted, bipartite constructions of Father and Son are among the earliest Christological understandings of the church.[223] When it comes to eschatological language, teachings that indicate Christ's actions over the history of revelation and salvation also depict early Christological understandings.[224] Thus, if the two

---

[219] D. A. Carson, "Matthew," in *The Expositor's Bible Commentary: Matthew, Mark, Luke*, vol. 8, Frank E. Gabelein, ed (Grand Rapids, MI: Zondervan Publishing House, 1984), 126.

[220] Fruchtenbaum, *Yeshua,* vol. 2, 280.

[221] Gary Smith, *Isaiah 40-66*, New American Commentary, vol. 15b (Nashville, TN: Broadman & Holman Publishers, 2009), 628.

[222] See the next section on Early Christological Concepts for more information.

[223] Cullmann, *The Earliest Christian Confessions,* 41.

[224] Cullmann, *Christology of the New Testament,* 9.

proposed Christological themes are found in the Beatitudes, then it can be said that the *logia* hold a connection to themes found in the earliest church.

Most assuredly, Jesus's ethical commands completely contradicted the commonly held beliefs of the age. A revolutionary spirit that desired the expulsion of the Romans from Israel was predominant in Israel at the time that Jesus lived.[225] The NT notes the desire of the people to appoint Jesus as a political ruler (John 6:15). Earlier in Matthew's Gospel, the evangelist focuses on Herod's attempt to execute the Messiah for fear that he would usurp his kingdom (Matt. 2:1–12) and the Holy Family's subsequent escape to Egypt (Matt. 2:13–15). The evangelist has already depicted the distinction between the current political foci and the future eschatological kingdom. As one engages the contents of the Beatitudes, one finds that the Beatitudes go much deeper than a set of ethical dos and don'ts.

Eschatology was a hot topic in first-century Israel. The people of Jesus's day associated resurrection with the eschaton. As N. T. Wright asserted, "the second-Temple Jews would see [the resurrection] in terms of the apocalyptic climax of their own history."[226] The idea that Yahweh would bring about a new kingdom for his people at the end of the age was not new concept, as it was the common belief of the day.[227] Yet the Beatitudes teach that, in some sense, the kingdom of God has already come. Jesus seems to suggest that entrance to the kingdom was readily available, saying, "Blessed are the poor in spirit, for the kingdom of heaven is theirs" (Matt. 5:3). The verb ἐστῖν is in the present, active, indicative case, indicating a person's present citizenship of the kingdom. Yet, as was clear in Jesus's day as well as the modern age, this kingdom is not fully actualized. Interestingly, R. T. France points out that the rewards spelled out in the Beatitudes, outside of verses 3 and 10, are in the future tense which suggests that the "best is yet to come, when God's kingdom is finally established and its subjects enter into their inheritance."[228] Jesus's message finds a correlation with the apocryphal *Psalms of Solomon* which describes God's vindication of the "poor in spirit." Ultimately, according to the writers of the *Psalms of Solomon,* God would "reveal the deeds of the men-pleasers, the deeds of such a one with laughter and derision; that the pious may count righteous the judgment of their God, when sinners are removed from

---

[225] Josephus, *Wars of the Jews* 4.132-133a, 670.

[226] N. T. Wright, *The Resurrection of the Son of God,* Christian Origins and the Question of God, vol. 3 (Minneapolis, MN: Fortress, 2003), 26.

[227] Ibid., 205.

[228] R. T. France, *Matthew,* Tyndale New Testament Commentaries (Grand Rapids, MI; Leicester, UK: Eerdmans; IVP, 1985), 109.

before the righteous."[229] Not only is the entrance of the kingdom unique in Jesus's eschatology in the Beatitudes, the person by whom this kingdom is ushered into the world is also that is particularly pertinent to one's Christological understanding of the passage.

A Father-Son bipartite formulation underlies Jesus's allusions in the text, as Jesus implied that he was the One who was in the process of delivering the Father's kingdom to earth, as predicted in Isaiah 61.[230] In fact, the Beatitudes are structured around a person's entry into this eschatological kingdom, contrasting the behaviors of a citizen of God's kingdom with that of a citizen of the world.[231] The early church may have used the Sermon on the Mount, particularly the Beatitudes, as an early pre-baptismal catechism for new believers. Jeremias suggests that the Matthean sermon was directed toward Jewish converts to Christianity, whereas the Lukan parallel was focused on new Gentile Christian converts, which could in part explain the differences in the two sermons.[232]

Getting back to the connection with Isaiah 61, it is important to give a brief word on the chapter in question. Isaiah 61 finds itself within a larger framework found within Isaiah 60 through 63, in which Yahweh describes the salvation that would be brought through an Anointed One, the transformation that would come to Zion, and the destruction of the wicked.[233] The larger context of oracles delivers four messages: 1) The glory of God will come to Zion (60:1–22), 2) Yahweh's Anointed One would announce God's favor (61:1–11), 3) the transformation of Zion (62:1–12), and Yahweh's judgment that would be brought upon wicked individuals and nations (63:1–6). These chapters also note that Israel and her children would be regathered (60:4, 9; 62:10), Yahweh would be glorified (60:16, 21; 61:3), Zion would also be glorified (60:7, 13; 62:2–3, 7), Jerusalem would be renamed (60:14, 18; 61:3;

---

229 *Psalms of Solomon* 4.8–9, in R. H. Charles, ed, *The Apocrypha and Pseudepigrapha of the Old Testament in English,* G. Buchanan Gray, trans (Oxford, UK: Clarendon, 1913), http://wesley.nnu.edu/sermons-essays-books/noncanonical-literature/noncanonical-literature-ot-pseudepigrapha/the-psalms-of-solomon/.

230 Fruchtenbaum, *Yeshua,* vol. 2, 280.

231 France, *Matthew,* TNTC, 109. This contrast would be later picked up by Augustine in his *City of God.*

232 Jeremias, *Jesus and the Message of the New Testament,* 29.

233 Smith, *Isaiah 40-66*, NAC, 607.

62:4, 12), and Yahweh's judgment would come on the day of his wrath (60:12; 61:2; 63:4–6).[234]

Of special interest is the work of the Anointed One in chapter 61.[235] The Anointed One in Isaiah 61:1–3 parallels the work of the Servant of the Yahweh in Isaiah 49:8–9[236] where the prophet says,

> This is what the Lord says: 'I will answer you in a time of favor and I will help you in the day of salvation. I will keep you, and I will appoint you to be a covenant for the people, to restore the land, to make them possess the desolate inheritances, saying to the prisoners, 'Come out,' and to those who are in darkness, 'Show yourselves.' They will feed along the pathways, and their pastures will be on all the barren heights."'

Throughout chapter 61, the Anointed One is the prominent speaker. The Anointed One proclaims,

> The Spirit of the Lord GOD is on me, because the LORD has anointed me to bring good news to the poor. He has sent me to heal the brokenhearted, to proclaim liberty to the captives and freedom to the prisoners; to proclaim the year of the LORD'S favor, and the day of our God's vengeance; to comfort all who mourn, to provide for those who mourn in Zion; to give them a crown of beauty instead of ashes, festive oil instead of mourning, and splendid clothes instead of despair. And they will be called righteous trees, planted by the LORD to glorify him (Isaiah 61:1–3).

Likened to the Servant of chapters 42 and 49, the Anointed One would heal the brokenhearted, rebuild the cities that were devastated by worldly powers, lead former enemy nations to restore the glory of Zion (61:4–7), judge the wicked, and bless the faithful with an everlasting covenant (61:8–9). Chapter 60 details how Yahweh would enforce the blessings previously announced in chapter 60 and alluded in the Servant of the Yahweh passages.

Due to the comparisons of the Beatitudes and Isaiah 61, Jesus is essentially revealing himself the Anointed One of Isaiah 61 and, more implicitly, to be the Servant of the Yahweh in previous chapters of Isaiah. This

---

234 Ibid., 610.

235 Isaiah 61 will play an important role in the interactions that Jesus holds with the disciples of John the Baptist in Matt. 11:2–19. See Chapter 5 for more details.

236 Smith, *Isaiah 40–66,* NAC, 607.

connection can be found in the numerous parallels found between Isaiah 61 and the Beatitudes.

First, Jesus connects the granting of the kingdom of God to the poor in spirit. Jesus said that the poor in spirit are blessed because they are given the kingdom of God (Matt. 5:3). Likewise, Isaiah notes that the people would be called the "LORD'S priests; they will speak of you as ministers of our God" (Isa. 61:6).

Second, Jesus describes the comfort found in God. Jesus said that those who mourned would be comforted by God (Matt. 5:4). Likewise, Isaiah said that the brokenhearted would be healed, and the captive would be freed (Isa. 61:1).

Third, Jesus said that the humble would inherit the earth (Matt. 5:5). Isaiah contends that the people of God would be given a crown of glory and would be called "righteous trees, planted by the LORD to glorify him" (Isa. 61:3). Fourth, Jesus denotes the blessings of God given to the righteous and the judgment brought against the wicked. Jesus argues those who thirst for righteousness would be filled, that the merciful will receive mercy, the pure in heart will see God, and that the peacemakers would be called the sons of God (Matt. 5:6-9). Isaiah holds that the people of God would be blessed (Isa. 61:9), would be wrapped in salvation (Isa. 61:10), and that the people of God would be rewarded with a "permanent covenant" (Isa. 61:8).

Fourth and finally, Jesus connects God's rectification of wrongs done to the saints of God with the Anointed One's work in Isaiah 61. Jesus draws attention to the persecuted and shows how that kingdom of heaven is theirs (Matt. 5:10-12). Likewise, Isaiah prophesies that "in place of your shame, you will have a double portion; in place of disgrace, they will rejoice over their share. So they will possess double in their land, and eternal joy will be theirs" (Isa. 61:7). Thus, one can comfortably claim that enough parallels are found to claim that Jesus is showing himself to be the Anointed One ushering in the new kingdom. Likewise, this new kingdom, while not fully actualized now, is now upon the world, allowing for a person's citizenship in this divine kingdom. Furthermore, and more importantly to the present task, Jesus connects himself as the ambassador of Yahweh's promises. By connecting himself with the Anointed One of Isaiah 61, he is essentially saying that he would be the instrument by which these eschatological promises would be delivered—as is also noted in Jesus's reading of the same passage at the synagogue in his hometown (Luke 4:17–21)..[237] Thus, one can find a bipartite connection

[237] One would think that Matthew knew of this story when penning the Sermon on the Mount.

(Yahweh-Anointed One) that is quite comparable to the already recognized early Christological themes.

The eschatological focus of the passage in corroboration with the bipartite theme makes the Beatitudes quite compelling. However, it must be noted that the text does not necessarily use any messianic titles. Even still, the messianic concepts are far more numerous in the text than this writer ever considered. As such, one can claim that an early overarching, underlying eschatological Christology is quite prominent in this text. Therefore, this passage receives a green light as it passes the second method. Thus far, the text has fared quite well passing the first two methods. If the text passes two more methods, the passage will enter into the yellow category of this research. But does the text find enough strength to pass it into the yellow or even the green? Time will tell as the study progresses. With the weighted scale, the text scores 5 points for this section, with 7 overall points at this juncture.

Theological Terminology Relating to Early Christological Concepts

The third method examines the theological terminology that is rooted in early Christological concepts. Problematically, there are no Christological titles in the section. If the method only looks for Christological titles alone, then the text is found wanting. However, that does not suggest that Christological themes are not found, as the previous section explained. As previously noted, there is some substance in Jesus's self-identification of himself found within the passage. Thus, while there are no Christological titles, Jesus's self-identification as found in early source material is quite prevalent in the text. Relating to early terminology connecting to Semitic concepts, two words prove useful to explore the early nature of this text—*μακάριος* and *βασιλεία*.

The most prominent word in the Beatitudes is *μακάριος*. The CSB translates *μακάριος* as "blessed" but is translated as "happy" in other translations such as the *Good News Bible*. The term is probably the Greek translation of the Hebrew *yrva* which denotes someone who should be congratulated because of one's mental and emotive state.[238] The term is used in the *2 Enoch* 52 where blessings and curses are spelled out. For instance, the text claims, "Blessed is he who opens his lips blessing and praising God" and "Blessed is he who implants peace and love. Cursed is he who disturbs those that love their neighbours."[239] However, the only problem with *2 Enoch* is that the date of his composition is unknown. Scholars have suggested dates anywhere from the

[238] France, *Matthew,* TNTC, 108.

[239] *2 Enoch* 52.3, 11–12, in *Pseudepigrapha of the Old Testament*, vol. 2, Robert Henry Charles, trans (Oxford: Clarendon Press, 1913), 460.

first-century AD to the 10th century AD.[240] It may be that the reference to *2 Enoch* is too late to hold any significance to denote early material from the Beatitudes. Nonetheless, it can be asserted that the terms *μακάριος* and *yrva* were used to denote similar theological concepts during the time of Jesus.[241]

A better usage of *μακάριος* is found in the LXX.[242] The form of affirmations associated with the term are found in Hellenistic literature as well as the OT as well as the rabbis.[243] The LXX uses the same format in Psalm 1:1; 2:12; 105:3; 118:1; Isa. 30:18; 31:9; 32:20; 56:2; *Baruch* 4:4; and Daniel 12:2. Rabbinic parallels are found in *b. Hag.* 14b and *b. Yoma* 87a. Intriguingly, the ὅτι clause is used uniquely in Matthew's Gospel, but it is rarely found in that structure outside of the NT.[244] Thus, *μακάριος* is deeply enriched theological term of Jesus's day. The term points to the eschatological bliss experienced by God's people in the end. But there is another term that holds an even deeper theological impact in the Beatitudes.

Βασιλείας is another theological term found in the Beatitudes with quite a profound depth. It was understood in antiquity that *βασιλείας* referenced "reign," "rule," or "authority."[245] While it was recognized that God currently ruled and reigned, a future day was anticipated when God's reign would be unchallenged by the global powers (Dan. 2:44-45; 7:14, 27).[246] In Matthew's Gospel, the phrase *βασιλείας τῶν οὐρανῶν* ("kingdom of heaven") is used instead of *βασιλείαν τοῦ θεοῦ*. ("kingdom of God"). Both phrases relate to the reality of God's rule over creation.[247] However, *βασιλείας τῶν οὐρανῶν* was preferable in Jewish circles as it did not evoke the name of God. As such, it was used as a

---

240 A. Chadwick Thornhill, "Enoch, Second Book of," *The Lexham Bible Dictionary,* John D. Barry, ed, et. al. (Bellingham, WA: Lexham Press, 2016), Logos Bible Software.

241 Another late reference using makarioV can be found in 4 Maccabees 12:1. However, here again, the document may prove too late to be of assistance as the document could also be dated to the first-century AD.

242 LXX is used to denote the Septuagint, a Greek translation of the Hebrew Scriptures.

243 Hagner, *Matthew 1–13*, WBC, 88–89.

244 Ibid.

245 Keener and Walton, eds., *NIV Cultural Backgrounds Study Bible*, 1616.

246 Ibid.

247 Joshua A. Crutchfield, "Divine Sovereignty," *Lexham Theological Wordbook,* Lexham Bible Reference Series, Douglas Mangum et al., eds, *Lexham Theological Wordbook* (Bellingham, WA: Lexham Press, 2014), Logos Bible Software.

circumlocution for *βασιλείαν τοῦ θεοῦ*.[248] Other examples of the replacement of "kingdom of heaven" for "kingdom of God" is found in Luke 6:20; Matt. 11:12 and Luke 16:16; Matt. 13:24.[249]

The kingdom of God was an important, if not central, theme of the gospel message.[250] In Matthew, Jesus teaches that the kingdom of heaven—the *βασιλείας τῶν οὐρανῶν*—belongs to the one who is persecuted for righteousness (Matt. 5:10). Furthermore, Jesus says, "You are blessed when they insult you and persecute you and falsely say every kind of evil against you because of me" (Matt. 5:11). Darrell Bock argues that the verse finds a close parallel to Luke's version which says, "Blessed are you when people hate you, when they exclude you, insult you, and slander your name as evil because of the Son of Man" (Luke 6:22).[251] Bock notes that while Luke is more sociologically focused, he is not without spiritual depth. Thus, it is quite possible that the two variations reference the same line of thought; regardless of whether the variation stem from a difference in the way the message was heard, or from the same message being repeated with a different emphasis. Jesus combines the Son of Man thinking with the *βασιλείας* in other passages.[252] For instance, Jesus notes that the "Son of Man will send out his angels, and they will gather from his kingdom [*βασιλείας*] all who cause sin and those guilty of lawlessness" (Matt. 13:41). Additionally, he says that "there are some standing here who will not taste death until they see the Son of Man coming in his kingdom [*βασιλείας*] "(Matt. 16:28). The term finds numerous connections with numerous passages in the LXX. Of particular interest is Daniel 7:14 which states that *καὶ ἐδόθη αὐτῷ* ("one like a human") was given *ἐξουσία αἰώνιος* ("eternal power") and a *βασιλεία αὐτοῦ, ἥτις οὐ μὴ φθαρῇ* ("a kingdom that will not perish").[253] The Beatitudes taken with Jesus's self-understanding of himself in Zechariah 9:9 from his entrance into Jerusalem portray Jesus's understanding

---

[248] Licona, *Why Are There Differences in the Gospels,* 245, fn 58.

[249] For a more complete list of references, see Licona, *Why Are There Differences in the Gospels,* 245, fn 58.

[250] Crutchfield, "Divine Sovereignty, *LTW,* Logos.

[251] Bock and Simpson, *Jesus According to Scripture: Restoring the Portrait from the Gospels*, 204.

[252] The Son of Man will be the emphasis of chapter 4.

[253] Unless otherwise noted, all quotations from the LXX come from Randall K. Tan, David A. deSilva, and Isaiah Hoogendyk, *The Lexham Greek-English Interlinear Septuagint: H.B. Swete Edition* (Bellingham, WA: Lexham Press, 2012), Logos Bible Software.

of himself as the Shepherd-King of Israel,[254] thus indicating that Jesus's kingdom was an antirevolutionary kingdom that found its root in a "peaceable kingly figure."[255]

Since a classic Christological title is not used in the passage, it may initially seem as though the Beatitudes would not be granted a green light. However, the concepts surrounding *μακάριος* and especially *βασιλείας* show forth an early understanding that was comparable to those of Jesus's day and earlier. Their usage finds a connection with the LXX and literature that predates the Gospels. However, it is of special interest to note the distinction found in Jesus's message. Contrary to the revolutionary spirit of the day, Jesus sees his new kingdom as one that would come peaceably and through him. The connections he makes with Isaiah 61 and Daniel 7 shows that the promised eschatological kingdom had come but would be fully actualized when God fully establishes it. Thus, the kingdom had come (Matt. 5:3, 10), but the blessings of the kingdom would come at the end (Matt. 5:4–9). When first approaching the text with the third methodology, it seemed as if the text would not pass the third methodology. However, the theology is rich and corroborates with early Semitic concepts while still holding unique aspects. Thus, the Beatitudes pass the third methodology and add 4 more points to the weighted tally. It can be said that the Beatitudes is at least in the yellow zone. But the study will continue to see whether enough can be shown to claim that the Beatitudes meet the conditions necessary to enter the green zone.

Mnemonic and Rhythmic Patterns

The fourth methodology seeks to see if there are any mnemonic and/or rhythmic patterns that serve as placeholders for oral material. Consider this much akin to the flow of a song's chorus. Due to its structure, the chorus of a song is more often remembered than the verses due to its compact and rhythmic pattern. The same is true for oral material. It was structured so that memorization would come easier. As such, texts that hold mnemonic devices and rhythmic patterns are likely to have been part of the material that was deemed so important that communities remembered it. The question at hand is this: do the Beatitudes hold any mnemonic devices and rhythmic patterns?

The Beatitudes possess a few characteristics that display a rhythmic nature to its content. First, the Beatitudes are set up according to what Dale

---

[254] F. F. Bruce, "The Book of Zechariah and the Passion Narratives," *BJRL* 43 (1961): 347; J. C. O'Neill, *Messiah: Six Lectures on the Ministry of Jesus* (Cambridge, UK: Cochrane, 1980), 57-58.

[255] Witherington, III, *Christology of Jesus,* 107.

Allision calls an "antithetical correspondence."[256] Antithetical correspondences contrast blessings and warnings from certain criteria. The Beatitudes serve as bookends describing nine eschatological blessings that come to the one who enters the messianic community (5:3–12) as contrasted with three warnings for those who do not (7:13–27). The core message of the Sermon on the Mount is given between the two placeholders (5:13–7:12).[257] As such, the blessings found in the Beatitudes are best understood with the warnings of 7:13–27.[258] Thus, the Beatitudes find a rhythmic pattern within the overall structure of the Sermon on the Mount. However, the Beatitudes also finds patterns within the text itself as will be noted in the following points.

Second, the Beatitudes include a similar structure in Matthew's Gospel as is found in Luke's. Luke condenses the Beatitudes to include the warnings with the blessings. Matthew sandwiches the blessings and warnings around the core of the message.[259] As such, the structure of the two versions, while differences do exist, find a common pattern. However, the evangelists structure the Beatitudes in differing forms to emphasize distinct aspects of the same message. Interestingly, a Christological focus is found in the sandwiched material.[260]

Third, the conditional nature of the Beatitudes exhibits a rhythmic pattern. Jeremias argues that the "sayings of Jesus that have been brought together in the Sermon on the Mount are part of the gospel. Each of these sayings reiterates that the old era is passing away. Through the proclamation of the gospel and discipleship, you are transferred into the new era of God."[261] The Beatitudes are structured around conditional claims. For instance, the phrase "Blessed are the poor in spirit" (Matt. 5:3a) serves as a consequence of the kingdom of heaven belonging to the individual (Matt. 5:3b). One's belonging to the kingdom of heaven itself serves as a consequent to one's previous acceptance into the messianic kingdom. Thus, the Beatitudes find a

---

256 Allison, "The Structure of the Sermon on the Mount," *JBL*: 431.

257 Ibid.

258 The warnings include an admonition to those who do not enter by the narrow gate (7:13–14), to those who are disingenuous in their commitment—or false teachers (7:15–20), to those who are not authentically part of the messianic community (7:21–23), and to those who do not act on the teachings of Jesus (7:24–27).

259 Kenneth E. Bailey, *Jesus Through Middle Eastern Eyes: Cultural Studies in the Gospels* (Downers Grove, IL: IVP Academic, 2008), 66.

260 Ibid.

261 Jeremias, *Jesus and the Message of the New Testament,* 33.

pattern that very well serves Jeremias's assessment well in arguing that the Sermon on the Mount was an early Christian catechism.[262]

Finally, the Matthean Beatitudes form an *inclusio* from the verbal tenses employed in the text.[263] The verb *ἐστιν* is found in the present active indicative tense in both verses 3 and 10. In both cases, the kingdom of heaven is shown to be in the current possession of those who are poor in spirit—that is, humble and dependent on God's power[264]—and those who are persecuted for righteousness. In contrast, every other verb in the Matthean Beatitudes is in the future passive indicative tense, with the sole exception of verse 8. The eighth verse notes that the pure in heart will be blessed *Ὅτι αὐτοὶ τὸν Θεὸν ὄψονται* ("because they will see God"). The verb *ὄψονται* is in the future middle indicative tense. The present tenses of the first and ninth beatitudes surround the future tenses of the second through eighth beatitudes, thus forming an *inclusio.*

This section presented four pieces of evidence to support the notion that the Beatitudes contain rhythmic patterns as found in early oral traditions. But the evidence provided is far from the only support that is found to support such a case. For instance, Matthew Black asserts that the first and third beatitudes should be taken together as the third is an "adaptation of Psalm 37:11.[265] Additionally, he finds evidence of synonymous parallelisms and synthetic parallelisms along with couplets that are evident of primitive traditions.[266] With the evidence provided and the additional support noted, it is safe to hold that the Beatitudes pass the fourth methodology, as they show rhythmic patterns associated with mnemonic devices, adding 5 more points to its score.

Aramaic/Hebraic Literary Characteristics

When speaking of the Aramaic literary characteristics of Q, John S. Kloppenborg Verbin contends that the evidence for a written version of an Aramaic Q, from which Matthew and Luke depend, is so weak that it nearly

---

[262] Ibid., 27–30.

[263] Hagner makes the same argument. See Hagner, *Matthew 1–13,* WBC, 89.

[264] Blomberg, *Matthew,* NAC, 98.

[265] Matthew Black, *An Aramaic Approach to the Gospels and Acts* (Eugene, OR: Wipf & Stock, 1967), 136.

[266] Ibid., 156–157.

stands at zero percent.[267] The evidence, however, seems to suggest otherwise, especially in the case of the Sermon on the Mount, particularly the Beatitudes. First, an Aramaic source can answer the translational variants between Matthew's presentation of the sermon and Luke's. Three examples can be given. First, Matthew's Gospel uses rejoice in the present imperative says to be glad, whereas Luke uses rejoice with the aorist imperative for the same statement. In Matthew's Gospel, the reward in heavens is used in the plural sense, whereas Luke uses it in the singular. Finally, Matthew emphasized the persecution of the prophets before the current generation, whereas Luke notes that the people's ancestors persecuted the prophets.[268] While two sources or traditions could have existed, even then the sources and/or traditions more likely stemmed from an Aramaic source which the interpreters translated into Greek in different ways. Jeremias notes that the case for an Aramaic original is strong when the Aramaic original could have been understood as an apposition in Matthew ("who were before you"), and by Luke as a subject ("their ancestors").[269] Even though Jeremias places Luke's source earlier than Matthew's, there is no reason to believe that both did not originate from the same tradition. It may have been a translational decision more than anything else.[270] The Aramaism of Matthew 5:12 is also noticed by Matthew Black. He argues that ἀγαλλιᾶσθε is associated with the word *wvud* (or, *dusu*) which describes "movement and dancing."[271] This exuberance is closely aligned with the thoughts of Isaiah 61:3.[272]

Second, the poetic form of the text strongly suggests an Aramaic underpinning. Parallels were noted earlier in the previous section, so there is no need to rehash the material once again. However, it is important to note that the parallelism and poetic form as found in the Beatitudes closely aligns

---

[267] John S. Kloppenborg Verbin, *Excavating Q: The History and Setting of the Sayings Gospel* (Minneapolis, MN: Fortress, 2000), 81.

[268] See Jeremias, *Jesus and the Message of the New Testament,* 26.

[269] Ibid.

[270] Translational decisions also account for the rewording of various texts in current Bible translations as well. For instance, the NIV decided against including John 3:16–21 as the words of Jesus, but rather the words of the evangelist, whereas most other translations continue to accept the text as Jesus's words. Better examples are found in the different wording of difficult texts.

[271] Black, *An Aramaic Approach to the Gospels and Acts,* 158.

[272] "to provide for those who mourn in Zion; to give them a crown of beauty instead of ashes, festive oil instead of mourning, and splendid clothes instead of despair. And they will be called righteous trees, planted by the LORD to glorify him" (Isa. 61:3).

with the format found in Aramaic and Hebrew literature. However, the poetic nature of the Beatitudes is found primarily in verses 3–10 and is not prevalent in verses 11 and 12.[273]

Third, the Beatitudes exhibit the practice of asyndeton which is noted to be "highly characteristic of Aramaic."[274] Asyndeton is the practice of omitting conjunctions between the parts of a sentence. C. F. Burney holds that the excessive use of asyndetons in the Gospel of John, particularly in the prologue, is evidence of the influence of an Aramaic original.[275] While the Gospel of Mark uses asyndetons more than Matthew, they are found frequently throughout Matthew 5:3–17.[276]

From evaluating the linguistic characteristics of the Beatitudes, it does appear that the text holds traits that point to a Semitic underpinning. Of particular interest is the text's use of asyndetons, which are not as prevalent in Matthew's Gospel as in Mark's. Additionally, the use of poetic form which is frequently used in Aramaic and Hebrew sources is found in the Beatitudes. Also, it has been noted that the variations between Matthew and Luke's presentation of the sermon can best be alleviated by a previous Aramaic original by which both translated according to their preference. There is something to the Aramaic nature of the Beatitudes. However, the text does not find a word order (VSO) that follows early material. The variants between Luke and Matthew actually fit well within the parameter of mistranslations—that is, while the evangelist did not necessarily mistranslate an Aramaic term, points of difference are found among the evangelists. Terms related to the kingdom of God are among the second-level words in Wellhausen's assessment.[277] While it would be preferable if there were additional lines of evidence from which to draw, the text provides enough linguistic connections to Semitisms to give clearance to the possibility that the text holds an Aramaic linguistic foundation, thus adding 5 more points to its already burgeoning score.

Semitic Cultural Concepts of First-Century Israel

If one is keeping count, then one acknowledges that if enough evidence can be found to link the Beatitudes with Semitic cultural concepts of

---

273 Black, *An Aramaic Approach to the Gospels and Acts,* 158.

274 Ibid., 36.

275 C. F. Burney, *The Aramaic Origin of the Fourth Gospel* (Oxford, UK: Clarendon, 1922), 26, 55; Black, *An Aramaic Approach to the Gospels and Acts,* 36.

276 Black, *An Aramaic Approach to the Gospels and Acts,* 37. Notice the form of the first beatitude. "Makavrioi oiJ ptwcoi; tw: pneuvmati, o{ti aujto:n ejstin hJ basleiva tw:n oujranw:n."

277 Wellhausen, *Einleitung,* 33.

the time, then the text stands strong with its link to an Aramaic original. But one must ask, does such evidence exist? Regarding the sixth method, the Beatitudes find at least a couple of connections to Semitic concepts of Jesus's day.

First, the Beatitudes relate back to the understanding that the prophets of the OT were persecuted. In verses 11–12, Jesus compares the persecution of the disciples as standing in line with the persecution that the prophets suffered. By this, Jesus is not saying that the disciples were prophets, but rather he is connecting them with the lineage of individuals who were persecuted for their stand for God.[278] While Bailey sees the possibility that Matthew could have later added the latter verses to comfort those who were being persecuted in his day,[279] there is just as good a possibility that Jesus forecasts the future persecution of the church as he realizes that the faithful through the Hebrew Bible were persecuted. Thus, because the prophets were faithful to God and were persecuted, those who stand for divine righteousness can expect the same.[280] In the first-century, the persecution of the prophets received a lot of attention. The pseudepigraphical book *The Martyrdom of Isaiah* expounds on the ministry of the prophet Isaiah of Amoz. The book states that Isaiah was sawn asunder while Balchira and false prophets laughed at him and accused him falsely. The text reads as follows:

> And he sawed him asunder with a wood-saw. [2] And when Isaiah was being sawn in sunder Balchîrâ stood up, accusing him, and all the false prophets stood up, laughing and rejoicing because of Isaiah. [3] And Balchîrâ, with the aid of Mechêmbêchûs, stood up before Isaiah, [laughing] deriding; [4] And Belchîrâ said to Isaiah: 'Say: "I have lied in all that I have spoken, and likewise the ways of Manasseh are good and right. [5] And the ways also of Balchîrâ and of his associates are good."' [6] And this he said to him when he began to be sawn in sunder. [7] But Isaiah was (absorbed) in a vision of the Lord, and though his eyes were open, he saw them [not]. [8] And Balchîrâ spake thus to Isaiah: 'Say what I say unto thee and I will turn their heart, and I will compel Manasseh and the princes of Judah and the people and all Jerusalem to reverence thee.' [9] And Isaiah answered and said: 'So far as I have utterance (I say): Damned and accursed be thou and all thy powers and all thy house. [10] For thou canst not take (from me) aught save the skin of my

[278] France, *Matthew,* TNTC, 112.

[279] Bailey, *Jesus Through Middle Eastern Eyes,* 86.

[280] Ibid.

body.' 11 And they seized and sawed in sunder Isaiah, the son of Amoz, with a wood-saw.[281]

Even though the Greek text of *The Martyrdom of Isaiah* is thought to have been written around AD 100, the original was probably written earlier in Hebrew or Aramaic.[282] The idea that Isaiah was sawn asunder is earlier than AD 100 due to a reference made to the same event in the book of Hebrews. The writer of Hebrews notes that the faithful were "stoned, they were sawed in two, they died by the sword, they wandered about in sheepskins, in goatskins, destitute, afflicted, and mistreated" (Heb. 11:37).[283] People of the day realized that persecution for one's faithfulness to God was a reality. Thus, Jesus's concept of one being persecuted for the sake of righteousness fits well within the cultural milieu of the day.

Second, Jesus countered the nationalistic spirit of his day. Some desired to see the second coming of Judas Maccabeus. Even among Jesus's accompaniment, at least one of the disciples was of the Zealot party—that is, Simon Zelotes (Matt. 10:4; Mark 3:18; and Luke 6:15). Notice that in Luke's account, the disciples were named and appointed before Jesus delivered the sermon. It is quite interesting that one of Jesus's own may have supported a nationalistic spirit that Jesus himself combated. Rather than taking back Israel by force, as was the desired tactic of the day, Jesus taught that the kingdom of God would come in a more peaceful manner, which could possibly explain Judas Iscariot's issues with Jesus.

In Jesus's understanding, the citizens of the kingdom of heaven would be met with persecution because the kingdom would be resisted by the enemies of darkness.[284] Jesus viewed the root problem behind the persecution of the saints as one that was spiritual. National and material problems stemmed from

---

[281] *The Martyrdom of Isaiah* 5.1–11, in *Pseudepigrapha of the Old Testament*, vol. 2, Robert Henry Charles, ed and trans (Oxford: Clarendon Press, 1913), 162.

[282] Chad Brand et al., eds., "Isaiah, Martyrdom Of," *Holman Illustrated Bible Dictionary* (Nashville, TN: Holman Bible Publishers, 2003), 841.

[283] The book of Hebrews was most likely composed prior to AD 70, although a range is possible between AD 60–100. *1 Clement* most likely quotes Hebrews, although some have questioned Clement's dependence on Hebrews. Nonetheless, if *1 Clement* does quote from the text, Hebrews cannot be dated any later than AD 96 as this was when *1 Clement* was composed. A better date for Hebrews is found to be prior to AD 67 as good evidence suggests that Paul held some influence on the book's composition. David L. Allen, *Hebrews,* New American Commentary, vol. 35 (Nashville, TN: B&H, 2010), 74–78.

[284] Bock and Simpson, *Jesus According to the Scriptures,* 202–203.

a battle in the spiritual domain.[285] Jesus's teachings are closely aligned with a rabbinical debate of the day. Early rabbinics debated the reasons behind the destruction of the two temples.[286] Rabbi Johanan argued that idolatry was the cause of the first temple's destruction and that "causeless hatred" led to the destruction of the second.[287] The prophets of the Hebrew Bible engaged in similar debates.[288] Habakkuk made the connection between the people's sin and their imminent destruction (Hab. 1:5–17). In like manner, Jeremiah noted that the evil and rebellion of Zedekiah and Jehoiakim led to the fall of Jerusalem and the sacking of the temple complex (Jer. 52:1–34). Stephen made a similar connection to the people's nationalistic sin (Acts 7:44–50), even linking their judgment to the execution of Jesus (Acts 7:51–53).[289] It was the latter connection that particularly led to his death. Stephen's sermon is considered one of the early sermon summaries of Acts, which gives his message an early connection to Jesus's concepts of the already-not-yet kingdom.[290]

Even though persecution would be a reality, the Beatitudes asserted that the people of God could take heart because of the "eschatological reversal,"[291] as Bock and Simpson termed it. The eschatological reversal would afford blessings to the persecuted to blessed and judgment to the persecutors. This concept finds a home in other Jesus traditions, particularly the Parable of the Rich Man and Lazarus (Luke 16:19–31). In an ironic historical twist, the

---

285 Michael Heiser gives numerous examples of the ancient dualist interpretation of reality. Noting the crossover between the spiritual and material domains, the biblical writers saw the conquest of Israel as one that was "at war with enemies spawned by rival divine beings." Michael S. Heiser, *The Unseen Realm: Recovering the Supernatural Worldview of the Bible* (Bellingham, WA: Lexham, 2015), 203. Seeing that Jesus held that the kingdom of God had come through him, then it is no major stretch to contend that Jesus also saw his work as holding practical applications on earth while flowing from the spiritual domain. In more ways than one, the spiritual impacts the material, whereas the material also impacts the spiritual dimension.

286 Bailey, *Jesus Through Middle Eastern Eyes,* 74.

287 *Kallah Rabbati* 54b.1.

288 This gives pause to consider that the destruction of the temple passages does not necessitate as late of a date as some might consider. Because the destruction of the temple had been linked to sinful behaviors in the people of the past, then it would be easy for a prophetic voice like Jesus to make a similar link to the problems of his day.

289 John B. Polhill, *Acts*, vol. 26, The New American Commentary (Nashville: Broadman & Holman Publishers, 1992), 204.

290 Max Wilcox, *The Semitisms of Acts* (Oxford, UK: Clarendon, 1965), 163.

291 Bailey, *Jesus Through Middle Eastern Eyes,* 203.

Pharisaical rabbis who espoused peace were spared when the Romans destroyed Jerusalem, whereas those who advocated sedition were executed.[292]

Other connections to Semitic cultural concepts could be made with the Beatitudes. Richard Bauckham notes that a third connection could be found in the communal standards of the Beatitudes with those of the Qumranic community.[293] For the purpose of this study, sufficient connections have been made to indicate that the Beatitudes find a home in early first-century Israel. Thus, it is suggested that the Beatitudes pass the sixth method which places the teaching in the green zone. Add 4 more points to its weighted score at this point. Even though the Beatitudes hold a strong connection to early Semitic residue, can the text pass all seven methodologies? The last method will serve as the deciding factor.

Similarities to NT Creeds, Summaries, and Early Literature

The final methodology will evaluate the link that each Matthean text holds with NT creeds and recognized sermon summaries. As previously noted, the creeds are based on five themes: 1) baptism and catechumenisms, 2) worship, 3) exorcism, 4) encouragements against persecution, and 5) polemics against heresies.[294] Observing the Beatitudes, it has already been noted that some evidence suggests that the early church used the Beatitudes—more to the point, the Sermon on the Mount as a whole—as a catechism for early converts before they were baptized. The Beatitudes do not necessarily find a correlation with the worship creeds or exorcisms. However, they do serve to provide encouragement against persecution as Jesus links his already-not-yet kingdom to the eschatological text of Isaiah 61. As already noted, Jesus's Beatitudes serve as a code of conduct for the citizens of this heavenly kingdom. This kingdom would be met with resistance. However, future blessings would come to the faithful who were persecuted when the kingdom was fully actualized. The Beatitudes do not necessarily serve as a polemic in general. But it could be said that Jesus stands opposed to the nationalistic spirit of his day, suggesting that the divine kingdom would come by peace rather than force.

Additionally, credal material is identified by three main characteristics: 1) single-statement declarations, 2) formulaic prose, or *homologiai,* and 3) hymns and poetry.[295] Outside of the use of *Ὅτι*, the Beatitudes do not hold the

[292] Keener, *Bible Background Commentary: NT,* 56–57.

[293] See Richard Bauckham, *The Christian World Around the New Testament* (Grand Rapids, MI: Baker Academic, 2017), 468.

[294] Cullmann, *Earliest Christian Confessions,* 18.

[295] Longenecker, *New Wine into Fresh Wineskins,* 7.

confessional nature as would be anticipated in credal material.[296] It is also difficult finding links to what is considered *homologiai.* One possible link is a possible *hapax legomena*[297] found in Jesus's usage of *μακάριος*, an unusual term found in both Matthew and Luke's presentation of the message. The stronger link to credal material is found in the poetic structure of the Beatitudes. Of the seven characteristics of poetic credal material, the Beatitudes match four of them.[298] It could be said that the presence of *inclusio* matches the parallel structures one would expect to find with poetic Hebrew structures. As noted, the *hapax legomena* found in the peculiar use of *μακάριος* also matches the criteria. The third link is found with the use of contextual dislocations, particularly concerning the conditional statements so prevalent in the Beatitudes to dictate kingdom ethical principles. Finally, the Beatitudes implicitly describe the work of Jesus as he is shown to be the Anointed One of Isaiah 61 who was ushering in the messianic eschatological community, albeit in the form of an already-not-yet format.

The Beatitudes hold significant parallels to the characteristics one would expect to find in early credal material. For the sake of this section, it can be said that the Beatitudes pass the seventh methodology. But what can be said of this passage of Scripture as it relates to early Semitic material? How did the text do in the examination that has been set forth? Before moving to the Lord's Prayer, the Beatitudes need to receive its color assignment and any concluding thoughts.

Conclusion and Color Assignment

The Beatitudes passed all seven methodologies, thus indicating that the text holds strong signs of Semitic residue. While bipartite Christological language which is so prevalent in early credal material is lacking, that does not remove the strong eschatological nature of the Beatitudes. The Beatitudes exhibit all the categories set forth by this study. When the study first began, the primary area of concern involved the theological language used by the text. Surely, *μακάριος* and *βασιλεία* indicate early theological language. However, they

---

[296] Better examples can be found in Mark 8:29b and Matthew 16:16 where Peter said to Jesus, "You are the Christ."

[297] Longenecker lists *hapax legomena* as one of 9 indicators of *homologiai.* Longenecker, *New Wine into Fresh Wineskins,* 15.

[298] The seven characteristics of Hebrew poetic devices include 1) parallel structures, 2) *hapax legomena,* 3) a preference for participles over finite verbs, 4) frequent usage of the relative pronoun o'V ("who") to begin the statements, 5) contextual dislocations set to a doctrinal or ethical section, 6) continuance of a lesson that ceases to remain relevant, and 7) the affirmation of a basic conviction pertaining to the work or person of Christ. Ibid., 10–11.

do not necessarily match the Christological focus understood to come from early Christian confessions. Or so it was thought.

As the research indicated, the text actually makes a stronger Christological connection than was previously expected. Making the connections to the Anointed One of Isaiah 61, the text portrays the person and work of Jesus in a manner that is linked eerily similar to the Son of Man Christology, as found in Daniel 7:13–14, and to other Synoptic material that makes similar connections (e.g., Jesus's reading of Isaiah 61 in the synagogue at Nazareth in Luke 6:17–21). The Beatitudes proved to hold strong Semitic residue as it passed all seven criteria and scoring a perfect score of 30 points. Therefore, the Beatitudes can be given a color designation of green, indicating that it is beyond a reasonable doubt that this material predates the composition of the Gospel of Matthew and most likely finds a home in the authentic *ipsissima vox* of Jesus himself. It passes both the tallied and weighted scales. Now that the Beatitudes have been completed. It is now time to investigate the other half of the equation concerning the Sermon on the Mount—The Lord's Prayer.

The Lord's Prayer (Matt. 6:9-13)

The second part of the investigation into early material found in the Sermon on the Mount focuses on the Lord's Prayer..[299] Most Christians know the prayer by heart and can easily recite it. Many liturgical churches recite the prayer as part of their normal weekly worship services. The prayer itself comes after Jesus's teaching on how to pray, which itself flows from his focused attention on ethical living. In the first part of chapter 6, Jesus tells his disciples that they were not to "practice [their] righteousness in front of others to be seen by them. Otherwise, [they] would have no reward with [their] Father in heaven" (6:1). He continues by emphasizing that the disciples' prayer life should not be conducted to be celebrated by others. But rather, they were to "go into your private room, shut your door, and pray to your Father who is in

---

[299] Sometimes called the "Model Prayer."

secret. And your Father who sees in secret will reward you" (6:6). Jesus then teaches the disciples to pray the following:

> Our Father in heaven, your name be honored as holy.
> Your kingdom come. Your will be done on earth as it is in heaven.
> Give us today our daily bread.
> And forgive us our debts, as we also have forgiven our debtors.
> And do not bring us into temptation, but deliver us from the evil one (6:9b–13).
> Some later manuscripts add "For your is the kingdom and the power and the glory forever. Amen."

Following the prayer, Jesus gives attention to the concept of forgiveness which was emphasized in the Lord's Prayer. Jesus goes so far as to say that "if you don't forgive others, your Father will not forgive your offenses" (6:15); something Jesus emphasized in other teachings..[300]

The Jesus Seminar was fairly kind to the Lord's Prayer. Verse 9 included three of the four colors. The words "Our Father" were highlighted in red, the highest color and one very rarely used by the Seminar, yet the words "in the heavens," or "in heaven," was listed as black..[301] Thus, the verse holds two extremes within the span of a few words according to the Seminar. The remainder of verse 9 is listed in pink. The Seminar believed that the phrase "in heaven" was an amplification by Matthew..[302] In verse 10, the first line of God's imperial rule was listed in pink, whereas the rest of the verse was in black..[303] All of verse 12 was viewed as pink and the first link of verse 13 was gray with the balance of the verse in black..[304] The Seminar accepted the majority of the Lord's Prayer as stemming from something that Jesus probably said even though they doubted a few lines in Matthew's presentation of the prayer..[305]

---

[300] A good example of this teaching is found in the Parable of the Unforgiving Servant in Matthew 18:21–35.

[301] Funk, Hoover, and the Jesus Seminar, *Five Gospels,* 148.

[302] Ibid., 148.

[303] Ibid.

[304] Ibid.

[305] The Seminar believes that the prayer should read as follows: "Father, your name be revered. Impose your imperial rule. Provide us with the bread we need for the day. Forgive our debts to the extent that we have forgiven those in debt to us. And please don't subject us to test after test." Ibid., 149.

This bodes well for the probability that Matthew 6:9–13 could contain Semitic residue from early Jesus traditions.

The Lord's Prayer has become a cherished passage of Scripture. It has nearly become institutionalized by its frequent recitations, which is not necessarily a bad thing. It has been observed that when many saints of God near death, they will recite the Lord's Prayer when they cannot think of anything else to pray. When it comes, however, to the concept of Semitic residue, does this cherished prayer find evidence that roots it back in the formal teaching of Jesus of Nazareth? Or is it a passage of Scripture that is loosely based on his teachings? Just as the Beatitudes were examined by the seven-fold methodology set forth in this research, so now it is time to turn the Lord's Prayer to the same scrutiny. The Beatitudes passed with flying colors, earning a green identifier. Will the same be true for the Lord's Prayer?

Unique Rabbinic Concepts

The fact that Jesus prayed does not make him unusual in the Jewish culture of his day. Jewish people of the first-century were people of prayer, especially the rabbis of the day. While the Lord's Prayer of Jesus finds similarities with the Jewish prayers of his day, the differences in focus between Jesus and the traditional prayers of his day cannot be avoided. Jakob Petuchowski and Michael Brocke describe a Jewish prayer of antiquity called the Kaddish. The Kaddish was prayed as follows:

> Exalted and hallowed be His great Name
> in the world which He created
> according to His will.
> May He establish His kingdom
> in your lifetime and in your days,
> and in the lifetime of the whole household of Israel,
> speedily and at a near time.
> And say, Amen..[306]

Likewise, the Talmud includes a great deal of information on prayer. In a few instances, one can find parallels between the Lord's Prayer and the thoughts of the rabbis. First, like the rabbis, Jesus emphasizes the importance of God's presence. Verse 10 of the Lord's Prayer is a fascinating passage in which Jesus petitions God to bring about his will through the lives of his disciples. The next section will examine Jesus's view of God's work through history in more detail. But for now, it should be noted that Jesus held that God's presence was actively involved with his people and in the world to meet

---

[306] Petuchowski and Brocke, *The Lord's Prayer and Jewish Liturgy,* 37, in Hagner, *Matthew 1–13,* WBC, 147.

present needs and to bring about his coming kingdom..[307] In a similar fashion, Rabbi Rabin, son of Ada, notes the importance of God's presence in a person's life, saying, "Whence do we derive the tradition that when even one studies the law, the Divine Presence rests with him? It is written, 'In every place where I shall permit my name to be mentioned, I will come unto thee and I will bless thee.'".[308] Rabbi Simon ben Jochai refers to the prayers of OT saints, saying, "The requests of three persons were granted before they had finished their prayers—Eleazar, Moses, and Solomon.".[309] It becomes clear that Jewish rabbis placed a great deal of emphasis on prayer. As one would expect, prayer held a major place in the lives of the Jewish rabbis as they were people of faith. However, as one will find, Jesus's focus on prayer was quite different from the rabbis in a few areas.

Before examining the differences between Jesus's teaching on prayer and the take of the rabbinics, the overall scope of Jewish prayer should be mentioned. Prior to AD 70, faithful Jewish individuals would recite the *Amidah* or *Sheoneh Eshreh*, the central prayer of the Jewish liturgy that included eighteen benedictions that were recited three times a day. On Shabbat, thirteen of the most central benedictions of the *Amidah* were recited. Kenneth Bailey notes that fifteen of these benedictions contain specific petitions, including 1) a prayer for knowledge, understanding, and intelligence; 2) a prayer to return to the Torah and divine service; 3) forgiveness; 4) divine help to fight one's battles; 5) healing from wounds; 6) a blessing on the year and harvest; 7) blowing the trumpet for liberation and a gathering of exiles; 8) restoration of judges and the establishment of innocence; 9) the cutting off of enemies; 10) mercy for the elders and converts; 11) prayer for a return to Jerusalem; 12) prayer for the strength (aka., the horn) of David to bring "victorious salvation;" 13) a petition to hear one's prayers; 14) petition to return the sacrifices to the altar of God; and 15) the granting of peace, happiness, and divine blessings to Israel and all her people..[310] As Bailey has rightly noted, the focus of Jewish prayers prior to AD 70 revolve around seven major themes: 1) an emphasis on Jerusalem and the temple; 2) knowledge built around Scripture; 3) the need for relief and restoration from the community's sufferings; 4) personal forgiveness, but not including the forgiveness of others; 5) an emphasis on the blessings of the

---

[307] Bailey, *Jesus Through Middle Eastern Eyes,* 115–117.

[308] H. Polano, trans, *The Talmud* (San Diego, CA: Book Tree, 1876, 2003), 265–266.

[309] Ibid., 267.

[310] Bailey, *Jesus Through Middle Eastern Eyes,* 106.

harvest; 6) a call to attack Israel's enemies; and 7) a focus on mercy and the need for peace and happiness.[311]

The first distinction is the means by which Jesus addressed God. For the most part, Jewish people addressed God as their "heavenly Father"[312] in their prayers. However, Jesus uniquely used the term *abba* (Gk: *πατήρ*, Aram: *abba*) to relate to God. *Abba* does not seem to appear in Jewish prayers until much later after Jesus's ministry. The term is virtually unparalleled in the first-century,[313] thus leaving the use of the term exclusively unique to the teaching and prayer life of Jesus of Nazareth. This holds a major impact on the current methodology, which bodes well for the Semitic and original nature of the text at hand.

The second distinction between Jesus and the rabbis' teaching on prayer is his focus on the kingdom of God being ushered in through him. Like the Beatitudes, Jesus places a major focus on the already-not-yet kingdom. While certain portions of the prayer focus more on daily living than the kingdom—such as the petitions for daily bread and assistance to overcome—other areas focus on the eschatological community that was already established in Jesus. One of the clearest examples of this focus is found in the petition "Hallowed be Your name. Your kingdom come. Your will be done, on earth as it is in heaven" (6:9b–10, NASB).[314] The second petition involves, as Hagner notes, the "consummation of God's purposes in history, the fulfillment of the prophetic pictures of future bliss (cf. Acts 1:6)."[315] The third petition continues the thought process of the second, requesting that the will of God would come to earth as it has been established and decreed in heaven.[316] R. T. France contends that the third petition is the most eschatological clause in the entire prayer.[317] As such, the eschatological focus of Jesus's prayer is much different than the modern prayers of the Judaism of his day.

The third difference between Jesus's prayer and the prayers of first-century Judaism was his lack of focus on Jerusalem and the Temple. As

---

[311] Ibid., 107.

[312] Keener, *NIVCBSB*, 1621.

[313] Blomberg writes, "Use of this intimate term for God (almost equivalent to the English "Daddy") was virtually unparalleled in first-century Judaism." Blomberg, *Matthew*, NAC, 119.

[314] Scriptures marked NASB come from the *New American Standard Bible* (La Habra, CA: Lockman, 2020).

[315] Hagner, *Matthew 1–13*, WBC, 148.

[316] Ibid. See also Blomberg, *Matthew*, NAC, 119.

[317] France, *Matthew*, TNTC, 134.

previously noted, Jewish prayers, such as the Kaddish and the *Amidah* mention Jerusalem, the Temple, and the people of God.[318] However, Jesus never mentions any of them in his prayer. The closest one could come to a reference to a temple of any kind is an implicit reference to God's throne in the third petition.[319] Yet the human Temple in Jerusalem, which could be a human representation of the divine throne in heaven, is never mentioned. Even more interesting is that when Jesus references the Temple, he often speaks of the Temple's destruction (24:2) and its corruption (21:12–13). Additionally, rather than focusing exclusively on the community of Israel, Jesus places his focus on the global work of God as he reaches all people on earth.

A fourth difference is found in the aspect of forgiveness. Jewish prayers often directed its attention to the forgiveness of the individual rather than connecting forgiveness to a relational status. In stark contrast, Jesus first directs a person's forgiveness to God—"forgive us our debts" (6:12a). But then he connects the divine forgiveness received to the forgiveness extended to other individuals (6:12b). This is a unique take. To a degree, the forgiveness received correlates to the forgiveness offered to those who have harmed us.[320] From what has been observed in the Jewish prayers analyzed, nothing compares to Jesus's inimitable view of forgiveness.

Saying that more could be said about the distinctions of Jesus's view of prayer from the Jewish prayers of his day is most certainly an understatement. Nonetheless, for the purpose of this first method, the Lord's Prayer passes with no reservation or hesitation adding 2 points to its weighted scale. Quite honestly, the unique nature of Jesus's prayer is far more thorough than was anticipated when this study began.

Early Christological Concepts

Like the Beatitudes, the Lord's Prayer finds a connection with unique eschatological viewpoint of Jesus. The early nature of Jesus's eschatological focus finds a strong consensus among NT scholars. Witherington argues that "Jesus sees himself not merely as a herald but as one who brings in the dominion of God."[321] Jesus saw himself as the *Shaliach* of God, which was one

---

318 This is true more of the *Amidah* than necessarily the Kaddish. Bailey, *Jesus Through Middle Eastern Eyes,* 106.

319 Blomberg agrees with this point. Blomberg, *Matthew,* NAC, 119.

320 Ibid., 120.

321 Witherington, *Christology of Jesus,* 203.

who was endowed with the power and authority of God.[322] With the exception of 1 Kgs. 14:6, the concept of the *Shaliach* is not so much found in the OT but is rather found in the later Jewish sources of the Mishnah.[323] T. W. Manson summarizes the nature and the function of the *Shaliach* by five characteristics: 1) The *Shaliach* is one who acts on behalf of another; 2) he does not act beyond the commission to which he is assigned; 3) he is one who possesses an untransferable commission; 4) his position is one of function over status; and 5) he operates within the borders to which he is assigned.[324] From his understanding of himself as God's *Shaliach,* Jesus may have seen himself as the incarnate embodiment of divine Wisdom in Proverbs 8 or even as the figure of the Son of Man as preserved in *1 Enoch*.[325] The early apostles may have been the agents of the *Shaliach,* who would have been known as the *shalihim*.[326] As such, they would have operated under the authority of the *Shaliach* of God.

Bruce Chilton, a more progressive historian and member of the Jesus Seminar, maintains that Jesus's unique understanding of the kingdom of God was not only a major theme of Jesus's ministry, it was one of the first inclinations that Jesus apprehended of God's kingdom; as "he had a direct intuition of how his *Abba,* moment by moment, was reshaping the world and humanity."[327] Two areas of the Lord's Prayer show Jesus's Christological focus on his unique eschatological system.

First, the way Jesus views God's work through history is of particular interest. Throughout time, the flow of history has been viewed in different ways. The first viewpoint maintains that history is meaningless. Greek philosopher Gorgias (483–378 BC) can be said to be the first nihilist. Though his work is now lost, Gorgias is noted as arguing that nothing exists, and even if it did, no one could know it.[328] To some degree, the Sadducees could be said

---

322 Ibid. See also the connections with the "finger of God" found in Exod. 8:15; Deut. 9:10; Psa. 8:3. More will be found on this topic in Chapter 4. See also Witherington, *Christology of Jesus,* 51.

323 Particularly, *m. Rosh Ha-Shanah* 4.9 which dates to around AD 80–120. Witherington, *Christology of Jesus,* 133.

324 T. W. Manson, *The Church's Ministry* (London, UK: Hodder and Stoughton, 1948), 43–44.

325 Witherington, *Christology of Jesus,* 51; Hurtado, *One God, One Lord,* 17–92.

326 Witherington, *Christology of Jesus,* 133.

327 Bruce Chilton, *Rabbi Jesus: An Intimate Biography* (New York, NY: Doubleday, 2000), 19.

328 See Sextus Empiricus's *Against the Logicians* and Pseudo-Aristotle's *On Melissus, Xenophanes, and Gorgias.*

to hold some form of a nihilistic view of history as they did not hold to a view of God's interactions with humanity and a rejection of an afterlife (Matt. 22:29–30). A second view of history holds that history is circular. The Greek philosophers of Jesus's day held this perspective.[329] The primary difference between this view and the third is that some claimed that history never reached a final climax. Rather, it merely repeated itself to infinity. Jesus's view tended to match the third, which viewed that history was linear and held meaning. In this view, history has a direction and purpose. God is driving history to the place where God's kingdom is actualized. This was the intention behind Isaiah 61 and other apocalyptic passages pertaining to the eschaton. Paul would later pick up on this theme when he wrote that "God cause all things to work together for good to those who love God, to those who are called according to His purpose" (Rom. 8:28, NASB).

Second, the imminent reign of God is shown in the Lord's Prayer. In the second petition, the Greek text reads "*ἐλθέτω ἡ βασιλεία σου,*" or "bring your eschatological kingdom."[330] As Hagner notes, "This refers to the eschatological rule of God expected and longed for by the Jewish people (cf. the central petition of the Kaddish, above v 9).[331] The Lord's Prayer finds a home in Jesus's recognizable eschatological focus on the already-not-yet kingdom. Jesus announced that he was the *Shaliach* of Yahweh, the one through whom God's kingdom would be brought to earth.[332] As noted previously, one finds a crossover between the spiritual and material domains in ancient biblical theology. The same is true in Jesus's theology. Jesus understood that the kingdom of God is God's desire to rule over all his creation—both the spiritual and material realms.[333] Because of the work of Jesus, God's divine council would now include a human presence found in the redeemed saints of God.[334] Nevertheless, the request to bring the eschatological kingdom was being answered through Jesus but would be fully completed at the end of history.

---

[329] Bailey, *Jesus Through Middle Eastern Eyes,* 114. Plato was an advocate of this circular pattern to history.

[330] Hagner, *Matthew 1–13,* WBC, 148.

[331] Ibid.

[332] This will be readdressed in Matthew 11:2–19. A great deal of similarity is found between the Sermon on the Mount and the interaction that Jesus holds with John's disciples. See Chapter 5 for more details.

[333] Heiser, *Unseen Realm,* 38.

[334] Ibid., 47.

Since the eschaton is a major element of early Christology, the Lord's Prayer finds a perfect home in Jesus's theological thinking.

While the Lord's Prayer is not totally focused on the eschatological kingdom, it does find a strong connection to the recognized early Christological themes of Jesus's ministry. It is most certain that Jesus connects the coming eschatological kingdom through his ministry. This connection is found in the first three petitions of the Lord's Prayer, that the already-not-yet kingdom has come through him. Hagner finds a connection between this prayer and the early credal prayer of 1 Corinthians 16:22 which simply states *Marana tha* ("our Lord come"). Due to the eschatological emphasis of the first three petitions of the prayer, the Lord's Prayer can be said to pass the second methodology as it matches the eschatological function of early Christology. For the weighted scale, add 5 points to its score.

Theological Terminology Relating to Early Christological Concepts

The difficulty with the Lord's Prayer and the third methodology is that, like the Beatitudes, no Christological title is found. However, in the previous entry concerning the Beatitudes, it was noted that *βασιλεία* and *μακάριος* pointed to early Christological concepts which supported the notion that the kingdom of God had come through the reign of Jesus. In like manner, the Lord's Prayer contains a term that, while not an official Christological title, does refer to Jesus's identification as the Son of God. That term is *Abba.*

Early Christological terminology can point to Christological titles without specifically stating the title. Oscar Cullmann similarly argued that "If Jesus' consciousness of sonship really has such great significance for the understanding of his person and work, then once more we may not limit ourselves to the few sayings in which the word 'Son' itself occurs."[335] Cullmann contends that due to Jesus teaching his disciples to pray "our Father" that he unconsciously, or even subconsciously, illustrates his understanding of the "special Son-relationship" that he holds with the Father.[336] The implicit nature of the Son-Father relationship may also help explain the Messianic secret found in Mark's Gospel as Jesus references the relationship without explicitly revealing it.[337]

While the Aramaic *Abba* does not necessarily find a connection to early terminology in the LXX, Jesus's unique usage of the term shows its distinct nature. Most certainly, Jewish people called God their Heavenly Father. However, they did not draw the connection to God as Jesus did. Jesus's unique

---

335 Cullmann, *Christology of the NT,* 289.

336 Ibid.

337 Ibid.

prayer finds three early connections in the church. First, because of the similarity that the Lord's Prayer holds with the Kaddish, the prayer comes from the earliest times of the church and, thereby, would not have been an invention of the later Gentile church..[338] Keener argues that the Lord's Prayer with the Kaddish argues for its authenticity..[339] Second, the *Didache,* a manual most likely written in the late first-century, quotes the prayer found in Matthew's Gospel..[340] The manual adds that Christians should fast on the fourth day and on the preparation.[341] and should recite the Lord's Prayer three times a day..[342] Lastly, the Lord's Prayer finds a fascinating parallel to Jesus's High Priestly Prayer in John 17. All but one of the petitions found in the High Priestly Prayer matches the Lord's Prayer..[343] As such, it may have been that Jesus used the Lord's Prayer as something of a guide to later prayers, which may have served as the reason behind the church's call to pray the Lord's Prayer three times daily.

---

[338] Keener, *The Historical Jesus of the Gospels,* 198.

[339] Ibid.

[340] *Didache* 8.2.

[341] Ibid., 8.1.

[342] Ibid, 8.2.

[343] Craig L. Blomberg, *The Historical Reliability of the New Testament* (Nashville, TN: B&H Academic, 2016), 220.

Our Father, who is in heaven, Hallowed be Your name. Your kingdom come. Your will be done, On earth as it is in heaven. Give us this day our daily bread. And forgive us our debts, as we also have forgiven our debtors. And do not lead us into temptation, But deliver us from evil (6:9–13, NASB).	Father, the hour has come; glorify Your Son, so that the Son may glorify You… I glorified You on the earth by accomplishing the work which You have given me to do… I have revealed Your name to the men whom You gave Me out of the world; they were Yours and You gave them to Me; and they have followed Your word… Sanctify them in truth… I am not asking You to take them out of the world, but to keep them away from the evil one (John 17:1, 4, 6, 13, 17, NASB).[344]

While there are no Christological titles in the passage, the Lord's Prayer, as was the case with the Beatitudes, finds a deep connection with early Christological concepts. In the case of the Lord's Prayer, Jesus's use of the Aramaic term *abba* when referencing the Father-Son relationship he holds with God connects to the Son of God Christological title, albeit in a much more implicit manner. Furthermore, the unique Father-Son relationship afforded in the passage matches the bipartite formulations identified in early creedal material.[345] Because of the Father-Son connection to the Son of God title and the early bipartite formulation, the Lord's Prayer passes the third method, adding 4 points.

Mnemonic and Rhythmic Patterns

The Lord's Prayer, by its very nature, holds a mnemonic and rhythmic pattern, even as evidenced by the large number of people who recite it in its traditional form.[346] One of the most intriguing rhythmic aspects of the Lord's Prayer is the use of what is called *parallelismus membrorum. Parallelismus membrorum*

344 Ibid.; William O. Walker, "The Lord's Prayer in Matthew and John," *New Testament Studies* 28 (1982): 237–256.

345 Cullmann, *Earliest Christian Confessions,* 36.

346 One such example is found in the 1979 *Book of Common Prayer* which calls for the recitation of the Lord's Prayer in morning and evening devotions, and even during ceremonies for the sick and dying.

is described as an "endeavor to produce parallelism in lines."[347] Jeremias notes that the parallels are found in "'Our bread for tomorrow/give us today'; 'Forgive us/as we forgive'; and 'And lead us not into temptation/but deliver us from evil.'"[348] The parallelisms are found in both Matthew and Luke's presentation of the Lord's Prayer. Luke's phrase "And do not lead us into temptation" (Luke 11:4, NASB) is an abbreviated form of Matthew's lengthier parallelism, which says, "And do not lead us into temptation, but deliver us from evil" (6:13, NASB). While the stylistic structure is carried out to greater lengths in Matthew's Gospel than in Luke's, the three "Thou-petitions" early in Matthew's prayer correspond with the three "We-petitions" in Luke's.[349]

The Lord's Prayer is more developed in Matthew's presentation of the Lord's Prayer than in Luke's. This has led some scholars to posit that Luke derives his information from an earlier source than Matthew's.[350] In part, this is due to the shorter text and parallels found in Romans 8:15 and Galatians 4:6 in Luke's Gospel. For instance, Matthew contains seven petitions compared to Luke's five.[351] However, while there are differences, many similarities are found. The first two petitions in both Gospels are in agreement, as does Matthew's sixth petition with Luke's fifth.[352] But do the differences in the rhythmic patterns of the Lord's Prayer in both Gospels detract from its Semitic residue?

In biblical scholarship, there is no general consensus on which text represents the earlier tradition. Some argue that the prayers derive from two traditions rather than one source.[353] While there is good evidence to suggest that this may be the case,[354] another option provides a possibility. Early churches viewed themselves as Christian synagogues, as is evident in the

---

347 Jeremias, *Jesus and the Message of the New Testament,* 46.

348 Ibid.

349 Ibid.

350 Ibid.

351 Luke does not add the petition where God's will is desired on earth as it was decreed in heaven.

352 Hagner, *Matthew 1–13,* WBC, 145.

353 Ernst Lohmeyer, *The Lord's Prayer* (London, UK: Collins, 1965), 293.

354 D. A. Carson, "Matthew," in *The Expositor's Bible Commentary: Matthew, Mark, Luke*, ed. Frank E. Gaebelein, vol. 8 (Grand Rapids, MI: Zondervan Publishing House, 1984), 168.

Didache and Ignatius's epistles.[355] The *Didache* adopted the Matthean version of the Lord's Prayer as the official prayer to quote three times daily.[356] Thus, the Matthean version held strong support in the early church. However, Luke's presentation of the Lord's Prayer and its parallels with Romans 8:15[357] and Galatians 4:6[358] may represent another tradition of the Lord's Prayer floating around in various churches. Michael Bird argues that these double traditions, while affirming the presence of a Q tradition, could originate from an "array of sources, oral and written, some of which found their way into Q."[359] If Bird is correct, then there is no reason to deny that the traditions could have derived from Jesus presenting the prayer in different locations and at different times. As was mentioned previously, it is entirely possible that the messages within the Sermon on the Mount represent sermon summaries of various messages given over a course of time instead of only one day. If true, then it is entirely possible that Jesus could have given the Lord's Prayer to different people on different days of his preaching series. If fixed liturgical traditions of the Lord's Prayer were found in the earliest church, and they identified themselves as Christian synagogues holding fast to their sacred traditions,[360] then there is no reason to doubt that both Matthew and Luke afford early varieties of the prayer and that both of the traditions could have arisen from the lips of Jesus himself.[361]

In conclusion, rhythmic patterns are found in both Matthew and Luke's versions of the Lord's Prayer. Since both Gospels present the prayer in a different way, many have felt the need to argue that one of the portrayals represents an earlier tradition than the other. However, these debates have proven futile as neither side can establish a clear-cut case to defend their position. A better way is to view both traditions as early, possibly coming from different oral traditions concerning the prayer. If one is to accept that the

---

355 The *Didache* adopted similar practices of fasting and the recitation of the Lord's Prayer as Jewish synagogues adopted from their own fasts and recitations of the *Amidah*. See the *Didache* 8.1–2.

356 Ibid.

357 "…we cry out, 'Abba! Father!'" (Rom. 8:15b, NASB).

358 "…crying out, 'Abba! Father!'" (Gal. 4:6, NASB).

359 Michael F. Bird, *The Gospel of the Lord: How the Early Church Wrote the Story of Jesus* (Grand Rapids, MI; Cambridge, UK: Eerdmans, 2014), 170.

360 Hagner, *Matthew 1–13,* WBC, 167–168.

361 While Keener holds that Luke's prayer represents an earlier tradition than Matthew, he agrees that Matthew most likely preserved the Lord's Prayer in his Gospel from an oral source rather than Q. Keener, *GMSRC,* 214.

Sermon on the Mount is a conglomerate of sermon summaries from Jesus's messages delivered on the mountainside, then it is quite possible that Jesus may have presented the Lord's Prayer in two similar but varied ways according to his audience's needs. If so, the audiences would have remembered the prayer in different ways. Despite their differences, both portrayals have more similarities than differences. For the purpose of this study, it is only necessary to note that rhythmic patterns are indeed found in Matthew's presentation of the Lord's Prayer and, thereby, pass the method. But, indeed, there are numerous issues that need to be worked through concerning the differences between Matthew and Luke's documentation of the Lord's Prayer. Yet a full exploration of these issues is beyond the scope of this work. Nonetheless, add 5 more points for the weighted scale.

Aramaic/Hebraic Literary Characteristics

The Matthean version, like the Lukan version, is replete with Aramaic literary characteristics. Already, it has been noted that Jesus's use of *πατήρ* stemmed from the original, yet unique, usage of the Aramaic term *abba*. The NT writers picked up on the usage in other passages of Scripture (Rom. 8:15; Gal. 4:6). Additionally, the term is used in Mark's Gospel, one that does not hold the Lord's Prayer, when Jesus prayed in the Garden of Gethsemane, saying, "*Abba,* Father! All things are possible for you. Take this cup away from me. Nevertheless, not what I will, but what you will" (Mark 14:36). One could even argue that the Matthean form of the prayer is found in Mark's Gospel as Jesus includes the petition to live out the Father's will on earth as it has been decreed in heaven, one of the few petitions missing in Luke's Gospel. Nonetheless, the use of *Abba* is not the only Aramaic characteristic found in the Matthean Lord's Prayer.

If one were to include verses 14 and 15 in the text, then it is held that verse 15.[362] contains an Aramaic imperfect which, according to Jeremias, would read, "But if you do not forgive others, neither can your Father forgive your trespasses.".[363] The text appears consistent with Jesus's other messages in the Gospel such as Matt. 18:35. The term *ἀφήκαμεν* in verse 12 is in the aorist tense, which affords the idea that the person has already been forgiven, which anticipates the actions of forgiveness to be given in verses 14 and 15..[364] It is possible that *ἀφήκαμεν* could be a Greek rendition of the Aramaic *perfectum praesens* which could possibly provide the idea that one forgives as one is being

---

[362] "But if you don't forgive others, your Father will not forgive your offences" (6:15).

[363] Jeremias, *Jesus and the Message of the New Testament,* 31.

[364] Hagner, *Matthew 1–13,* WBC, 150.

forgiven.[365] R. T. France notes, the teaching does not imply that forgiveness is a precondition to divine forgiveness, but rather that "Like all God's gifts, it brings responsibility … To ask forgiveness on any other basis is hypocrisy."[366] But for the purpose of this research, it should be noted that there is a strong possibility that the text holds an Aramaic trait as it links with the usage of a *perfectum praesens.*

Correlating with the pattern noted in a previous method, the Lord's Prayer also uses a four-beat rhythmic pattern that is quite common to Jesus's didactical teaching style. The 4+4+2 occurs in the Lord's Prayer, particularly in the Aramaic.[367] A two/four-stress rhythm and rhyme is found in the Aramaic version of Luke's version, as well. Jeremias translates the Lukan prayer as the following:

> *'Abbâ*
> *yitqaddáš š*^{e}*mâk / tētḗ malkūtâk*
> *laḥmán d*^{e}*limḥár / hab lán yōmā dḗn*
> *uš*^{e}*bōq lán ḥōbtḗnan / k*^{e}*diš*^{e}*báqnan l*^{e}*ḥayyābtḗnan*
> *w*^{e}*lā ta'ēlínnan l*^{e}*nisyṓn.*[368]

While Jeremias contends that the Lukan version derives from an earlier tradition, he also argues that the Matthean's wording is preferable.[369] If one either accepts the variances that were permitted within oral traditions stemming from one source, which Matthew's version has already been linked to an early oral tradition, or if one holds to a dual tradition stemming from two variations that Jesus himself used for the prayer; then, there is no reason as to why one could not accept both the Lukan and Matthean traditions of the prayer as early. But that the Lord's Prayer contains Aramaisms and Aramaic traits are undeniable.

One final example of an Aramaism encompasses the petition found in verse 11, particularly around the Greek word *ἐπιούσιον*. Jerome, the early church father, noted that the *Gospel of the Nazareans,* a book now lost except for a few excerpts, used the word *mahar* which is understood to designate future

---

365 Ibid.

366 France, *Matthew,* TNTC, 142.

367 Joachim Jeremias, *New Testament Theology*, John Bowden, trans (London: SCM, 1971), 23.

368 Ibid., 196.

369 Ibid.

eschatological bread.[370] The *Gospel of the Nazareans* was not an Aramaic original, but more likely an Aramaic translation of the Gospel of Matthew.[371] Nevertheless, the use of Jesus's eschatological slant throughout the Sermon on the Mount in addition to the dominance of the eschatological understanding of the petition for bread throughout the first few centuries of the church, found in both the East and West,[372] provides a strong case that ἐπιούσιον could have originally been uttered and understood as *mahar*, a prayer that the eschatological bread of tomorrow would be given today.

With the evidence provided in this section along with what has been given prior, it is beyond a reasonable doubt that the Lord's Prayer contains a strong Aramaic undertone. As such, it is very reasonable to hold that the Lord's Prayer passes the current method with flying colors. Even though the Beatitudes were strong in their Aramaic characteristics, the text could be said to be eclipsed only by the Lord's Prayer in its level of Aramaisms. Freely add 5 more points to its weighted scale.

Semitic Cultural Concepts of First-century Israel

Given the previous data provided for the Lord's Prayer, particularly with its relationship with the Kaddish and the *Amidah,* the Lord's Prayer already holds strong parallels to the cultural concepts of its time by default. There is no reason to regurgitate the parallels between the Lord's Prayer and the Kaddish at this time.[373] However, there is a cultural concept implicitly noted by Jesus's use of the term "name" (Gk. ὄνομά) when referencing Yahweh's divine name.[374] This was a form of circumlocution used by ancient Jews to avoid

---

[370] Jerome, *Commentary on Matthew 6:11*, in E. Klostermann, *Apocrypha II* (Berlin: KIT, 1929), 7.

[371] Jeremias, *NT Theology,* 199.

[372] Ibid.

[373] It is, however, interesting to note the translation of the Kaddish that Jeremias provides at this juncture. The following is Jeremias's presentation of the Kaddish:

> "Exalted and hallowed be his great name
> in the world which he created according to his will.
> May he let his kingdom rule
> in your lifetime and in your days and in the lifetime
> of the whole house of Israel, speedily and soon.
> Praised be his great name from eternity to eternity.
> And to this, say: Amen." Jeremias, *NT Theology,* 198.

[374] Robert H. Stein, *The Method and Message of Jesus' Teachings,* revised ed (Louisville, KY: Westminster John Knox, 1994), 64.

saying God's divine name. The disallowance of uttering the divine name extends back to the pre-Christian era, given to prevent any chance that the second commandment would be broken (Exod. 20:7; Deut. 5:11).[375] While Jesus does occasionally mention the name God, Jeremias lists 18 areas where Jesus uses a *periphrase* to avoid the name. "*Πάτερ ἡμῶν*" in Matthew 6:9 is one such example. Nonetheless, the resemblances between the Kaddish, *Amidah,* and the Lord's Prayer in addition to Jesus's circumlocution all find a home in the cultural setting of the time. Additionally, the three "Thou-petitions" and the four "we-petitions" have been compared to the arrangement of the Decalogue.[376] Much more could be given. But sufficient evidence has been given in this section, along with the material given previously in this research, to closely align the Lord's Prayer with the cultural context of Jesus's day. As such, this material can be said to derive from the early Jewish setting of Jesus's time and not a later invention of the Gentile church, adding 4 more points to its score.

Similarities to NT Creeds, Summaries, and Early Literature

Thus far, the Lord's Prayer has seen the same strength as the Beatitudes when it comes to its Semitic residue. It is not anticipated that the rest of the researched *logia* will hold the same level of strength. Nevertheless, as the Lord's Prayer is already defaulted into the green light, it needs to be seen whether the Lord's Prayer can pass all seven methods as did its Sermon on the Mount colleague—the Beatitudes.

Before exploring the Lord's Prayer's similarities to the NT Creeds and Summaries, it needs to be noted that the comparisons that the prayer holds with early literature have already been described. As previously mentioned, Jesus's prayer finds great similarities with the Jewish Kaddish and *Amidah* prayers. The Matthean version is also the official prayer of the early church, as noted by the *Didache*. The *Didache* called for the Matthean version of the prayer to be recited three times daily. Additionally, Peter quotes the Lord's Prayer[377] in his first epistle. The petition of Matthew 6:9 finds a reference point in 1 Peter 1:17, as do other teachings of Jesus preserved in Matthew's Gospel.[378] Thus, with the mounting cumulative evidence, one can say that the Matthean version of the Lord's Prayer finds good support with the early literature of the time

375 Jeremias, *NT Theology,* 9.

376 Keener, *GMSRC,* 214.

377 Assuming that Simon Peter is the author of the epistle.

378 Blomberg, *Historical Reliability of the NT,* 481.

prior to Jesus's teaching, during the time of Jesus's teaching, and subsequent to Jesus's teaching.

As a reminder, the NT creeds are based on five themes: 1) baptism and catechisms, 2) worship, 3) exorcisms, 4) encouragement against persecution, and 5) polemics against heresies.[379] As previously noted, the Sermon on the Mount was used as a catechism for the early church. The Lord's Prayer was an integral part of the Sermon and meets the criteria of being an early catechism. With the integration of the Lord's Prayer in the everyday worship of the early church, as noted by the *Didache,* then one can hold that the Lord's Prayer was part of the worship dynamic held by early creedal systems. If one holds to the eschatological nature of the Lord's Prayer, as the link between ἐπιούσιον and *mahar* implies, along with the last petition's focus on standing strong against evil, then it can be said that the prayer could offer encouragement against present persecution. There are no apparent links to exorcism and polemics against heresies in the Lord's Prayer.

Of the three characteristics of early material—1) single-statement declarations, 2) formulaic prose/*homologiai,* and 3) hymns and poetry,[380] the hymnic characteristic is most prominent in the text. As was previously noted, the Lord's prayer uses parallelism in both the Matthean and Lukan accounts. Jeremias notes the four-beat pattern of the prayer, which, as he noted, was a popular teaching method of Jesus.[381] The parallel structures of the Lord's Prayer find a connection with the early creedal material.[382] The prayer not only contains parallelism, but it also affords a unique *hapax legomena* with Jesus's usage of *Abba.* The unique convictions of the prayer which stand in contrast with the Kaddish and *Amidah* also meet the criteria of the text's affirmation of basic Christian convictions.[383]

Outside of the similar traits that *homologiai* share with hymnic creedal patterns, the Lord's Prayer does not necessarily match the *homologiai* and does not appear to hold any traits aligning with the single-statement affirmations. However, due to the prayer's alignment with the hymnic creedal pattern, the links it holds with early material, and the three themes it shares with early material, then the *logia* of Matthew 6:9–13 can be said to pass the final method.

---

[379] Cullmann, *Earliest Christian Confessions,* 18.

[380] Longenecker, *New Wine into Fresh Wineskins,* 7.

[381] Jeremias, *NT Theology,* 23.

[382] Longenecker, *New Wine into Fresh Wineskins*, 9.

[383] For instance, the bipartite relationship between Jesus and Yahweh along with the ongoing theme of the already-not-yet kingdom. Ibid., 11.

Like the Beatitudes, the Lord's Prayer scored a perfect score of 30 on the weighted test.

Conclusion and Color Assignment

Like the Beatitudes, the Lord's Prayer passes all seven methodologies. While there are some distinctions between Luke's presentation of the prayer and Matthew's, one does not necessarily need to place one as an earlier tradition over the other. Due to the nature of oral traditions and the possibility that Jesus may have formulated the prayer more compactly for different audiences, one is justified to hold Michael Bird's assessment that the two prayers may represent a double-tradition..[384] Since the *logia* passed all seven criteria in this research and upheld a perfect score of 30, the Lord's Prayer can be said to maintain a strong green designation. The cumulative case presented in this work has shown that it is beyond a reasonable doubt that the Lord's Prayer holds strong Semitic residue, which most likely indicates that the prayer was not an invention of the church but rather represents the very voice of Jesus himself.

Conclusion

This chapter has investigated two passages of Scripture from the Sermon on the Mount. Both the Beatitudes and the Lord's Prayer fared very well against the criteria established by this research. Not only did both the Beatitudes and Lord's Prayer find themselves with the green light designations, but their color tone of green also ran quite dark as both passed every method placed before them. The ongoing theme of Isaiah 61 was found in the Beatitudes and Lord's Prayer, albeit to a mildly lesser degree. If the Sermon on the Mount consists of sermon summaries from various messages that Jesus delivered on the mountainside during the days or weeks that he was there, as this research suggests, then it is quite possible that the eschatological theme of Isaiah 61 served as the major teaching point from which the varied messages arose. Most intriguingly, Jesus portrayed an already-not-yet portrayal of the kingdom of heaven. The kingdom was arriving through him, but it would not be fully actualized until the final glorification at the eschaton. While many other passages deserve treatment through the Sermon on the Mount, there is sufficient evidence to suggest that the entire series of messages in the Sermon may hold the same Semitic residue that the Beatitudes and Sermon on the Mount possess. Therefore, the research suggests that the entire Sermon on the Mount could hold a green light for containing high levels of Semitic residue. But to know for sure, it would be necessary to run all the texts of Matthew 5:3–

---

384 Bird, *The Gospel of the Lord,* 170.

7:29 through the prescribed methods. Such an effort is beyond the limitations of this current research.

CHAPTER THREE
MATTHEAN PARABLES OF JESUS

One of the most distinctive traits of Jesus's teaching is his frequent use of parables. Parables are understood to be stories that portray a spiritual truth in common settings. J. Robertson McQuilkin holds that parabolic teaching is in the general category of "figures of comparison."[385] Jesus was not the only person of antiquity who recognized the power and need of parables in teaching. Galen (AD 140), the first nonbeliever to document positive things about Christians, wrote, "Most people are unable to follow a demonstrative argument consecutively; hence they need parables, and benefit from them ... just as now we see the people called Christians drawing their faith from parables [and miracles] and yet sometimes acting in the same way [as those who philosophize]."[386]

All the Synoptic Gospels heavily emphasize the parabolic teaching ministry of Jesus. However, as Bock has noted, it may be that the Evangelists only provide a sampling of Jesus's messages while he traveled the region.[387] Matthew's Gospel affords 23 parables in his text, compared to Mark's 10 and Luke, who holds the most, with 24. Examining the Semitic residue of all 23 Matthean parables would go beyond the spatial limitations of this project. However, three have been chosen which hold certain attributes that would make them more inclined to meet the criteria set forth by this research.

The parables chosen all contain either a high eschatological or Christological focus. The first parable is the Parable of the Harvest found in Matthew 13. Coinciding with the primary parable in chapter 13, a mini-parable can be found in Matthew 9:37–38. This parable notes the comprehensive nature of the end-times judgment as the wheat is separated from the weeds.[388] The wheat, in this case, represents the people of God, whereas the weeds represent those who reject God's grace. Its intrinsic Christological focus surrounds Christ as the catalyst which delineates the mark between the two.

The second parable also contains an eschatological flavor but is more Christocentric in nature. The Parable of the Compassionate Employer (20:1–16) primarily emphasizes the graciousness of God. The parable tells the story of a landowner who seeks to hire help for the day. He calls workers at various

---

[385] J. Robertson McQuilkin, *Understanding and Applying the Bible* (Chicago, IL: Moody Press, 1983), 153.

[386] Galen, *Summary of Plato's Republic,* in James Stevenson, ed., *A New Eusebius* (London, UK: SPCK, 1957), 133.

[387] Bock and Simpson, *Jesus According to Scripture,* 284.

[388] Bock and Simpson, *Jesus According to Scripture,* 291.

times during the day. However, Jesus's emphasis on the last being first and the first being last (20:16) indicates that there may be some sense of an eschatological focus to the teaching, particularly when referencing a person's entrance into the kingdom.

The third parable is found in Matthew 25 and is entitled the Parable of the Wise and Foolish Young Women. This parable holds both eschatological and Christological themes which one would think would bode well for the methodological system set in place. In symbolic fashion, the parable denotes the imminent return of Christ who is likened to the groom. The young women represent people, some of whom were ready for the groom's arrival, whereas others were not. The groom comes for the bride. The readied women entered the feast, and the unprepared women were left out.

One of the biggest questions of this section is whether the parable meets the criteria for holding early Semitic residue which is indicative of early theological and linguistic material. However, another question inquires as to whether the entire parable represents the voice of Jesus or whether a few portions of the parables provide seeds upon which the remainder of the parable is built. A potential problem for this section of Scripture is due to the flexibility of the parable. As previously noted, oral traditions can hold a bit of flexibility so long as the core essence of the material is the same. One could imagine that Jesus's parables could maintain a bit more flexibility due to the ease by which the stories are memorized.

Parable of the Harvest (Matt. 13:24–30, 36–40)

The role of harvest plays an important role in the teachings of Jesus. In an agrarian society, Jesus's metaphor would have been particularly compelling. Jesus uses the harvest to represent salvation and its blessings..[389] Two such examples of Jesus's focus on the harvest are found in Jesus's teaching of the Lord of the Harvest (9:37–38)—which is technically not a parable in the strictest sense—and the Parable of the Harvest (13:24–30, 36–40). The former section finds itself within the *logia* of Jesus's teaching campaign. Jesus taught in various towns and villages and was "preaching the good news of the kingdom, and healing every disease and every sickness" (9:35). Jesus noted the abundant people's need for a shepherd. Then, he noted to the disciples, "The harvest is abundant, but the workers are few. Therefore, pray to the Lord of the harvest to send out workers into his harvest" (9:37–38).

The latter portion of Scripture is found in the third block of teachings found in Matthew's Gospel..[390] The section has been called the "kingdom

---

[389] Jeremias, *NT Theology,* 106.

[390] Blomberg, *Matthew,* NAC, 211.

parables."[391] Interestingly, Morris finds a contrast with the earlier passage. Whereas Jesus had been teaching in the synagogues, he now finds himself teaching the people outdoors on a beach and increasingly using parables in his didactical system.[392] Jesus increasingly abandons the synagogue for the outdoors to reach the masses.[393] In the Parable of the Harvest, sometimes called the Parable of the Wheat and the Weeds,[394] Jesus tells the story of a wicked individual who plants a darnel[395] in a landowner's field. The wheat and darnel are allowed to coexist with one another until the time of the harvest. If the darnel is removed before the harvest, the wheat would be damaged (13:29). The Jesus Seminar holds that the first part of the text derives from some of the Jesuan thought. Nonetheless, they believe that Matthew has heavily redacted the parable according to his interpretation. The gray category is given to Matthew 13:24–30, whereas verses 37–40 are listed in black.[396] The Seminar believes Jesus probably taught something comparable to the parable but that the interpretation is solely the evangelist's explanation.[397]

To investigate this particular parable, one will need to extract the major theological themes in the parable. The main theme is that of the eschatological harvest. To a degree, one could note the problem of theodicy in the parable. The enemy plants darnel among the wheat which will be ultimately separated at the end of harvest. Additionally, the use of parables and the themes found therein will be useful to examine whether the parable contains the Semitic residue being explored in this research. Of special interest in this parable is the

---

391 Ibid.

392 Leon Morris, *The Gospel According to Matthew,* Pillar New Testament Commentary (Grand Rapids, MI; Leicester, UK: Eerdmans; IVP, 1992), 333.

393 Ibid.

394 Hagner, *Matthew,* WBC, 381. Bock gives the parable the title of "The Parable of the Wheat and the Darnel," which may be a better choice of the two. Bock and Simpson, *Jesus According to Scripture,* 291.

395 Darnel is a weed that looks so much like wheat that it is difficult to decipher the two during the earlier stages of growth. Ibid.

396 Funk, Hoover, and the Jesus Seminar, *Five Gospels,* 196.

397 Ibid., 196.

use of the title Son of Man, which is an extremely important Christological title..[398]

Unique Rabbinic Concepts

Jesus's use of parables was not in itself unique. Parables were used in the Old Testament and by rabbinical teachers. The Talmud notes in the teachings of Rabbi Meir, he taught with "one-third *halakha,* one-third *haggada,* and one-third parables.".[399] Rabbi Yohanan later notes that Rabbi Meir gave "three hundred parables of foxes, and we only have three.".[400] While Jesus's use of parables is not unique, the level of frequency in which he used parables was unique to him. However, this is not necessarily what is needed for the parables to pass the first method. A further investigation must be given regarding the content of the parable itself to dictate whether it passes the first criterion.

The primary message of the parable is that while God sows on the earth, the enemy also sows. Because of the enemy imitation of God's works, the true test of a person's faith is found in one's fruit. At the Great Harvest at the eschaton, the angels of God will separate the wheat (the saints of God) from the darnel (the followers of the enemy). Fruchtenbaum avers that the parable makes three points—"True sowing will be imitated by counter-sowing; the true and the false will develop side by side …; and the judgment at the end of the mystery kingdom will separate the two.".[401] Jesus's eschatological viewpoint is unique and seems to find a home more in the Jewish apocalyptic literature of the day rather than the Talmud. For instance, *2 Ezra* describes the eschatological harvest which will distinguish the "evil seed … sown in Adam's heart from the beginning, and how much ungodliness it has produced until now—and will produce until the time of threshing comes.".[402] The Talmudic rabbis mentioned the harvest, but primarily denoting the typical agrarian and relational definitions encompassing the religious festivals of Judaism. Thus, from what this researcher has found, there are no parallels to Jesus's usage of the eschatological harvest as found in this harvest. Therefore, the parable does not pass the first method. One slight parallel can be found in his usage of the Son of Man title, as will be noted in a future section. However, since the

---

[398] The Son of Man title will be explored in more detail in Chapter 4.

[399] *Sanhedrin* 38b, *Sefaria.org,* https://www.sefaria.org/Sanhedrin.39a.1?lang=bi.

[400] Ibid.

[401] Fructenbaum, *Yeshua,* vol. 3, 443–444.

[402] *2 Ezra* 4:30. All quotations from the Apocrypha comes from the *New Revised Standard Version* (New York, NY: National Council on the Churches of Christ, 1989).

primary theme deals with the eschatological harvest, there is not sufficient evidence to connect the parable to the first method.

Early Christological Concepts

One of the most central themes of Jesus's public proclamation was on the reign of God.[403] As was noted in the previous chapter, Jesus described an "already-not-yet" kingdom. This was a kingdom that had already come through him but would find itself fully actualized in the eschaton. However, the bipartite connection is not as strong as it was in the Sermon on the Mount. Even still, there is a slight intrinsic connection found throughout the parable. In the explanation of the parable (13:36–43), Jesus uses third-person language to show that the Son of Man is the sower (13:36) and the "chief harvester."[404] He even makes a connection with Zephaniah 1:3[405] by showing how people who cause sin and those who commit evil will be the objects of God's judgment at the eschaton. Earlier in the Gospel, Jesus makes the startling claim that even those that had thought themselves to be at the Messianic banquet because of their national identity would not be assured a place in the kingdom because of their lack of faith.[406] This aspect of the kingdom was startling as it was commonplace to think that "no descendant of Abraham could be lost."[407]

The key Christological identifiers are found in the parable's interpretation, especially identifying the Son of Man with the harvester and the eschatological judgment to come. One of the questions concerning the parable, and all the parables of Jesus in general, is whether Jesus provided the interpretation as found in verses 36 through 43. It is often assumed that the parable's interpretation stems from the early church rather than Jesus.[408] While there may be some validity to the argument in some cases, there is no reason to argue that the content did not belong to Jesus in this particular parable,

---

[403] Jeremias, *NT Theology,* 96.

[404] France, *Matthew,* TNTC, 229.

[405] "I will sweep away people and animals; I will sweep away the birds of the sky and the fish of the sea, and the ruins along with the wicked. I will cut off mankind from the face of the earth. This is the LORD'S declaration" (Zeph. 1:3).

[406] France, *Matthew,* TNTC, 160.

[407] Joachim Jeremias, *Jesus' Promise to the Nations* (London, UK: SCM, 1958), 48.

[408] Morris, *Matthew,* PNTC, 344.

primarily due to the usage of the title Son of Man.[409] Although the *Gospel of Thomas* includes an abbreviated version of the parable—which is interesting considering that the parable does not find a parallel in the other Gospels—the *Gospel of Thomas* most likely relies on the Gospel of Matthew as its source.[410] Furthermore, arguments against the authenticity of the interpretation of parables are not as robust as one might think. R. T. France asserts that the objections brought against the parables' interpretations are moot when examining the common usage of interpretations in Jesus's teachings and the absence of any Judaic requirements that parables must be instantly explained.[411] Gundry does not accept the interpretation as stemming directly from Jesus's lips, but he does hold that the "singularity of the expressions in Jesus' teaching may derive, however, from the singularity of the parable itself and therefore carry little weight concerning the authenticity or inauthenticity of the interpretation."[412] Therefore, even if the literal interpretation did not come from Jesus as it has been preserved, the essence of the interpretation would have still been found in Jesus's original parable. Thus, the interpretation captures the essence of Jesus's original message. To claim otherwise, as Morris contends, is to avow that the earliest disciples did not understand the message of Jesus.[413] Granted, it is true that the disciples often struggled with the message of Jesus during his earthly ministry, to the point of incomprehension at points (Mk. 4:40; 6:51–52; 8:4, 14–21; 8:33;9:2–10; 14:68–72). Nonetheless, Jesus patiently instructed them throughout his ministry and especially after his

---

[409] Jeremias argues that the "apocalyptic Son of Man sayings which we have recognized as the earliest stratum must in essentials go back to Jesus himself." Jeremias, *NT Theology,* 267.

[410] Another reason for this explanation is the curious absence of the title "Son of Man" outside of the canonical Gospels. Apart from Acts 7:56; 13:21–22; Hebrews 2:6; Revelation 1:13; and Revelation 14:14, the early church never uses the title Son of Man. For this reason, the early church preserved the title as part of Jesus's didactical system but did not use the title outside of Jesus's teachings. The absence of the title in the *Gospel of Thomas* could speak in favor of the Gospel of Matthew's connection to early material.

[411] France provides answers nine objections to the authenticity of the parables' interpretation. R. T. France, "The Authenticity of the Parable of the Sower and Its Interpretation," *Gospel Perspectives: Studies of History and Tradition in the Four Gospels,* vol. 1, R. T. France and David Wenham, eds (Eugene, OR: Wipf & Stock, 1981), 169.

[412] R. H. Gundry, *Matthew: A Commentary on His Literary and Theological Art* (Grand Rapids, MI: Eerdmans, 1982), 261; Morris, *Matthew,* PNTC, 345.

[413] Morris, *Matthew,* PNTC, 344.

resurrection (i.e., Lk. 24:27) to the point that they would have understood at least the essentials of his own theology.

Even if Jesus did not instantly provide the interpretation before the people to whom he preached, he could have easily interpreted the parable to the disciples privately. Therefore, the themes found in the parable's interpretation link with the earliest understanding of the parable, thereby the interpretation summarizes and distinguishes the players in Jesus's story.

While the Christological themes are not as airtight as in other passages already discussed in this research, the parable still houses some of the eschatological themes identified with early Christology. The Son of Man title will receive further attention in the following section and even more extensive attention will be given to the title in the next chapter. Nonetheless, so far as it pertains to the Christological aspect of the parable, the title affords an incredible precedent when it comes to Christology and the parables, as the title is most assuredly Christological. Oscar Cullmann argues that the title Son of Man "embraces the total work of Jesus as does almost no other idea."[414] Due to the title Son of Man, the Christologically-centered eschatology found in the parable, and due to the interpretation finding a home within the message of Jesus, the parable meets the criteria of early Christology. Therefore, the parable passes the second methodology. So far, the parable passed one methodology but failed the first. Since it passed the second test, the text receives 5 points for its early Christological connections. The journey ahead will prove interesting for this one.

Theological Terminology Relating to Early Christological Concepts

Concerning theological terms and titles that indicate early Christological concepts, the interpretation of the parable uses the title Son of Man twice in verse 37 and verse 41. The title Son of Man is among the most important Messianic titles used by Jesus.[415] and was one of his most preferred titles..[416] It should be noted that there is a bit of overlap between this criterion and the previous one as the themes overlap with the eschatological title in this parable. Since the previous section discussed the aspects concerning the authenticity of the parable's interpretation and alluded to the nearly exclusive use of the title by Jesus concerning himself, there is no need to restate that information again in this section, outside of noting that the essence of the

---

[414] Cullmann, *Christology of the NT,* 137.

[415] See Hurtado, *One God, One Lord,* 55.

[416] Jesus seems to prefer the title "Son of Man" over that of "Messiah." Stein, *Method and Message of Jesus' Teachings,* 40.

interpretation finds a home in the teaching of Jesus for a variety of reasons.[417] Additionally, a full exposition of the nature of the Son of Man title will be presented in Chapter 4, as the chapter will engage teachings where the Son of Man takes center stage.

One of the most important questions pertaining to this methodology is whether the interpretation is authentic. The Christological titles and terminology are all found in the interpretation. If the interpretation is found to be Matthean, then the parable fares far worse at this juncture. But even if the interpretation is largely Matthew's, the Son of Man title is almost exclusively found in Jesus's teachings, representing his self-understanding. Thus, there could be said to be at least some essence of Jesus's voice in the interpretation. Concerning the current parable and the third method, sufficient evidence has been granted to show that the use of the Son of Man title, along with the concept of the *basileia ton ouranon* (13:24),[418] is enough to allow the parable to pass, at least in its essence. Thus far, the parable is 2 for 3. However, a word of caution must be granted. If the interpretation is shown to be an exclusive Matthean invention not based on earlier traditions, then the parable could find itself with potentially only one passing grade, if any. Yet one could still argue that the interpretation encapsulates the essence of the parable's message while keeping in mind Morris's argument concerning the disciples' ability to interpret Jesus's parables.[419] Therefore, since it passed the third test, the parable scored an additional 4 points, tallying 9 points overall thus far.

Mnemonic & Rhythmic Patterns

The structure of Matthew 13 is constructed as an extended chiasmus, or inverted parallelism.[420] In an extended chiasmus, the elements of the first half are paralleled in reverse in the second half.[421] The prophets used chiasmus to their advantage to not only show variety but to contribute to the meaning of

---

417 France, "The Authenticity of the Parable of the Sower and Its Interpretation," *Gospel Perspectives: Studies of History and Tradition in the Four Gospels,* France and Wenham, eds, 169.

418 The importance of the *basileia ton ouranon* was noted in Chapter 2.

419 Morris, *Matthew,* PNTC, 344.

420 Craig Blomberg, *Matthew*, New American Commentary, vol. 22 (Nashville: Broadman & Holman Publishers, 1992), 213.

421 "Chiasmus—the sequence of the parallel elements in a line is reversed (a b/ b' a'//). This produces a 'crossover' effect (the word is derived from the Greek letter 'chi," which is cross-shaped." Philip P. Jenson, "Poetry in the Bible," in *New Bible Commentary: 21st Century Edition*, 4th ed, D. A. Carson et al., eds (Leicester, England; Downers Grove, IL: Inter-Varsity Press, 1994), 454.

the text, particularly to emphasize a certain point or to use the central point as a means to unlock the meaning of the other text.[422] Amos 6:4b–6a and Isaiah 55:8–9 are a couple of examples of chiasmus in the OT prophetic writings. In Matthew 13, the two halves of the outline indicate a division between those outside and those inside of the kingdom.[423] The Parable of the Sower and the Parable of the Harvest contrast the distinction between the saints of God and the unbelieving citizens of the world. After the interpretation of the Harvest parable, Jesus likens those who find the kingdom of heaven to a person who found a great treasure, a great pearl, and a homeowner who brings out the "storeroom treasures" (13:52). Wenham proposes the following chiasmus in chapter 13.

A. Parable of the Sower (13:1–9).
    B. Disciples ask why Jesus used parables and the interpretation of the Parable of the Sower (13:10–23).
        C. Parable of the Harvest (13:24–30).
            D. Parable of the Mustard Seed and Leaven (13:31–33).
                E. Conclusion of the Crowds and Interpretation of the Harvest (13:34–43).
            D'. Parable of the Treasure and Pearl (13:44–46).
        C'. Parable of the Net (13:47–50).
    B'. Jesus's Q&A with the disciples (13:51).
A'. Parable of the Homeowner (13:52).[424]

If the chiasmus holds, then not only is the interpretation of Jesus held as authentic, but it is also shown to be the interpretive key to unlocking the other parables.[425] This may bode well for the parable as it pertains to rhythmic patterns.

However, there are two problems with the chiasmus provided by Wenham as it pertains to the methodology proposed. First, it is evident that the body of parables represents an early body of Jesus's teaching preserved by oral tradition. The parallelism for the entire body of parables in chapter 13 could indicate that the entire body of kingdom parables was memorized as one unit. Dunn contends that prominent features of parallelism, alliteration, assonance, and paranomasia can all be "justly regarded as aids to

---

422 Ibid.

423 Blomberg, *Matthew,* NAC, 213.

424 D. Wenham, "The Structure of Matthew XIII," *NTS* 25 (1979): 517–518.

425 Blomberg, *Matthew,* NAC, 213.

remembering."[426] The collection of parables coheres with Kenneth Bailey's *informed controlled oral tradition* model which permits both flexibility, as noted by the Bultmannian school, and the formally controlled information, as noted in the Scandinavian school.[427] Of those materials retained in *informal controlled* settings, parables find a home with the kind of material preserved in such a manner.

Second, it is difficult to find any form of rhythmic pattern in the parable itself. In and of itself, that may be grounds for dismissing the parable from the current methodological test. However, since the parable is found in a larger collection of parables, constructed in a chiastic parallelism with the interpretation of the parable being given center stage, then the parable's rhythmic pattern takes on new life. It could potentially be the case that Matthew placed a previously existing interpretation of the parable as a key to interpreting the entire structure.

One question that impacts not only this parable, but all parables in general, is whether redactional involvement by the evangelist[428] demerits the antiquity and authenticity of the parable or its interpretation. Kenneth Bailey observes three levels of flexibility in *informal controlled* oral settings. The first level allows for no flexibility.[429] Poems and proverbs are found in this category.[430] The second level allows for some flexibility within a strict paradigm. This level does not permit the central facts and data points to be changed but does allow room for personal reflection and interpretation.[431] Parables and historical narratives[432] are found in this category.[433] The third level allows for complete flexibility with no control points. This level includes joke-telling, tragedies from other areas, and reports of everyday events that hold no important bearing on

---

[426] Dunn, *The Oral Gospel Tradition,* 238.

[427] Kenneth E. Bailey, "Informal Controlled Oral Tradition and the Synoptic Gospels," *Themelios* 20, 2 (1995): 5.

[428] I.e., the writer of the Gospel.

[429] Ibid., 7.

[430] Ibid.

[431] Ibid.

[432] Bailey observed that Middle Eastern cultures preserved proverbs, story riddles, poetry, parables/stories, and historical narratives in an informal yet controlled manner. As such, the core, key elements were retained even though some flexibility may be granted. Ibid., 6–7.

[433] Ibid., 7–8.

the community or its history.[434] Thus, with this parable, some redactional involvement is anticipated as the evangelist constructs the biography of Jesus, preserving the teachings of Jesus, and adding explanatory data that would have been taught to the evangelist by Jesus.[435] Yet, given the test set forth in this methodology, does the parable itself match the rhythmic pattern that is so frequently attributed to early material?

Given the station of chiastic parallelism in which the current parable finds itself, particularly the interpretation, it seems that Matthew meticulously arranged the parables to lend the interpretation as the key to unlocking the remaining parables. One cannot deny the redactional involvement of Matthew at this juncture. If Matthew was indeed an eyewitness, as church tradition suggests, then Matthew was well within his right to interpret the Parable of the Harvest as Jesus would have trained him to do. However, since neither the parable nor the interpretation holds a rhythmic pattern within the texts, the Parable of the Harvest cannot be said to pass the fourth test. Thus, the Parable of the Harvest now scores a 2 for 4.

Aramaic/Hebraic Literary Characteristics

The fifth methodology is a bit of a paradox concerning the Parable of the Harvest. On the one hand, the parable in question has a considerable amount of evidence supporting its connection to an Aramaic original. On the other hand, the parable's interpretation (13:36–40) is a bit more problematic as the terms used are a bit more complicated to connect to Aramaic terminology. First, evidence in favor of the Aramaic nature of the parable (13:24–30) will be examined before considering the interpretation.

The main body of the parable has five characteristics that denote a possible connection to an Aramaic original. First, the term oJmoiwvqh, translated as "compared," is in the aorist, indicative, third person tense. Black recognizes the verb as an Aramaic Semitic Perfect,[436] which stands among the more prominent cases as opposed to the three aorists in Luke 11:52.[437] Hagner

---

[434] Ibid., 8.

[435] This is not only found in the teachings of Jesus, but, as Bailey noted, some redaction can be anticipated in historical narratives. Licona notes that the evangelists used three kinds of chronology. 1) Floating—free-floating without any specified timeframe, 2) implied—when a time is implied but not specifically detailed, and 3) explicit—when an absolute timeframe is given. Licona, *Why Are There Differences in the Gospels?,* 190–191.

[436] Black, *Aramaic Approach to the Gospels and Acts,* 129.

[437] Ibid.

notes that the term reflects the "Aramaic formulaic *le*,"[438] or *de*, which means "it is the case with."[439] The verb form is fluently found in the Aramaic language, which could show that the verb was translated, or adapted, from earlier Semitic material.

Second, the subordinate clause often shows an Aramaic source. This often surrounds the Aramaic particle *de* which is often translated as oJti, o}ti, o|te, or w}ste.[440] Black argues that the Aramaic subordinate clause *de* brought about four difficulties.[441] First, the Aramaic *de*[442] was difficult to translate into Greek, giving rise to unintentional mistranslations.[443] Second, the distribution of the evidence[444] of the translations, and sometimes mistranslation, of *de* speaks to the existence of an Aramaic sayings-tradition behind the teachings of Jesus in the Synoptic Gospels, and even for some of the sayings in the Gospel of John.[445] Third, the influence of the Aramaic circumstantial clause behind the Gospel translations support an earlier Jesus sayings tradition.[446] Finally, and interestingly, textual variants of D and the Vulgate often occurred around the usage of *de*. Concerning the current parable, the Aramaic term *kadh*, which is identified as a compound of *ke*[447] and *di*,[448] frequently occurs in the Aramaic narrative.[449] However, the evangelists often differ on which Greek word they choose. Matthew and Mark prefer *hote* while Luke fancies the term *hos*.[450]

---

438 Hagner, *Matthew 1–13,* WBC, 383.

439 Ibid.

440 Black, *Aramaic Approach to the Gospels and Acts,* 70.

441 Ibid., 91.

442 Meaning "this," "when," or "one another."

443 Black argues that the mistranslations are merely "deliberate Greek renderings of a meaning possible in the original. The Greek Gospels in this respect are not just literal renderings of Aramaic originals, but to some considerable extent original Greek compositions incorporating interpretations of Aramaic sources." Black, *Aramaic Approach to the Gospels and Acts,* 91.

444 See Ibid., 70–91.

445 Ibid., 91.

446 Ibid., 92.

447 Meaning "as."

448 Black, *Aramaic Approach to the Gospels and Acts,* 90.

449 Ibid.

450 Ibid.

Matthew employs the same usage of *hote* in Matthew 13:26 as he does in other areas where the presence of *de* or *kadh* is most prevalent (Matt. 9:25; 13:26; 13:48; and 21:34).[451] Thus, most likely the Aramaic temporal conjunction *kadh* undergirds Matthew's temporal conjunction o}te in verse 26.

Third, verse 26 finds another link to an Aramaic substratum. The term *karpon epoinsen* ("produced grain," CSB) is linked to the Hebrew/Aramaic use of *'asah* ("to make" or "to yield").[452] The LXX uses a derivation of the term *karpon epoinsen* in Genesis 1:11–12; 2 Kings 19:30; Jeremiah 12:2, 17:8; and Ezekiel 17:23.[453] The Semitic term is only used eight times in the NT (Matt. 3:10, 7:17–19, 13:26; Luke 3:9, 6:43, 8:8, 13:9; and Revelation 22:2. The aorist active indicative version of the phrase is only used in Matthew 13:26 and Luke 8:8.[454] Thus, the interesting format of the phrase could possibly indicate the presence of a Semitic source anchoring the phrase.

Fourth, verses 28 through 30 exhibits no less than three Aramaic asyndetons.[455] An asyndeton is the omission of a conjunction word between two connecting thoughts.[456] Asyndetons were practiced more in Semitic languages than in Greek because of the disdain that popular Hellenistic culture had for the practice.[457] It was for this reason that Luke often avoided using asyndetons as opposed to other Gospel writers.[458]

Fifth, an interesting idiom is used in 13:28, which is identified as a Semitism. The one who planted the seeds is called an *ekthros anthropos* ("an enemy man"). Of the idioms found in the NT, the vast majority of them are found in the Gospels and most frequently in Mark and Q.[459] Black asserts,

---

451 Ibid.

452 Ibid., 138.

453 Ibid.

454 *Kai heteron epesen eis ten gen ten agathen, kai phuen epoiesen karpon hekatonpanlasiona tauta legon ethonei. Ho echo nota akouein akoueto* (Luke 8:8). "Still other seed fell on the good ground; when it grew up, it produced fruit: a hundred times what was sown" (Luke 8:8, CSB). The focused term has been bolded in both translations.

455 Black, *Aramaic Approach to the Gospels and Acts,* 57.

456 An example of an asyndeton is Julius Caesar's classic phrase, "I came. I saw. I conquered."

457 Jeremias, *NT Theology,* 57.

458 Ibid. Interestingly, Black also finds an Aramaic distributive in the text, as well. See Black, *Aramaic Approach to the Gospels and Acts,* 59.

459 Ibid., 107.

"The idiom in the Gospels must therefore be strictly described as a Semitism, though its origin in most cases is almost certainly Aramaic."[460]

As noted, good evidence suggests that the body of the parable holds Aramaic characteristics that link it to early Semitic material. Earlier, it was noted how the parable's interpretation finds a home in the center of an extended chiasmus that extends throughout the 13th chapter. However, Jeremias casts doubt on the antiquity of the interpretation. Giving 37 oddities and "linguistic peculiarities"[461] in the interpretation that are either not found in Jesus's other teachings or were not used by the early church, Jeremias concludes that the parable's interpretation "is the work of Matthew himself"[462] and an allegorization. However, there is a bit of an oddity in Jeremias's approach. Several of the terms he lists as peculiarities hold the same Aramaic characteristics that he would consider early in other areas.[463] Additionally, some of the terms he lists as peculiar in this case, such as *basilena* in verse 38, he affirms as one of the central themes of Jesus's message in other areas.[464]

Is there a solution to this conundrum? While space does not permit a full examination of the anomalies that Jeremias posits in his *Parables of Jesus*, the research conducted may provide two possible explanations. First, the *informal controlled* transmission of oral traditions would allow for some flexibility in transmitting the parable and, especially, its interpretation.[465] Bailey later argues that the *informal controlled* transmission continued prior to AD 70 when a more formally controlled format had to be adopted.[466] Post AD 70, only eyewitnesses could serve as the *huperetes tou logou* (Luke 1:2) of the Jesus traditions. If one adopts the traditional interpretation that the apostle Matthew recorded, or at least preserved, the material found in the First Gospel, then the unique expressions can coexist with the Semitic nature of the terms and chiastic structure that tends to bolster the interpretation's authenticity.

Second, the early disciples' training would allow them to interpret Jesus's messages, as Jesus spent time training the disciples. The text notes that Jesus privately explained the parable to the disciples in one of their homes,

---

460 Ibid., 106.

461 Joachim Jeremias, *The Parables of Jesus,* 2nd ed (Upper Saddle River, NJ: Prentice Hall; SCM, 1972), 85 n89.

462 Ibid., 85.

463 One instance is the *casus pendens* of ou'toi in verse 38.

464 Jeremias, *NT Theology,* 34–35.

465 Bailey, "Informal Controlled Oral Tradition and the Synoptic Gospels," *Themelios* 20, 2 (1995): 5–6.

466 Ibid., 10.

most likely the house of Simon Peter. It is within the realm of possibility that Jesus would have used unique terms with the disciples that he did not use with the public. If true, then the parable represents what the early church would have understood Jesus to have said even if it employs the Matthean vernacular. Many of the anomalies that Jeremias posits are not unique to Matthew and are not as unique to the NT as he notes.

Despite some difficulties with the interpretation, the parable itself finds a good deal of Aramaic qualities that permits it to pass this fifth methodology. Even though the parable struggled initially, add 5 more points to its weighted score. Admittedly, this parable fared better in this category than was anticipated given the nature of parables themselves. Thus far, the Parable of the Harvest has passed 3 of the 5 tests. But it will be interesting to see if the parable passes the next two criteria to make it into the yellow zone for the tallied score.

Semitic Cultural Concepts of First-Century Israel

The parable, like many of those uttered by Jesus, uses agrarian concepts. There is nothing unique about the cultural concepts found in the parable outside of the unique term used for weeds. Hagner notes that the word "ζιζάνια, 'weeds,' found in the NT only in Matt 13, refers to a kind of darnel, a common weed (*Lolium temulentum*; thus Jeremias, *Parables*, 224) that plagued grainfields."[467] However, darnel was not unique to Israel. It was also found throughout North Africa, Asia, and parts of Europe. As such, the concept of wheat, weeds, and the dangerous entanglement of the two were well known among those in both Semitic and Hellenistic cultures.

While the text holds some cultural concepts of the time, it is nearly impossible to see how the parable's agrarian concepts differ in any substantial means from information also known by Hellenistic culture. Thus, while the parable does hold Semitic cultural concepts, it cannot be said to hold the distinctive nature this method pursues. There are simply not enough distinctions in the text to distinguish between the Semitic and Hellenistic cultural concepts of the time. Therefore, the parable cannot be said to be strictly Semitic in its cultural concepts. Thus, the parable does not pass the 6th methodology, leaving the parable at 3 for 6. Mathematically, the parable cannot pass into the green zone even if it passes the last method. Nonetheless, the last

---

[467] Hagner, *Matthew 1–13*, 383.

method is still important to evaluate the level of strength the parable holds in the yellow zone.

Similarities to NT Creeds, Summaries, and Early Literature

Concerning the last methodology, it is difficult to see any of the traits of early credal material in the Parable of the Harvest. The parable does not match the theme of baptism and catechumenisms, worship, exorcisms, and does not offer a polemic against heresy. One could argue that the parable could, in some sense, offer encouragement against persecution. But even that is not conclusive. The parable also does not offer any single-statement declarations, formulaic prose, or a hymn and prose that is so prevalently found in early credal material.

However, there is some evidence that the parable contains a sermon summary. But since the text is a parable, it must be acknowledged that parables afford a mild degree of flexibility within the established central threads, those which cannot be altered.[468] In his book *The Semitisms of Acts,* Max Wilcox asserts that the Semitisms throughout the sermon summaries and historical narratives point to Aramaic sources available to Luke.[469] However, he also readily accepts that Luke interacted with the material to add his own personal touch.[470]

In like manner, the Parable of the Harvest shows some signs of Semitisms. As previously noted, the main body of the parable shows strong signs of Aramaic features, whereas the parable's interpretation suggests having more Matthean involvement than the main body of the text. This does not remove the possibility that the parable's interpretation predated the Gospel. But it does make it much more difficult to single out what parts of the interpretation belonged to Jesus alone. However, concerning the main body of the parable, the text is found in other early works. The *Gospel of Thomas* adopts many of the kingdom parables, but in a much more abbreviated version. The Parable of the Harvest is one such example. It is dramatically reduced. The parable reads as follows in the *Gospel of Thomas*:

> The Kingdom of the Father is like a man who had [good] seed. His enemy came by night and sowed weeds among the good seed. The man did not allow them to pull up the weeds; he said to them, 'I am

---

[468] Bailey, "Informal Controlled Oral Tradition and the Synoptic Gospels," *Themelios* 20, 2: 7.

[469] Wilcox, *The Semitisms of Acts,* 174.

[470] Ibid., 176–177. For example, when speaking on Acts 15:6, Wilcox notes that the text "shows signs of Lukan activity, both in the connecting material and in the speech ascribed to Peter." Ibid., 177. Thus, the evangelistic involvement does not detract from the Semitic sources from which he obtained his material.

> afraid that you will go intending to pull up the weeds and pull up the wheat along with them.' For on the day of the harvest the weeds will be plainly visible, and they will be pulled up and burned.[471]

As one may notice, the parable is far more condensed in the *Gospel of Thomas*. This does not necessarily indicate that the parable must have been first delivered as brief as the *Gospel of Thomas* suggests. The non-canonical Gospel relates thirteen of the parables of Jesus in the book, eleven of them are found in the Synoptic Gospels.[472] Nine of the eleven parables are greatly abbreviated and streamlined in the *Gospel of Thomas*. Blomberg asserts that the abbreviations and details show a tendency to be "conscious, Gnostic redaction or secondary developments in the continuing oral tradition."[473] Additionally, the parable in Matthew finds comparisons in its portrayal of the harvest to 2 Ezra, 4 Ezra 4:30-32; 2 Baruch 70:2; Isa. 32:13-15; Jer. 31:27-28; Hos 2:21-23; 6:11; 1 Enoch 54:6; 98:3; 4 Ezra 7:36.[474]

The Parable of the Harvest finds good support in its correlations with other early texts. The fact that the *Gospel of Thomas* copies and abbreviates the parable seems to suggest that the Matthean Gospel's presentation is much earlier, even though it is longer and more detailed. The gist of the parable does seem to show signs of being a sermon summary. However, the interpretation, though it holds more early Christological language than the main body of the parable, seems to be a summary, Matthew's hands were most certainly involved in its shaping. Due to the lack of credal traits and themes, there just is simply not enough current evidence to permit the parable to pass the seventh method. Granted, it is believed that there are traits to suggest that the parable is a sermon summary. But to what level and degree will require a much lengthier investigation beyond what this current research can afford.

Conclusion and Color Assignment

As a recap, the parable failed the first method. While Jewish literature often viewed the harvest through an eschatological lens, the Talmud did not. Thus, the parable could not be linked with unique rabbinical concepts, as the harvest was only viewed through its application to Jewish festivals. The parable passed the second test, as the interpretation of the parable afforded early Christological concepts. Though the interpretation holds some concerns as to the evangelist's involvement with its shaping, the connection with the main

---

[471] *The Gospel of Thomas* 57, in Blomberg, *Historical Reliability of the Gospels,* 267.

[472] Blomberg, *Historical Reliability of the Gospels,* 267.

[473] Ibid., 267–268.

[474] Keener, *IVPNT,* 84.

body of the parable is undeniable. The parable also passed the third method. Here again, the parable and its interpretation contained some language that correlates the material with early Hebraic and Aramaic concepts, particularly with early literature and its usage in the LXX. The parable nearly passed the fourth test, not that the parable itself held mnemonic and rhythmic patterns. Due to its connection with the overall body of chiastic material in Matthew 13, the general flow of the parables found a rhythmic pattern, but the parable itself did not. The main body fared very well with the fifth test. Ironically, the main body of the parable showed at least five traits that one would expect to find in early Semitic material. The interpretation has a complicated connection with early Semitic characteristics. But if one were to accept even Gundry's middle ground viewpoint, then one could accept that at least the core fundamentals of the interpretation come from early material. According to Bailey, this is what one would expect with parabolic oral transmission. The parable did not fare well on either the sixth or seventh tests. The parable obviously retains cultural concepts. Yet one could not necessarily find separation from these concepts as both wheat and darnel was found in Semitic and non-Semitic cultures. Concerning the last test, the parable holds certain traits that suggest it is a sermon summary, but not enough credal characteristics to connect it to what the test requires.

With all said and done, the Parable of the Harvest passed 3 of the 7 tests. Therefore, the parable finds itself in the red zone with the cumulative tallied scale. Oddly enough, given the weight of the tests that the parable did pass, the parable finds itself in the yellow zone with the weighted scale.

This indicates that the parable mildly holds some traits that connect it with earlier Semitic materials related to oral Jesus traditions. Originally, I noted that there just simply is not enough to make a strong case for semitic residue for the oral tradition undergirding the parable. However, after weighing the tests that the parable did pass, I think it seems likely that the parable itself holds a good case for stemming from original Jesuan material. However, the interpretation seems to belong more to Matthew's lips than necessarily Jesus's. Granted, it seems evident that Matthew is pulling from previous material even with his interpretation. Matthew's redactional involvement with the shaping of the material clouds one's ability to dissect the tradition from its retelling primarily with his interpretations of the parable. But to clarify, the parable itself appears to belong to Jesus. The interpretation belongs to Matthew. Yet remember that Matthew was trained by Jesus, meaning that Matthew reflects Jesus's instruction even through his own rewording.

A further word concerning the parable must be given here. If the interpretation were to be completely dismissed, then the parable would find itself passing only one test. The main body of the parable most assuredly passes the fifth test regardless. However, the early Christological and theological concepts are displayed more in the interpretation than the parable's main body. Yet, if Matthew was correct in his interpretation—which it is held that he was—then the early Christological concepts were in fact communicated in the main parable itself, although shrouded by Jesus's parabolic language. Some may argue that this potentially strengthens the case for the parable's connection with early Jesus traditions. As such, one could claim that the interpretation only puts to pen what Jesus intended to teach.

It is here that Bailey's research is of utmost importance. Since some flexibility is permitted in the transmission of parabolic information in Middle Eastern cultures, then Matthean shaping does not override the tenability of early Semitic material, as the *informal controlled model* required that the central threads of history and parables are maintained to retain accuracy. Therefore, even if Matthew was involved in the shaping of the parable, especially the interpretation, this does not remove the earlier material from which he drew both the interpretation and the parable. The beauty of the informal *controlled* method is if either the parable or interpretation were outside the bounds of the early oral traditions of Jesus, the community would have called for a correction. Thus, the parable, so far as this researcher is concerned, fits comfortably within the yellow zone as is noted by the weighted scale. The parable scored 14 points on the weighted scale, even though it only passed 3 tests, which placed it in the red zone according to the tallied scale. The weighted scale only further highlights my original thoughts about the parable in that there is some semitic residue found in the parable itself.

It will be of interest to see how the other two parables fare. Is the yellow zone indicative of parabolic material in general, or does this speak only of the characteristics of this parable alone? In either case, the answer will be interesting.

Parable of the Compassionate Employer (Matt. 20:1–16)

The next parable to be investigated is called the Parable of the Compassionate Employer. This parable finds itself within a body of messages that Jesus gave after departing Galilee and entering the Judean region (Matt. 19:1–2). During this phase in Jesus's ministry, the Pharisees' inquisition into Jesus's message intensified. The parable tells the story of a landowner who went out early in the morning to "hire workers for his vineyard" (20:1). The landowner went out at 9 AM, noon, 3 PM, and 5 PM. The landowner paid each group of workers the same amount, according to what he had promised at the outset. Some of the workers who began in the early morning complained that they should be paid more than the workers who started late in the day, especially since they had worked much longer (20:11–12). The landowner noted that it was his money to give, and that he had the right to be generous if he so desired (20:15).

This parable is fascinating for several reasons. First, the parable is one of those that are unique to Matthew and is, thereby, distinct from the Markan material.[475] Second, the parable has a connection with an independent *logion* that is found in the *Epistle of Barnabas*, which says "Again I will shew the how the Lord speaketh concerning us. He made a second creation at the last; and the Lord saith; Behold I make the last things as the first. In reference to this then the prophet preached; Enter into a land flowing with milk and honey, and be lords over it."[476] Finally, a similar parable is found in rabbinical teachings, although Jesus's version has a major twist when compared with the rabbinical version.[477] At face value, it would seem that this parable would fare better than the one previously examined due to its link with early literature and rabbinic concepts. To see how well it fares, it must be placed under the scrutiny of the seven-fold methodology of this research.

Unique Rabbinic Concepts

One of the primary messages of Jesus's Parable of the Compassionate Employer is that the kingdom is not based on seniority, but rather on the grace and love of the Father. The key theme is condensed in the last line of the parable, where Jesus says, "So the last will be first, and the first last" (20:16). Interestingly, the Parable of the Compassionate Employer finds a parallel in several rabbinical teachings. For instance, Rabbi Raba Mezi'a is noted as saying, "Go out and find some occupation in the barn, that your wages may not be payable until then; since wages are not payable until the end [of one's task], and it is only then that they make you the gift."[478] Similarly, another Talmudic parable is found in the following:

> To what may R. Bun bar Chaya be compared? To a king who hired many laborers. One of them was extremely proficient in his work. What did the king do? He took him and walked with him the lengths and breadths [of the field]. In the evening the laborers came to take their wages. But [to the one with whom he had walked—the king] gave

---

[475] Donald A. Hagner, *Matthew 14–28,* Word Biblical Commentary, vol. 33b (Dallas, TX: Word, 1995), 569.

[476] *Epistle of Barnabas* 6.13, in Joseph Barber Lightfoot and J. R. Harmer, *The Apostolic Fathers* (London, UK: Macmillan, 1891), 274.

[477] Arnold G. Fruchtenbaum, *Yeshua: The Life of Messiah from a Messianic Jewish Perspective*, vol. 3 (San Antonio, TX: Ariel, 2018), 196–197.

[478] *b. Baba Mezi'a,* 73a.

> a full day's wage. The laborers murmured and complained, "We worked all day long, but [the king] has given this one who only worked two hours a full wage like us." The king answered them, "He has done more in two hours than what you did for the entire day!" Thus though R. Bun labored only twenty-eight years, he did more than a learned scholar could have studied in a hundred..[479]

While the two parables hold similarities, there are distinct differences. Though the worker was hired late in the day in the rabbinic parable, he performed more work than the preceding laborers. However, the key distinction between Jesus's parable and the rabbinical version is that the rabbinic parable emphasizes the importance of production during the time that a laborer was working. Jesus does not say whether the later laborers worked harder than the previous ones or not. The emphasis seems to be on the grace of the landowner rather than the rate of manufacture of the workers.

One may be tempted to claim that all rabbinic parables were work-based in nature. Yet that would be unfair. Another parable by Rabbi Simeon ben Eleazar tells the following tale:

> To what may the matter be compared? To a king who hired two workers. The first worked all day and received one denarius. The second worked only one hour and yet he also received a denarius. Which one was more beloved? Not the one who worked one hour and received a denarius! Thus Moses our teacher served Israel one hundred and twenty years and Samuel [served them] only fifty-two. Nevertheless both are equal before the Omnipresent! As it is said, "Then the LORD said to me, 'Though Moses and Samuel stood before me'" (Jer. 15:1); and thus He said, "Moses and Aaron were among his priests, Samuel also was among those who called on his name" (Psalm 99:6); concerning them and others like them He says, "Sweet is the sleep of the laborer whether he eats little or much" (Eccl. 5:12)..[480]

Jeremias casts Jesus's message of grace in stark contrast with the message of works in the rabbinical period, leading him to aver that "this apparently trivial detail lies in the difference between two worlds: the world of merit, and the world of grace; the law contrasted with the gospel.".[481] However, the Rabbi Eleazar's parable presents a much more grace-filled message.

---

[479] *j. Ber.* 5c., ch. 2, halakah 8. See also Brad H. Young, *The Parables: Jewish Tradition and Christian Interpretation* (Grand Rapids, MI: Baker Academic, 1998), 76.

[480] Semachot de-Rabbi Chiyah 3:2, in M. Higger, *Masekhet Semachot* (Jerusalem, IL: Makor Foundation, 1970), 220–221; Young, *Parables,* 75.

[481] Jeremias, *Parables of Jesus,* 136–139.

However, it must be noted that Rabbi Chaya lived nearly 300 years after Jesus, whereas Rabbi Eleazar lived nearly 500 years apart from Jesus. Could these parables, as Jeremias suggests, represent an earlier teaching upon which both rabbis are drawing, even that of Jesus's though they may not have realized from whence it came?[482] Both options are a possibility. Pertaining to the conflict between the Judaism of Jesus's day and the message of Jesus, Brad Young resolves the distinction better than Jeremias. He contends that the sources from the Second Temple period and early Christianity "portray a compassionate God who is willing to receive the outcast."[483] The problem then was the same as it is with modern religion—a distinction between proclamation and practice.[484] The proclamation of Second Temple Judaism and Christianity held that God sought to accept all people into covenant relationships.[485] While that may have been the proclamation, the practice did not always follow.[486] A modern example of the difference between proclamation and practice is views of race. Modern Christian believers know that God will receive people from all races into his kingdom. However, most congregations across the United States remain largely segregated.[487]

Jesus's parable does hold a great distinction that makes his message unique. Only Jesus mentions God's desire to extend his love to sinners, as particularly contrasted with the literature of Qumran.[488] Even with Rabbi Eleazar's parable, which extends far more grace than Rabbi Chaya's, only those who were faithful to God were mentioned. Jesus describes God's compassion

---

[482] Ibid., 138.

[483] Young, *Parables,* 73.

[484] Ibid.

[485] E.g., Gen. 12:1–4, 22:18; and Jon. 1:16, 3:1–4:2. Also consider the *Community Rule* of the Dead Sea Scrolls.

[486] A good example of early differences between proclamation and practice can be found in Paul's rebuttal of Peter's unwillingness to dine with Gentile believers, out of fear of his Jewish compatriots. See Galatians 2:11–21.

[487] In fairness, location can attribute to this separation in certain areas.

[488] Jeremias, *NT Theology,* 121.

of those who were willing to provide grace to the one who comes and follows him.[489]

Even though the rabbinic parables mentioned stemmed from a much later time than Jesus, it could be assumed that they represent earlier stories preserved by the Jewish oral traditions. Nonetheless, it can be said that Jesus's parable holds similar themes to rabbinic material, but it is unique enough to demonstrate a contrast between Jesus's message of grace to sinners compared to the rabbinic demonstration of God's grace to his followers. As such, the Parable of the Compassionate Landowner can be said to pass the first test earning 2 points.

Early Christological Concepts

The Parable of the Compassionate Employer does not contain any overt Christological titles. The parable does not necessarily connect to any of the major Christological concepts that relate to the earliest credal material, such as the divine-human nature of Jesus, the oneness of that nature, and existing as one person.[490] However, it does contain a thread that is thoroughly Christological; that is, Jesus's proclamation that the love of God benefited all people, particularly the poor. This thread is so strong that Jeremias contends that "the gospel accounts of Jesus's proclamation of the good news to the poor cannot be derived either from Judaism or from the earliest church. They reproduce the *ipsissima vox* of Jesus."[491]

The parable does, however, find a bipartite relationship between the Father and Son, particularly with the advent of the Father's kingdom being ushered in through Jesus. Remember, that bipartite relationships between the Father and Son are among the earliest confessions of the church.[492] First, the bipartite relationship between the Father and Son is found in the parable's connection with the earlier teaching in Matthew 19:28–30. One would make a grave hermeneutical mistake if one were to examine the parable without the larger context in mind. The term *gar* connects the parable to the previous material. As Morris notes, "It is because of what Jesus has just said about those

---

[489] "The new parable impresses these lessons, but adds an even more important one—God acts toward us in sheer grace. There is no question of salvation being an arithmetical process, adding up the good deeds and the bad ones and coming out with salvation or loss according to whether the balance is on the credit or debit side. That is not the way to understand the dealings of a gracious God." Morris, *Matthew,* PNTC, 499.

[490] Oden, *Classical Christianity,* 299.

[491] Jeremias, *NT Theology,* 121.

[492] Cullmann, *Earliest Christian Confessions,* 39.

who would follow him giving up everything for the kingdom of heaven's sake and because of the reversals implied in the first being last and the last first that Jesus proceeds to this parable."[493] Prior to the parable, Jesus had a series of interactions with people from various socio-economic backgrounds. The Pharisees attempted to test Jesus, indicating their rejection of the Father's kingdom through Jesus (19:1–12). Jesus rebuked the Pharisees, individuals who were thought to be nearest to God, but then accepts young children who were often neglected, and seen by some as second-class citizens (19:13–15).[494] Then, a rich young ruler approaches Jesus to ask how he can enter the kingdom of heaven.[495] Jesus tells him to keep the commandments, but then he tells him to sell everything to come follow him, which the ruler was unable to do (19:16–22). Finally, Peter asks about the position they will have in the kingdom since they left everything to follow Jesus (19:27). To which Jesus responds, noting that the Son of Man[496] will sit on his throne, the disciples will sit on twelve thrones, and that everyone who follows him would "inherit eternal life" (19:28–29). Jesus ends the message in the same manner that he ends the parable, saying, "many who are first will be last, and the last first" (19:30). The parable immediately after the previous message, which could indicate that the two are part of the same message, as there is no narrative break between the two.

Second, the parable begins with *Homoia gar estin he basileia ton ouranon* (20:1).[497] The *Basileia ton ouranos* is mentioned frequently throughout the Gospel of Matthew and finds a similar structural pattern in Matthew 13:31, 33, 44, 45, and 47. As previously noted in this work, the already-not-yet kingdom is a frequent theme in the teaching of Jesus and is an early Christological theme.[498] But what is shocking in this parable is the graciousness of the master figure, as

---

[493] Morris, *Matthew,* PNTC, 499.

[494] "Children were socially powerless and dependent. Some people in the Old Testament would lay hands on others to bestow a blessing in prayer. Insensitive disciples trying to keep from the master those seeking his help might remind Jewish hearers of Gehazi, a disciple of Elisha who eventually lost his position (2 Kings 4:27; 5:27)." Keener, *IVPBBC:NT,* 97.

[495] Bock views the parable as a reinforcement of his discussion about the rich young ruler. Bock and Simpson, *Jesus According to the Scripture,* 402.

[496] An important Christological title whose usage belongs almost exclusively to Jesus. Jeremias, *NT Theology,* 267.

[497] "For the kingdom of heaven is like…," personal translation.

[498] Since the Christological aspects of the *basileia ton ouranos* has been previously covered in this work, there is no reason to rehash the data again here.

was the case with the Parable of the Prodigal Son (Luke 15:11–32), and the Parable of the Banquet (Luke 14:16–24; Matt. 22:1–14).[499]

Even though some contend that the present-day entrance into the eschatological kingdom may not have dated to the pre-Easter sayings of Jesus,[500] the OT is replete with examples of retribution theology (e.g., Gen. 6:18; 17:1–14; Exod. 19:3–8; and Deut. 30:15–20), where God promises to bless or judge according to the people's faithfulness to or rejection of his covenant.[501] Additionally, numerous OT texts speak of God's reign over Israel (Isa. 43:15), that his reign extends beyond Israel's boundaries (Psa. 103:19), and that God would comprehensively reign over all creation at the eschaton (Obad. 21). Individuals are said to have a peaceful relationship with God and each other (Zech. 9:9–10; Zeph. 3:14–20). Daniel 7:13–14 speaks extensively of one like a son of man, coming from the throne of the Ancient of Days, who will rule over all creation. Second Temple Jewish literature also speaks of the Messiah defeating demons and evil (*1 Enoch* 55:4),[502] and putting an end to Satan (*Ascension of Moses* 10:1).[503] Thus, Jesus's interpretation of the Son of Man escorting the messianic kingdom into the world is not all that unique considering the literature of the time. What does make Jesus's message stand out is that he claims that the messianic kingdom has come through him, and that any and everyone is allowed access, as this parable alludes. Additionally, the exclusive nature of Jesus's usage of the Son of Man sayings[504] along with their eschatological implications, the Son of Man's tie to Daniel 7:13–14, and Jesus's extensive use of the already-not-yet kingdom motif[505] speaks highly in favor of the theme originating with the authentic pre-Easter *ipsissima vox* of Jesus. That is to say, the Son of Man sayings provide access into Jesus's

---

499 See Blomberg, *Historical Reliability of the NT,* 123–124.

500 Witherington, *Christology of Jesus,* 206.

501 D. Brent Sandy, *Plowshares & Pruning Hooks: Rethinking the Language of Biblical Prophecy and Apocalyptic* (Downers Grove, IL: IVP, 2002), 85.

502 "Yet mighty kigns who dwell on the earth, ye shall have to behold Mine Elect One, how he sits on the throne of glory and judges Azazel, and all his associates, and all his hosts in the name of the Lord of Spirits." *1 Enoch* 55:4.

503 "And then His kingdom shall appear throughout all His creation, and then Satan shall be no more, and sorrow shall depart with him." *Assumption of Moses* 10.1.

504 Jeremias, *NT Theology,* 267.

505 Ibid.

understanding that the kingdom was being brought through him and would finally be actualized in the eschaton.

Tying the previous two points together, it would appear that the parable indeed holds early Christological themes. If one connects the parable to the previous teachings of Matthew 19, a point to which both Morris and Bock contend,[506] then the Christological themes are intensified. Therefore, the parable passes the second test and scores and additional 5 points. Thus far, the Parable of the Compassionate Employer has fared better than the Parable of the Harvest, scoring 2 for 2.

Theological Terminology Relating to Early Christological Concepts

While there are certainly Christological concepts, as noted in the previous section, outside of Jesus's implicit connection with the *Basileia ton ouranos*, there are no notable theological terms or titles in the parable proper. However, if the parable includes the introductory teaching of Matthew 19:28–30, then the text would contain a Son of Man title. Interestingly, the passage is flanked by another Son of Man statement, where Jesus says, "See, we are going up to Jerusalem. The Son of Man will be handed over to the chief priests and the scribes, and they will condemn him to death. They will hand him over to the Gentiles to be mocked, flogged, and crucified, and on the third day he will be raised" (20:18–19). Matthew 20:19 has been linked to Hosea 6:2.[507] and could be an Aramaic paraphrase..[508] Thus, the parable is wedged between two bookends that contain theological titles and terminology that would match this test. Thereby, it may be said that the parable could allude to theological titles and themes by default. However, since the parable itself does not contain any of these characteristics, then the parable cannot pass the test at hand. Therefore, this leaves the parable with a score of 2 for 3.

Mnemonic & Rhythmic Patterns

Looking through the parable's structure and pattern, there are no mentionable characteristics that match the fourth methodology. As with any parable, there are some mnemonic traits. The closest parallel that this parable has to any mnemonic or rhythmic patterns is found in a particular rabbinic

---

[506] Bock and Simpson, *Jesus According to Scripture,* 402; Morris, *Matthew,* PNTC, 499.

[507] Which reads, "He will revive us after two days, and on the third day he will raise us up so we can live in his presence" (Hos. 6:2).

[508] Craig A. Evans, "Jesus' Dissimilarity from Second Temple Judaism and the Early Church," *Memories of Jesus: A Critical Appraisal of James D. G. Dunn's Jesus Remembered,* Robert B. Stewart and Gary R. Habermas, eds (Nashville, TN: B&H Academic, 2010), 150.

teaching style. Birger Gerhardsson argues that the parables match the rabbinic teaching style known as *meshalim*.[509] *Meshalim* (plural of *mashal*) are described as "short, carefully formulated text[s], which could be many different kinds: a maxim, a proverb, a riddle, a taunt … as well as a brief narrative, an illustration, a parable … all distinguished by their skilful [sic] formulation from flat everyday speech."[510] Gerhardsson counts 55 *meshalim* in the Synoptic Gospels—five in Mark, 21 in Matthew, and 29 in Luke.[511] Of the 21 *meshalim* counted in Matthew's Gospel, the Parable of the Merciful Landowner, which he terms the "The Labourers in the Vineyard," is counted as one.[512] The *meshalim* characteristic does not, however, necessitate a mnemonic and rhythmic pattern. Thus, the parable cannot be said to pass the fourth test. However, since the *meshalim* could be said to hold some characteristics comparable to a similitude, the connection between the two is not entirely clear.[513] As it stands, the parable sits at a score of 2 for 4.

Aramaic/Hebraic Literary Characteristics

When evaluating the Aramaic characteristics of the Parable of the Compassionate Employer, the parable proves to be quite formidable. The parable holds Aramaic characteristics in no less than four instances. The first Aramaic trait is found in 20:1. Drawing from the analysis of Julius Wellhausen, Black builds a case that the replacement of the word τις with the word ἀνθρώπῳ is an idiom, which should be, as Black denotes, "strictly described as a Semitism, though its origin in most cases is almost certainly Aramaic."[514] The phrase in 20:1, which reads "Ὁμοία γάρ ἐστιν ἡ βασιλεία τῶν οὐρανῶν ἀνθρώπῳ οἰκοδεσπότῃ ὅστις," uses the term ἀνθρώπῳ in the manner that Black describes. In an interesting twist, the noted idiom most frequently occurs in the teachings of Jesus, especially in those texts found in Mark and the theoretical Q.[515]

Second, the use of ἐποίησαν in Matthew 20:12 is of notable mention. The term is a derivation of the word *poiema.* The tense and style of the word

---

[509] Birger Gerhardsson, "Illuminating the Kingdom: Narrative Meshalim in the Synoptic Gospels," *Jesus and the Oral Gospel Tradition,* Journal for the Study of the New Testament Supplement Series 64, Henry Wansbrough, ed (Sheffield, UK: Sheffield Academic, 1991), 266.

[510] Ibid.

[511] Ibid., 267.

[512] Ibid., 268.

[513] Ibid., 272.

[514] Black, *Aramaic Approach to the Gospels and Acts,* 106.

[515] Ibid., 107.

are only used in the Greek NT 15 times; most cases are found in the Gospels.[516] There is some comparison to the term's use with Exodus 36:1 in the LXX[517] and Proverbs 31:13. However, the iteration found in 20:12 is unique and has been linked with similar usage in rabbinical Aramaic.[518]

Third, Matthew 20:16 contains a parallelism, which reads, "οὕτως ἔσονται οἱ ἔσχατοι πρῶτοι καὶ οἱ πρῶτοι ἔσχατοι" (20:16).[519] The phrase coheres to the style of antithetic parallelism. Antithetical parallelisms are a Semitic trait as they are extensively used by both the OT writers[520] and the Talmud. The Jewish leaders of Jesus's day used antithetical parallelisms to construct ethical, moral, and theological teachings.[521] Examples of rabbinical teachers using antithetical parallelism in their teaching include *b. Arak.* 16,[522] *j. B. K* 6c.20f, *R. Gamaliel* II.c90, and *b. Er.* 13b.[523] Even though rabbinical teachers used antithetical parallelism, it is a preferred teaching method of Jesus as noted by the numerous times it is found in his teachings.[524] Even though it is a preferred didactical tactic by Jesus, it serves as a Semitism.

The fourth Aramaic characteristic is found in the Old Syriac Gospels. Black notes that certain aspects of the usage of the adjective *allos* points to the Syriac of Jesus's day and less like the Edessene Syriac from which the Gospels

---

[516] Matt. 17:12; 20:12; 21:36; 26:19; 28:15; Mark 6:30; 9:13; Luke 9:10; 9:15; John 12:2; 12:16; 19:23; 19:24; Acts 8:2; and Acts 11:30.

[517] "Καὶ ἐποίησεν Βεσελεὴλ καὶ Ἐλιὰβ" (Exod. 36:1). All quoted texts from the Greek LXX come from Randall K. Tan, David. A. DeSilva, and Isaiah Hoogendyk, *Lexham Greek-English Interlinear Septuagint: H. B. Swete Edition* (Bellingham, WA: Lexham, 2012).

[518] E.g., *Erub.* 8:2 and *Shabb.* 19:5. Black provides a parallel between the usage and that of *Bikkurim* 1:6. See Black, *Aramaic Approach to the Gospels and Acts,* 302.

[519] "Thus, the last will be first and the first last." Author's translation.

[520] One such example is found in Proverbs 10:1–15:33.

[521] Jeremias, *NT Theology,* 19.

[522] "The reason is that your friend has a friend, and your friend's friend has a friend." *j. Arakhin* 16a, https://www.sefaria.org/Arakhin.16a.2?lang=bi&with=all&lang2=en.

[523] "Your name is the same as my name, and your wife's name is the same as my wife's name." *b. Eruvin* 13b, https://www.sefaria.org/Eruvin.13b.1?lang=bi&with=all&lang2=en.

[524] Jesus's use of antithetical parallelisms can be found in the following instances: Matt. 5:17; 6:2–4; 7:3–5, 24; 6:14; 11:18, 23; 12:27; 23:12; 25:46; Mark 6:10; 7:8; 8:12, 35; 10:18, 25, 34; 12:44; and 13:20.

arose.[525] The term is found in the form and spelling that derives from an Aramaic source. It not only occurs in 20:9, but it is also found in Matt. 15:22; 21:40; 22:7; Luke 8:13; 12:37; John 4:38; and John 4:43.[526]

From the four examples given above, it can be deduced that the Parable of the Compassionate Employer does indeed possess Aramaic characteristics that permit it to pass the present test. Because of this, the parable earns an additional 5 points. The depth of the Semitic characteristics is quite compelling. Therefore, the parable finds itself passing 3 of the 5 tests and sits at 12 points thus far, already placing it in the yellow zone of the weighted scale. Another passing grade will elevate this parable to a higher status than the first parable examined.

Semitic Cultural Concepts of First-Century Israel

The Parable of the Compassionate Employer contains some themes that make better sense in Middle Eastern Semitic settings than necessarily those of later Hellenistic environs. For instance, first, the setting of the parable reflects the economic conditions of the oppressed laborers, who seek to find employment to provide for the needs of their families. The denarius was not a great deal of money, but it was enough to provide food for the laborer and his family.[527] As Young notes, the denarius was "considered fair compensation for a day's work. The day laborer is on the bottom of the economic ladder."[528] While there were certainly impoverished people in Hellenistic culture who tried to do the same, the flow of the story seems to fit the agrarian lifestyle of Jesus's time.

Additionally, the context of the story seems to place Jesus in the mainstream teaching of Second Temple Judaism. Young argues that Jesus served as "an activist who sought renewal of the people by shaking the foundations of complacent belief without corresponding action … Like other Jewish teachers of the period, Jesus called the people to live up to the high spiritual values and ethical requirements of the Torah."[529] Young's interpretation is quite compelling. He does make an interesting parallel between the rich young ruler's rejection of Jesus's invitation to discipleship to the compassionate generosity of the landowner. However, there is a theological element to Jesus's teaching that seems unavoidable. Perhaps it is best to

525 Black, *Aramaic Approach to the Gospels and Acts,* 283.

526 Ibid., 283–284.

527 Young, *Parables,* 70.

528 Ibid., 70.

529 Ibid., 72.

conclude that Jesus's ethical implications were interwoven in his theological construct.

Third, Jesus connects the vineyard of God with the kingdom of God which is a connection most often made in Semitic contexts. In verse 1, Jesus connects the βασιλεία τῶν οὐρανῶν.[530] with the οἰκοδεσπότῃ..[531] The laborers were hired to work in the ἀμπελῶνα..[532] Thus, the kingdom of heaven is connected to the vineyard. The vineyard motif is frequently used as a symbol for Israel in the OT..[533] For instance, the prophet Isaiah declares that the "vineyard of the LORD of Armies is the house of Israel, and the men of Judah, the plant he delighted in" (Isaiah 5:7)..[534] The prophet Jeremiah uses the same symbolism. For Jeremiah, he contends that many "shepherds have destroyed my vineyard; they have trampled my plot of land. They have turned my desirable plot into a desolate wasteland" (Jer. 12:10).

Likewise, the parable presents the view of an upside-down kingdom, something that is unique to Jesus and replete throughout Jesus's didactic..[535] That is, God will right the wrongs of the world in eternity by allowing those who were the least to have places of high authority. One of the greatest examples of the upside-down kingdom is found in the Parable of the Rich Man and Lazarus (Luke 16:19–31). The interpretation flows from a Semitic pattern of divine justice, as God rights the wrongs of humanity in the eschaton. Habakkuk is a good example of this kind of thinking. Though wondering about the depravity of the people of his day and finding himself even more disturbed about the notion of an enemy nation invading, Habakkuk rested on the assurance that God would judge all people in the end. The prophet was able to conclude by saying, "Though the fig tree does not bud and there is no fruit on the vines … yet I will celebrate in the LORD; I will rejoice in the God of my salvation" (Hab. 3:17a, 18).

Finally, the ancient custom of seeking extra workers throughout the day to obtain the necessary help needed to accomplish a task is something that continues to this day. During his time in the Middle East, Kenneth Bailey

[530] "kingdom of heaven."

[531] Literally, the "master of the house."

[532] "vineyard."

[533] Hagner, *Matthew 14–28,* 570.

[534] The total reference can be found in Isaiah 5:1–7.

[535] Bauckham, *Christian World Around the NT,* 465–466. Other examples of Jesus's upside-down kingdom are found in Matt. 18:23–27 and Luke 12:37.

observed a similar practice outside the Damascus Gate in East Jerusalem.[536] Employers drive up in vans to scout five to ten young workers among the throngs of individuals seeking work. Bailey reflected on the matter and said, "I usually looked the other way when I passed, trying not to think about the humiliation those young men suffered and the quiet desperation that their presence reflected."[537] He also notes that the parable's ending matches Middle Eastern storytelling.[538] The ending is missing so as to allow the listener to think through the morals of the story on an even deeper level. Another great example is found in the Parable of the Prodigal Son (Luke 15:11–32) as one is not told how the conflict between the eldest son and the father is resolved.

The Parable of the Compassionate Employer holds some cultural traits that are ancient enough to fit within the timeframe of Jesus and unique enough to match the Semitic culture of the day. With the four unique cultural characteristics already mentioned, it would seem acceptable to permit the parable to pass the sixth test. Add 4 more points to the parable's score. Having now passed 4 of 6 tests, the Parable of the Compassionate Employer automatically fares better than the Parable of the Harvest. Also, since the parable passed four lines of testing, the parable enters the yellow zone of confidence with both the tallied and weighted tests.

Similarities to NT Creeds, Summaries, and Early Literature

Like the Parable of the Harvest, it is difficult to find any characteristics in the Parable of the Compassionate Employer that matches the criteria for NT creeds. The parable is not engaged with any of the major themes associated with creeds--baptisms, catechumenisms, worship, exorcisms, or encouragements against persecution.[539] One could argue that Jesus could have given a scathing polemic against the Pharisees' failure to heed the ethical and moral teachings of the Torah.[540] This is reinforced by the Mishnah's emphasis on genuine love. Antigonus of Socho writes, "Be not like servants who serve the master for the sake of receiving a reward, but be like servants who serve the master not on condition of receiving a reward. And let the fear of heaven be upon you."[541] The term פרס, translated as "just reward," is conveyed in

---

536 Bailey, *Jesus Through Middle Eastern Eyes,* 358.

537 Ibid.

538 Ibid., 357.

539 Cullmann, *Earliest Christian Confessions,* 18.

540 Young, *Parables,* 72.

541 *Abot* 1.3b, in Jacob Neusner, trans, *The Mishnah: A New Translation* (New Haven, CT: Yale University Press, 1988), 673.

Antiogonus's phrasing. In like manner, piety seeking to serve God out of one's love and reverence for God is a major emphasis in Jesus's teaching (e.g., Matt. 5:12, 46).[542] But even if this should be the case, Jesus's appeal is ethical rather than speaking against theological heresy. Thus, the parable does not match the polemical theme of credal material.

Likewise, the parable does not hold any of the structural materials found in credal material. Single-statement declarations, formulaic proses, and hymnic traits are all missing. There is one possible exception found in verse 16. As previously noted, verse 16 contains a parallelism that is a reversal of a similar teaching in 19:30, where Jesus says, "But many who are first will be last, and the last first" (Matt. 19:30).[543] Whereas the last verse is of substantial interest, it is difficult to permit the entire parable to pass because of the interesting traits of the last verse. As such, the parable cannot be said to pass the seventh test. Therefore, the parable can be said to pass 4 of 7 tests.

Conclusion and Color Assignment

The Parable of the Compassionate Employer finds a bit more connection to early Semitisms than the Parable of the Harvest. Passing four of the seven tests, the parable rests in the yellow zone. According to the weighted scale, the parable scores a comfortable 16 points. As such, there are some good reasons to think that the parable contains traits that connect it with earlier pre-NT materials. However, the evidence is not beyond a reasonable doubt. It may be that since the parables are memorized stories, there may be some more flexibility than in regular teachings from the Jesus tradition. But this will be revisited at the conclusion of this chapter. For now, the research continues with the final parable to be investigated—the Parable of the Wise and Foolish Young Women.

Parable of the Wise & Foolish Young Women (Matt. 25:1–13)

The final parable to be examined in this chapter is entitled The Parable of the Wise and Foolish Young Women[544] as found in Matthew 25:1–13. The

---

[542] Young, *Parables,* 73.

[543] Interestingly, Jesus's message finds another rabbinic parallel at this juncture. Rabbi Aboda Zara wrote, "Some obtain and enter the kingdom in an hour, while others reach it only after a lifetime." *b. Abod. Zar.* 17a, in Hagner, *Matthew 14–28,* WBC, 572.

[544] Sometimes the parable is called The Parable of the Ten Virgins or the Parable of the Ten Bridesmaids. The parable may be referenced as the Parable of the Ten Bridesmaids in this chapter for simplicity's sake.

story describes ten bridesmaids.[545] who anticipate the arrival of the groom who would escort them to the marriage festival. The groom came at night, which surprised them all. Five of the women were prepared as they had purchased extra oil, whereas the other five were foolish because they failed to prepare for a lengthy wait. The five that were prepared were allowed access into the wedding festival. Those who were unprepared were denied entry. They asked the master to open the doors. However, the master told the women that he did not know them (25:11–12). The parable ends with an admonition to be alert, "because you don't know either the day or the hour" (25:13).

Most interesting about this parable is not only the intriguing nature of the story, but rather its inclusion in the eschatological didactic found in the Olivet Discourse. The Olivet Discourse occurs after Jesus told the disciples that the stones of the buildings in Jerusalem would not be found standing (Matt. 24:1–2), which points to the coming destruction of Jerusalem by the Roman army in AD 70. Afterward, Jesus sat privately with his disciples on the Mount of Olives. The disciples inquired, "Tell us, when will these things happen? And what is the sign of your coming and of the end of the age?" (Matt. 24:3).

The message is thoroughly eschatological in nature..[546] Throughout verses 4–14, Jesus describes the signs that accompany the future time of tribulation. This time includes the rise of apostasy (24:4–5, 11), wars (24:6–8), apathy (24:12–12), and times of affliction (24:9–26, 29). Additionally, Jesus discusses his return (24:27–51). Before beginning the parable, Jesus advises the disciples that to be alert, saying, "since you don't know what day your Lord is coming … This is why you are also to be ready, because the Son of Man is coming at an hour you do not expect" (24:42, 44). There is a definitive connection between the Parable of the Ten Bridesmaids and the previous teachings of Jesus within the overall didactic of the Olivet Discourse. After the parable, Jesus provided two other eschatologically focused parables—respectively the Parable of the Talents (25:14–30) and the Parable of the Sheep

---

[545] Or "virgins" as noted in the CSB. The term "virgins" best translates the term παρθένοις which depicts young women who are "beyond puberty but not yet married and a virgin." 9.39 παρθένος, Louw Nida, 108. While the term "virgin" most accurately describes παρθένοις, the overall thrust of the term depicts the concept of a bridesmaid.

[546] As noted previously, the eschatological significance of Jesus's message and ministry cannot be overemphasized. Dunn notes that "there need be little doubt that Jesus was regarded as a prophet by many, that he saw himself in the tradition of the prophets, and probably also that he claimed a(n eschatological) significance for his mission (and thus himself) which transcended the older prophetic categories." Dunn, *Jesus Remembered,* 666.

and Goats (25:31–46). The latter teachings include the illustrious Son of Man title which is exclusively tied to the teachings of Jesus.[547]

For the Jesus Seminar, the parable finds some connection to the teaching of Jesus. But like the previous parables, they held that the parable had been largely altered by the evangelist's interpretation. The entire parable, except for verse 13, is listed in gray.[548] The committee believed that the parable was largely an invention of the evangelist for two reasons. First, they argue that the parable is dissimilar to other parables of Jesus. Second, the parable is more apocalyptic than the team preferred.[549]

Thus far, the parables have fared worse than the segments of the Sermon on the Mount in Chapter 2. Yet it remains to be seen whether the eschatological aspects of the Parable of the Ten Bridesmaids bolster the parable to a higher standing than the two parables previously mentioned. Thus, the parable will need to be examined under the same scrutiny, to unveil the level of certainty that one can connect the parable with early Jesus traditions.

Unique Rabbinic Concepts

The Parable of the Ten Bridesmaids, or Parable of the Wise and Foolish Bridesmaids, finds an interesting parallel between rabbinic literature. Both the Mishnah and the Apocrypha relay information concerning the wedding process, even though some of the precise concepts are not fully known.[550] It is generally agreed that the ancient Israeli wedding ceremony comprised four parts. First, there was the initial arrangement, a time when the father and groom paid the dowry for the bride. The marriage contract was valued at 200 half-shekels, called *zun*.[551] virgins, widows, divorcees, those who severed previous ties through *halisah*,[552] converts, captives, and slave girls.[553]

The second phase was called the "fetching of the bride."[554] This was a time when the groom greeted the bride to take her to the wedding party. The

[547] This will receive further attention in Chapter 4.

[548] Funk, Hoover, and the Jesus Seminar, *Five Gospels,* 253–254.

[549] The second assessment is a bit odd, because many of the messages of Jesus are apocalyptic and eschatological in nature. Ibid., 254.

[550] Morris, *Matthew,* PNTC, 621.

[551] *m. Ketuboth* 1.1c., in Neusner, trans, *Mishnah,* 378.

[552] According to Deut. 25:7–9, this is a ceremony that breaks the bond between a man and his brother's widow, when the brother died childless.

[553] *m. Ketuboth* 1.2a–i., in Neusner, trans, *Mishnah,* 378–379.

[554] Fruchtenbaum, *Yeshua,* vol. 3, 371.

waiting period between the arrangement and the retrieval of the bride could be as long as a year, if not longer.[555] The groom did not necessarily have a set time to escort his bride to the ceremony. It is this period that represents the uncertain and anticipated time that the bridesmaids awaited the groom's arrival. *1 Maccabees* describes the wedding procession of the time. While the text discusses an ambush that occurred during the celebration, the procession itself is shown to be a time of great celebration as the "bridegroom came out with his friends and his brothers to meet them with tambourines and musicians."[556]

The wedding ceremony marked the third phase.[557] This part of the wedding process is not surprising. For this was the time that the wedding vows were made, and the ceremony was administered. One interesting aspect is that the bride was led to a *mikveh,* a baptismal pool, for ritual cleansing.[558] However, the *mikveh* shows no relevance to the story, but only shows the practice of the time.[559]

Finally, the last phase is the wedding feast which immediately followed the ceremony. The wedding festivities normally lasted for seven days and were an important event for the community. In John's Gospel, Jesus is shown to have performed his first miracle at a wedding feast in Cana of Galilee (John 2). To keep the headwaiter and family from experiencing public embarrassment and shame, Jesus changed water into wine (John 2:9). The miracle occurred later in the week as the headwaiter said, "Every man serves the good wine first, and when the guests are drunk, then he serves the poorer wine, but you have kept the good wine until now" (John 2:10, NASB).

Relating to the overall theme of the Parable of the Ten Bridesmaids, the message of the story finds three interesting parallels to rabbinic thought. First, the concept of wish and foolish individuals either using or misusing items is found in the teachings of *b. Shabbath.* A story is told of a king who distributed apparel to his servants. After a period of time, the king required that the servants give back the garments that he gave to them. The wise servants returned the garments, ensuring that they were immaculately clean. However, the foolish servants returned the garments soiled and dirty. The king said that the wise servants could go home in peace, whereas the foolish servants were imprisoned. The rabbi connects the story with the Holy One, who would say

---

555 Ibid., 372.

556 *1 Macc.* 9:37.

557 Fruchtenbaum, *Yeshua,* vol. 3, 372.

558 Ibid.

559 Granted, some of the aspects of the ancient wedding protocol will be revisited in the methodology devoted to cultural concepts.

to the righteous, "He entereth into peace, they rest in their beds,".[560] and to the unrighteous, "There is no peace saith the Lord, unto the wicked.".[561] Additionally, the spiritual connotations of marriage were conveyed by the rabbinics, particularly one's spiritual devotion to God. For instance, Rabbi Berakhot encouraged grooms to recite the *Shema* on the first night after his wedding..[562]

Second, Matthew 25:13 parallels an interesting teaching found in the Talmud. Rabbi Eleazar is quoted as saying, "Repent one day before your death.".[563] His disciples asked him how one is to know the timing of one's death. The rabbi replied, "All the more reason to repent today, lest he die tomorrow, and hence his whole life should be spent in repentance.".[564] Compare Eleazar's teaching with Jesus, who said, "Therefore, be alert, because you don't know either the day or the hour" (25:13).

Finally, the parable finds a connection to the wisdom literature found in the book of Proverbs, as well as the Qumranic book of 1QS..[565] Thus, with the three parallel lines of comparison, the parable is firmly rooted in rabbinic understanding. The difference between the Talmud and Jesus's teaching is that he seems to direct the uncertain timing not to one's death but rather to the eschatological immediacy of the kingdom of heaven.

The customs and themes of the Parable of the Ten Bridesmaids find some connections and parallels to rabbinic thought. It is imagined that even deeper parallels could be found between the rabbinic literature and the Parable of the Ten Bridesmaids if one were to further explore the issue. Suffice it to say, enough parallels have been found to sufficiently connect the parable to rabbinic concepts. Thus, the parable passes the first test and earns 2 points.

Early Christological Concepts

The Parable of the Wise and Foolish Bridesmaids is a bit problematic to pinpoint whether it contains early Christological concepts or not. Clearly, as the previous test concerning the rabbinic material and the tests that follow will show, the parable finds some connection with the teachings of Jesus. However, it is unclear whether Jesus is providing a story relating to a real wedding of his

---

[560] *b. Shabbath* 152b.

[561] Ibid.

[562] *m. Berakhot* 2.7c, in Neuser, trans, *Mishnah,* 6.

[563] *b. Shabbath* 153a.

[564] Ibid.

[565] N. T. Wright, *Jesus and the Victory of God* (Minneapolis, MN: Fortress, 1996), 315.

time and was interpreted by the early church as eschatological,[566] or if he intended the story to be taken as eschatological by nature. A plain reading of the text in correlation with the overall emphasis of the Olivet Discourse definitely suggests such an eschatological interpretation. However, the interpretation must be read into the parable rather than being something extracted from the text. Lengthy interpretations that identify specific players in the eschaton, while fascinating, are not something that can be authenticated from the text.[567]

Previously, eschatological concepts permitted the parables to pass the second test as they presented a bipartite relationship between the Father and Son. The Parable of the Ten Bridesmaids certainly finds itself within those parameters. However, it must be admitted that this parable does not explicitly denote the bipartite relationship as other parables have. It could be that the appearance of Yahweh could be substantiated as much as the return of the Son of Man.[568] Further complicating the issue is that none of the Christological titles for Christ are found in the parable. Some translations, such as the *New King James Version,* include the phrase "in which the Son of Man is coming" (25:13, NKJV).[569] However, the oldest Greek texts do not contain the last phrase, thereby leaving the parable without a firm connection to a Christological title. Yet to maintain consistency, the parable could be connected

---

[566] Jeremias, *Parables of Jesus,* 52–53.

[567] One such example of an overreach is in Arnold Fruchtenbaum's commentary on the Parable of the Wise and Foolish Bridesmaids. Fruchtenbaum argues that the arrangement of the wedding refers to the sacrifice of the Son (Eph. 5:22–33), the fetching of the bride references the rapture (John 14:1–3), the wedding will occur in heaven before Jesus's Second Advent (Rev. 19:6–8), and the wedding feat denotes the Millennial Reign of Christ. Fruchtenbaum, *Yeshua,* vol. 3, 372. While Fruchtenbaum's interpretation very well may be accurate, it is a bit of an exegetical overreach to imply that the text teaches as much.

[568] In 2 Peter, the author references the eschaton by suggesting that the elements of creation will be melted away at the Lord's coming. The text reads, "But the day of the Lord will come like a thief, in which the heavens will pass away with a roar and the elements will be destroyed with intense heat, and the earth and its works will be discovered" (2 Pet. 3:10, NASB). Does κυρίου represent Yahweh or Jesus? It is not necessarily clear.

[569] Scripture passages marked NKJV come from the *New King James Version* (Nashville, TN: Thomas Nelson, 1982).

to the already-not-yet kingdom, depending on how one views the women.[570] Even if it does not, the imminency of the day of the Lord is in view, and, when taken in context with the surrounding passages, the kingdom's arrival through the Son is certainly implied. Indeed, Jewish literature never seems to link the Messiah with a bridegroom, but teachings such as the Parable of the Wise and Foolish Bridesmaids suggest that Jesus saw himself fulfilling such a role.[571] Thus, the parable can be said to pass the second test, albeit with some reservation, earning 5 points. So, the parable can be said to pass the first two tests placed before it.

Theological Terminology Relating to Early Christological Concepts

As noted in the previous section, the Parable of the Ten Bridesmaids poses a problem connecting it with early theological terminology due to its lack of Christological titles. That is not to say that there are no Christological concepts found in the text. However, they are far too implicit to claim with any certainty that they hold any certifiable link, outside of the βασιλεία τῶν οὐρανῶν motif. While some translations contain the title Son of Man, the oldest and most trustworthy manuscripts do not include the title. If the earliest Greek manuscripts represent those documents most closely aligned with the original texts, as is assumed by the vast majority of NT scholarship, then one is left without any titles or terminology that construes early Christological language. Therefore, since the parable fails to afford anything from which to build a case to connect it with early Christological language or Christological titles, then it may be initially thought that the parable fails the test at hand.

However, the use of the wedding in connection with the call to γρηγορεῖτε[572] for the bridegroom's appearing provides a connection with an early Christological motif that cannot be denied. Keener notes that Jewish parables may at times refer to the wedding of Israel and the Torah.[573] In like manner, the OT frequently depicts Yahweh as the groom to his people. Isaiah writes, "Indeed, your husband is your Maker—his name is the LORD of Armies—and the Holy One of Israel is our Redeemer; he is called the God of the whole earth" (Isa. 54:4–6). In other passages, Yahweh pledges his love for the people, his beloved, as a husband loves his wife (Eze. 16:7–34). Undeniably,

---

[570] If the women are viewed as those in the kingdom and that the foolish women identify those who lose faith in Christ, then an already-not-yet kingdom could be in view. If the women are seen as representing all individuals of the world, then the foolish women are those who reject Christ's salvific covenant.

[571] Witherington, *Christology of Jesus,* 212.

[572] I.e., "to be watchful."

[573] Keener, *GMSRC*, 595.

the bridal motif is found in Hosea, where Yahweh, speaking to his people, says, "I will take you to be my wife forever. I will take you to be my wife in righteousness, justice, love, and compassion" (Hos. 2:19). The theoretical document Q is generally held to be among the earliest tradition of Jesus sayings. Though this claim could be debated, it is intriguing that the Markan and Q portrayal of Jesus is that of a prophetic leader who is leading a covenantal renewal movement.[574] Jesus's appeal to γρηγορεῖτε for the eschatological kingdom, along with the refusal to allow the foolish access, seems to fit within this overarching theme. Additionally, the marriage motif also matches the Hallelujah cries of Revelation 19 which are considered to be early hymns.[575] Of particular interest is Revelation 19:7, which says, "Let us be glad, rejoice, and give him glory, because the marriage of the Lamb has come, and his bride has prepared herself" (Rev. 19:7). Revelation 19:7 is appealingly comparable to the message given in the Parable of the Wise and Foolish Bridesmaids.

At first glance, the parable did not appear to hold any theological language that matched Christological titles, particularly given the absence of the Son of Man, or כְּבַר אֱנָשׁ, in 25:13. However, the overarching language of God's wedding to his people finds a home in both the OT and the early hymn of Revelation 19:7.[576] Due to nature of the parable's link with early themes associated with Christological titles such as Son of God and Son of Man, then it can be said that the parable passes the present test, receiving 4 additional points. Therefore, the parable currently stands at 3 for 3.

Mnemonic & Rhythmic Patterns

The parable does not contain any notable rhythmic patterns or mnemonic devices throughout the totality of the message. However, it does contain a few antithetical parallelisms that correspond with the teaching style of Jesus. It has been estimated that Jesus used antithetical parallelisms so extensively in his teaching ministry that they are found well over a hundred

---

574 Eve, Horsley, and Draper hold this view. See Eve, *Behind the Gospels,* 118; Richard A. Horsley and Jonathan A. Draper, *Whoever Hears You Hears Me: Prophets, Performance and Tradition in Q* (Harrisburg, PA: Trinity Press International, 1999), 195–227.

575 Hurtado, *One God, One Lord,* 106.

576 As a caveat, it should be noted that Revelation was one of last, if not the final, book to have been written in the NT. Early, in this sense, points to a tradition predating the written text and could possibly have come from the earliest church. Dating the tradition in Revelation is a bit trickier since the book was composed so late in the first-century.

times in the teachings of Jesus.[577] Antithetical parallelisms, just as in the OT's usage of the rhythmic pattern, are used to provide wisdom material, ethical and doctrinal truths, and axiomatic concepts.[578] In contrast, synonymous parallelisms are used more often for devotional literature.[579] However, as Jeremias notes, it must be noted that one is hard-pressed to find a great deal of evidence concerning the use of the antithetical parallelism in Jesus's day.[580] While antithetical parallelism can be found in OT literature (e.g., Psa. 37:9; 146:9; and Prov. 15:1), if it is shown that many, or even most, did not use the poetic device in Jesus's day, then it could be said that this is an exclusive preference of Jesus. This could possibly speak even more to the originality of Jesus's teaching style and strengthen texts which maintain the poetic device. The structure of the parable appears to be an antithetical parallelism as the wise and foolish bridesmaids are compared. But more explicitly, verses 2 through 4 provide an example of the device.[581]

While not a poetic device, the structure of verse 13 finds parallels in other Gospels.[582] Mark 13:35–36 is of particular interest, stating, "Therefore be alert, since you don't know when the master of the house is coming—whether in the evening or at midnight or at the crowing of the rooster or early in the morning. Otherwise, when he comes suddenly he might find you sleeping" (Mark 13:35–36).[583] Also, Luke 12:37[584] provides an alteration of the same message while Revelation 3:20 alludes to the same concept.[585] Could the simple appeal of Jesus calling for watchfulness serve as the mnemonic reminder

---

577 Jeremias counted 30 antithetical parallelisms in the Gospel of Mark, 34 in Matthew and Luke, an additional 44 found in the original sayings in Matthew but unshared by Luke, and an additional 30 in the original sayings of Luke that are unshared in Matthew. Jeremias, *NT Theology,* 14–16.

578 Ibid., 19.

579 Ibid.

580 Ibid., 16–17.

581 Ibid., 15.

582 Jeremias, *Parables of Jesus,* 54.

583 "γρηγορεῖτε οὖν, οὐκ οἴδατε γὰρ πότε ὁ κύριος τῆς οἰκίας ἔρχεται, ἢ ὀψὲ ἢ μεσονύκτιον ἢ ἀλεκτοροφωνίας ἢ πρωΐ, 36 μὴ ἐλθὼν ἐξαίφνης εὕρῃ ὑμᾶς καθεύδοντας" (Mark 13:35–36).

584 "Blessed will be those servants the master finds alert when he comes" (Luke 12:37a).

585 "See! I stand at the door and knock. If anyone hears my voice and opens the door, I will come in to him and eat with him, and he with me" (Rev. 3:20).

of the parable and for the church? Perhaps. But even if the verse does not necessarily contain mnemonic devices, as such, the simplicity of the message is easy enough to remember that it could serve as a seed to bring to memory other teachings of Jesus which call for an eschatological alertness. Two options arise for how the teaching found itself repeated in various contexts. On the one hand, the tradition may have been circulated in different versions..[586] Churches may have duplicated the messages of Jesus using the core data. This corresponds with the informal controlled method advocated by Bailey..[587] On the other hand, the similarities could be the result of the text's duplication which derived from similar or duplicate forms..[588] As one would anticipate, a teacher would retell and recast his messages in various contexts and to different audiences depending on the circumstances and situations..[589] Disciples, having heard the message duplicated numerous times, could easily recite and recall the information that their teacher proclaimed due to its repeated use. But even if this is the case, the entire parable shows signs of a *modified* prophetic template..[590] Such a structure finds a firm foundation in the Hebrew tradition..[591]

The parable shows the necessary signs to pass the current test. Add 5 more points to the parable. Verses 2–4 provide an antithetical parallelism. Additionally, verse 13 links the parable to other eschatological messages given by Jesus. Even if verses 1 and 5–12 did not arise from the original Jesus

---

[586] Dunn, *Oral Gospel Traditions,* 135.

[587] Bailey, "Informal Controlled Oral Tradition and the Synoptic Gospels," *Themelios* 20, 2: 7.

[588] Dunn, *Oral Gospel Traditions,* 135.

[589] Ibid., 136.

[590] The *modified* prophetic template includes seven stanzas in which the climax is focused in the center. In this case, the proclamation of the bridegroom's appearance would serve as the centerpiece. Interestingly, the wise and foolish bridesmaids are contrasted in stanzas 2 and 6. Bailey, *Jesus Through Middle Eastern Eyes,* 269.

[591] Ibid.

tradition,[592] they most assuredly flesh out the message that Jesus provided. Thus, the totality of the message most reasonably represents the *ipsissima vox* of Jesus. Since the parable passes the present test, it now stands at 4 for 4, placing it in the yellow zone of probability.

Aramaic/Hebraic Literary Characteristics

The previous test noted the antithetical parallelisms that also relate to literary characteristics that are prevalent in Semitic literature. Thus, the parable already has some traits that speak to an earlier message which could relate to an early Jesus tradition. However, the parable also shows a couple of other aspects which could be linked to earlier material. In addition to the parallelisms of verses 2–4 and the likely mnemonic teaching of verse 13, Matthew 25:1 and 8 are of interest.

Matthew 25:1 shows similarities with the inchoative[593] and auxiliary verb form which corresponds with Semitic conventions.[594] Black holds that the inchoative and auxiliary verbs do not hold any significance in and of themselves, but they rather point to the main verb.[595] The introductory verse of Matthew 25 finds itself in Black's list, which he borrowed from Jeremias, finds itself among an impressive list of 35 occurrences.[596] The term λαβοῦσαι,[597] which appears and is used in this sense, is often used in this manner.

In his list of Aramaisms, Matthew Black also includes Matthew 25:8 as finding a home with Semitic usage.[598] ἐκ is a preposition used in the partitive sense. Black concedes that the construction is paralleled in Koine Greek, but later states that "its source in the New Testament is almost certainly

---

592 While verses 5–12 do not necessarily match the parallelism found in verses 2–4, there is no reason to deny their authenticity. It may be that certain teachings of Jesus served as triggers which recalled the totality of the teaching in mind. This practice is comparable to remembering acronyms such as "Please Excuse My Dear Aunt Sally" to remember the priority in solving mathematical equations (parentheses, exponents, multiplication, division, addition, and subtraction), or "Oh, Be a Fine Girl/Guy, Kiss Me" when remembering the Harvard Spectral Classification Scheme (OBFGKM).

593 Inchoative verbs describe a change of state.

594 Black, *Aramaic Approach to the Gospels and Acts,* 125.

595 Ibid.

596 Ibid.

597 Ibid.

598 Ibid., 108.

Semitic."[599] The ἐκ of Matthew 25:8 is listed as one among 12 instances of the partitive sense used in the NT.[600] While the nuances between Koine Greek and an Aramaic underpinning can be debated, the fact that the verse holds indicators linking it with the partitive sense makes the verse one of interest in the current investigation.

Since the parable shows good signs of an Aramaic bedrock, then it can be said that the parable passes the fifth test. Add an additional 5 points to the parable's growing score. Combining the last test with the current one, verses 1–4, 8, and 13 all hold signs that an Aramaic tradition preceded the current text as it stands. This would leave only seven verses out of thirteen that hold no Aramaic connotation.[601] Thus, the parable stands at 5 for 5.

Semitic Cultural Concepts of First-Century Israel

Unfortunately, ancient writers did not provide a great deal of information concerning ancient wedding practices.[602] While it is admittedly true that first-century rabbis were not overly persuaded to document the practices of weddings of the time, modern researchers still have enough evidence to contend that the Parable of the Wise and Foolish Bridesmaids is rooted in the cultural concepts of the day due to the continued wedding practices of the area. Weddings in Middle Eastern cultures normally occur in the seven warmest months of the year.[603] Even today, women of the Middle East carry lamps in front of their faces so that people will know their identity.[604] The parable notes that the wedding occurred at midnight, or the μέσης δὲ νυκτὸς[605] (25:6). While midnight might be an odd time to hold a ceremony,[606] weddings were generally held closer to the evening hours, and torches were

---

[599] Ibid., 107.

[600] Ibid., 108.

[601] 46% of the parable can be connected to an Aramaic characteristic of some sort and 53% does not. While the percentage of Aramaic characteristics are higher than its negative counterpart, the percentage of Aramaisms is quite high for this *logion* in comparison to textual percentages of the other parables in this study.

[602] Morris, *Matthew,* PNTC, 620.

[603] Bailey, *Jesus Through Middle Eastern Eyes,* 272.

[604] Ibid.

[605] I.e., "middle of the night."

[606] Perhaps this was a way in which Jesus illustrated the unexpected time of the groom's appearing. That is, the groom would appear at a time when people least expected him.

used as part of the bridal procession.[607] Likewise, torches most likely only burned for around fifteen minutes before the oil-soaked rags had to be replaced.[608] Since the foolish women did not have enough oil for their torches combined with the closure of stores being that the festivities were in the middle of the night, then it would not be surprising if the gatekeepers were unable to identify the women when they approached the gate. The gatekeeper had no choice but to say, "I don't know you."[609] However, since wedding feasts continued for seven days, then it would seem as if the bridesmaids would be allowed access the next day.[610] Something deeper must be going on. It is much more likely that the unpreparedness of the bridesmaids insulted the bride, the groom, and those hosting the party.[611]

The parable's presentation of wedding cultural concepts matches the practices of the time so closely that some have inquired as to whether Jesus had an actual wedding he observed when first delivering the story. Some have even suggested that the parable should not be considered allegorical as Jesus most likely used the story of an actual wedding didactically to direct his listeners' attention to an imminent eschatological crisis.[612] It was the church, not Jesus, who reshaped the story into its current parabolic form.[613] Given the inclination of Jesus to use parables to teach spiritual truths and his favorability to the parable in his overall didactical instruction, such arguments are not persuasive. It very well may be that Jesus observed a genuine wedding in which the groom came to obtain his bride at an unusually late and most unfavorable hour. The odd timing caught some of the bridesmaids off-guard. Due to their unpreparedness, they were not permitted inside to participate in the wedding festivities. Like modern preachers who use real-life illustrations to proclaim spiritual truths, Jesus may have used this story, if true, as an example of the soon-to-come eschatological kingdom. However, Jesus acknowledges that

---

[607] Keener, *IVPBBC: NT,* 110.

[608] Ibid., 111.

[609] Bailey makes the same argument. He also notes, "In the Middle East the word *no* is never an answer, rather it is a pause in the negotiations." Bailey, *Jesus Through Middle Eastern Eyes,* 273.

[610] Guests arrived during the days of celebration subsequent to the wedding ceremony. See *Safrai* 76b; *b. Ketub.* 7b–8b; *p. Ketub.* 1:1.

[611] Keener, *GMSRC,* 598–599.

[612] Jeremias, *Parables of Jesus,* 171–172.

[613] Ibid.

there may be a span of time before the kingdom is actualized. Because of the uncertainty of the time, people need to remain alert—or γρηγορεῖτε (25:13).

Because of the strength of the wedding concepts of the time, the parable passes the sixth test, adding an additional 4 points to its tally. One word of caution should be given. It is not known to this researcher whether Greco-Roman weddings were cast in the same traditions as were first-century Jewish weddings. There may not be sufficient evidence to distinguish the parable's Jewish wedding customs from later Hellenistic practices without further research. Even still, the richness and depth of the cultural concepts found in the parable overwhelmingly shine in the parable's favor. Therefore, the Parable of the Wise and Foolish Virgins is the only parable that finds itself in the green zone of probability, scoring 6 for 6 in the tallied test and 25 points in the weighted scale.

Similarities to NT Creeds, Summaries, and Early Literature

Like the other parables in this study, it is difficult to find anything in the Parable of the Wise and Unwise Bridesmaids that matches the themes and materials of the early creeds. The parable does not match the themes of baptism, worship, exorcisms, or polemics against heresies.[614] Yet it is possible that the parable could be used to encourage individuals against pending times of persecution. The watchfulness, or γρηγορεῖτε, could call individuals of Jesus's day, Matthew's, and end-time believers to remain steadfastly committed to the Lord even in times of peril. The subsequent parable the Parable of the Talents (25:14–30) along with the Son of Man's separation of the sheep from the goats (25:31–34) speak to the importance of faithfulness to the end, along with God's division of the saints from the sinners. While this could be the case, the primary objective of the parable seems to be more on the call for the disciples to be γρηγορεῖτε rather than encouraging them to endure persecution. There just is not enough evidence in the text to press the issue.

Considering the types of materials found in early creeds and summaries, the parable does not contain any of the attributes of *homologiai* or single-statement affirmations as described by Longenecker.[615] Nevertheless, the parable does show some compelling comparisons to credal hymns. The parable is most certainly not a hymn. Even still, like the credal hymns, the parable has been shown to exhibit antithetical parallelisms which are a favored teaching style of Jesus.[616] As previously noted, the parable exemplifies what many scholars term the *modified* prophetic template, which is frequently

---

614 Cullmann, *Earliest Christian Confessions,* 18.

615 Longenecker, *New Wine into Fresh Wineskins,* 13–23.

616 Jeremias, *NT Theology,* 14–16.

employed in the Hebraic tradition, particularly the OT prophets.[617] But the parable does not exhibit these traits throughout the entire section. Verses 1–4, 8, and 13 are of particular interest.

The Parable of the Wise and Foolish Bridesmaids is among the most compelling of the Matthean parables examined. Some traits in the parable suggest that at least portions of it may align with the characteristics of early hymns. Yet the parable remains elusive as to how much the parable could be aligned with early hymnic patterns, if at all. It may be better served to say that certain portions of the parable were mnemonic portions remembered by the early Jesus tradition, which Matthew used to flesh out the parable. As it stands for the present test, the best that can be said is that the parable holds interesting characteristics that are worth further exploration. But it does not hold enough to warrant a passing grade for the final test.

Conclusion and Color Assignment

The Parable of the Wise and Foolish Bridesmaids is by far the most compelling of the parables examined. The parable passed 6 of the 7 tests set before it and scored 25 points out of 30 on the weighted scale. Therefore, the parable is said to be in the green section on both tests—that is, it is beyond reasonable doubt that the parable holds traits that place it within the early Jesus traditions that predate the NT texts. The parable serves as an interesting case study for the early Semitic residue found in the parables. This will be discussed in greater depth at the conclusion of this chapter. The Parable of the Wise and Foolish Bridesmaids is the best-attested example of early material of the three that have been examined. The only test that the parable did not pass was the seventh one, and even then, it was noted that the parable exhibited some traits that were sought out by the examination.

Conclusion

The parables of Jesus presented some challenges for the study at hand. Unlike the Sermon on the Mount, the parables did not fare as well overall. However, this was not something that dismissed the thesis. Rather, three models of oral transmission were unveiled. The Bultmannian informal, uncontrolled model was shown to be deficient as it did not cohere with traditional practices in ancient Middle Eastern societies.[618] Additionally, Bultmann's model presupposes an antisupernatual bias that is foreign to biblical times. The second school is the Scandinavian school which promotes the formal controlled model. Birger Gerhardsson is among the scholars who

---

[617] Bailey, *Jesus Through Middle Eastern Eyes,* 269.

[618] Bailey, "Informal Controlled Oral Tradition and the Synoptic Gospels," *Themelios* 20, 2 (1995): 4–5.

advocate this model. This position holds that the primitive church held strict devices in place that transmitted material verbatim. Gerhardsson writes, "All historical probability is in favor of Jesus' disciples, and the whole of early Christianity, having accorded the sayings of one whom they believed to be the Messiah at least the same degree of respect as the pupils of a Rabbi accorded the words of *their* master!".[619] Kenneth Bailey presents a third model which holds the traits of the Scandinavian school but allows for some flexibility in the tradition's transmission. He calls his approach the informal controlled model..[620] Bailey's model permits some flexibility on the non-essential details of a story, but nothing greater than 15 percent of the story could be changed..[621] The flexibility of the model would permit the keeper of the tradition to add personal reflections and interpretations of the material to assist with the memorization of the material. Thus, the preserver was not allowed to falsify any of the information, though he could shape the material for the intended audience. The parables exhibit signs of the informal controlled model to varying degrees..[622]

The Parable of the Harvest was the weakest of the three parables. It contained Christological concepts, theological terminology, and Aramaic characteristics. However, the parable did not hold any substantial connections to rabbinic material, mnemonic devices and rhythmic patterns, early cultural concepts, or characteristics found in early credal material. Thus, the parable contains points of contact that connect it to early material, but the interpretation showed more redaction from the hands of Matthew than in other

---

[619] Gerhardsson, *Memory and Manuscript,* 258.

[620] Bailey, "Informal Controlled Oral Tradition and the Synoptic Gospels," *Themelios* 20, 2 (1995): 5.

[621] Ibid., 7.

[622] Gerhardsson's model is not as distant from Bailey's as some might suppose. Gerhardsson is also open for some flexibility in the transmission of material. Gerhardsson writes, "It is possible that skilled mishnah teachers could add an explanatory commentary to the difficult text: a sort of targum or simply a sort of elementary Talmud; that part of the process of instruction was however missing or rudimentary in the teaching of the average mishnah teacher: so much is clear." Gerhardsson, *Memory and Manuscript,* 115–116. Though, Gerhardsson does warn that pushing the issue too far is dangerous as it exhibits the practices of the Hellenized West rather than that of the Middle East. He writes, "The art of reproducing another person's statements in one's own words, and of abstracting points of view and ideas from someone's words, has been carried to considerable lengths in the Hellenized West. But the art was not practiced in ancient Israel. A person's views were conveyed in his own words. Authentic statements contained the authority and power of the one who uttered them; this we know from the Old Testament." Ibid., 130.

portions. Again, this should not trouble the one who holds to the inerrancy of Scripture as Matthew maintains the key points of Jesus's message even though it was the first *logion* to find itself in the red zone of probability.

The Parable of the Compassionate Employer passed four tests. The parable found connections with rabbinic material, early Christological concepts, Aramaic characteristics, and early cultural concepts. However, it failed to pass the tests for theological terminology, mnemonic and rhythmic patterns, and early credal materials. The parable fared better than its predecessor, passing four tests, and finding itself in the yellow zone of probability when connecting with early Semitic residue.

The Parable of the Wise and Foolish Bridesmaids was the most compelling of the three parables examined. Verses 1–4, 8, and 13 are especially aligned with these young traditions aligned with the teaching of Jesus. Verses 5–7 and 9–12 could be Matthew's expansion of the message that he learned from Jesus. Even if this were to be the case, Matthew, who would be among those who were the "apostolic custodians"[623] of the Jesus tradition and one who was impacted by Jesus's "historical impact and historical intention,"[624] would be able to accurately convey the message of Jesus. With these verses serving as markers, the parable shows signs of the *informal controlled* model described by Kenneth Bailey.[625] Matthew, who was one of the more highly educated of the disciples, could have employed early rabbinic learning practices that would have qualified him even further to transmit and accurately interpret the information that Jesus first uttered.[626] As with the interpretation portion of the Parable of the Harvest, the inerrantist should not fear. Matthew was fully capable of shaping the teachings of Jesus and preserving his message, especially if one holds that the author was an eyewitness.

Using Bailey's model as the primary method of oral transmission while remaining open to Gerhardsson's model, the researcher would be well served

---

[623] Dunn, *Jesus Remembered,* 180–181.

[624] Markus Bockmuehl, "Whose Memory? Whose Orality?: A Conversation with James D. G. Dunn on Jesus and the Gospels," *Memories of Jesus: A Critical Appraisal of James D. G. Dunn's Jesus Remembered,* Robert B. Stewart and Gary R. Habermas, eds (Nashville, TN: B&H Academic, 2010), 42.

[625] Bailey, "Informal Controlled Oral Tradition and the Synoptic Gospels," *Themelios* 20, 2 (1995): 7.

[626] Birger Gerhardsson notes an early midrash collection entitled Torat Kohanim which tells of Resh Laqish who hears that the son of Pedat knows the Torat Kohanim, goes to him, and "learns to repeat the traditional collection in *three days,* after which he spends *three months* penetrating the meaning and usage of the material he has learned." Gerhardsson, *Memory and Manuscript,* 117.

to examine the other Matthean parables not covered by this research. From what has been observed thus far, the parables contain lines that are stronger than other sections, as particularly detected in the latter parable. These sections could have been seeds of Jesus's teachings which acted as a springboard to help the evangelist flesh out the remainder of Jesus's messages. It would not be the least bit surprising to find this detected phenomenon in other preserved parables.

CHAPTER FOUR
THE SON OF MAN SAYINGS

Thus far, this research has frequently referenced the Son of Man sayings and how they would be engaged in Chapter Four. Now the waiting is over. The title Son of Man (Gk. ὁ0 υἱὸς τοῦ ἀνθρώπου; Aram. בַּר אֱנָשׁ) is referenced no less than 82 times in the canonical Gospels, 84 percent occurring in the Synoptic Gospels..[627] The distribution of the Son of Man sayings is found, respectively, 37 percent in Matthew, 17 percent in Mark, 30 percent in Luke, and 16 percent in John..[628] Outside of the title κύριος, the title בַּר אֱנָשׁ is perhaps the most important of all the titles used by Jesus, as it relates to his messianic self-identification and his relationship with the Father, at least as it pertains to the way he understood the mission afforded to him.

The level of strength that the title holds with early Jesus traditions has led many otherwise skeptical scholars to deduce that the Son of Man sayings represents the "earliest stratum [dating back to] Jesus himself.".[629] Bart Ehrman, self-proclaimed atheist-leaning-agnostic, concedes that the Son of Man sayings is to be found "on the lips of Jesus in the early Gospels.".[630] Thus, even though Jeremias is a believer and Ehrman is not, both agree that the Son of Man *logia* is considered to have been an early, Christological understanding that Jesus had of the messianic role.

Two pericopes of Jesus traditions will be examined in this chapter as they both contain a heavy influence on Jesus's Son of Man title. Matthew 12:22–40 will be the first text examined. This text contains the בַּר אֱנָשׁ title in connection with a rebuttal of Jesus being associated with Beelzebub, the prince of demons, pertaining to his practice of exorcisms, along with his teaching on the unpardonable sin. Additionally, the chapter will research Matthew 24:27, 30–44, which contains the most frequent use of the בַּר אֱנָשׁ title in the Gospel

---

[627] Jeremias, *NT Theology,* 259.

[628] To be exact, the title ὁ υἱὸς τοῦ ἀνθρώπου is found 35 times in Matthew, 14 times in Mark, 25 times in Luke, and 13 times in John. Percentages were rounded. Ibid., 259, fn 9.

[629] Ibid., 266–267.

[630] However, it must be noted that Ehrman does not look at the Son of Man saying in the same vein of thought as conservative evangelicals. Ehrman holds that Jesus sees a future Son of Man figure coming to bring about God's kingdom in the eschaton, to which later Christians ascribed this role to Jesus. Thus, the Son of Man sayings would have been pre-Easter sayings, whereas the apocalyptic application of the title to Jesus would have been a post-Easter understanding. Bart D. Ehrman, *Did Jesus Exist? The Historical Argument for Jesus of Nazareth* (New York, NY: HarperOne, 2012), 305.

of Matthew. This *logion* speaks to the coming of the Son of Man and is, thereby, thoroughly eschatological.

Before peering into the two test cases in Matthew's Gospel, a brief defense needs to be given for the Son of Man title..[631] In this excursus of sorts, the בַּר אֱנָשׁ will be shown to be an important Christological title. The title's origins will be examined in Daniel 7:13–14. The paper will then defend the notion that the בַּר אֱנָשׁ was understood to be a heavenly redeemer rather than the popularized notion that the title refers to the people of Israel. This distinction cannot be fully covered in this paper. Nevertheless, the most essential aspects of the argument will be discussed. Finally, the paper will afford a few good reasons to accept the usage of the title בַּר אֱנָשׁ as one stemming from a pre-Easter setting rather than being a post-Easter invention of the church. Pay close attention to the lack of references to the בַּר אֱנָשׁ outside the Gospels, something that speaks in favor of its Jesuanic usage and early dating.

As it will be shown, בַּר אֱנָשׁ makes the best sense of Christian teachings and early creeds that point to the ascension, heavenly work, and returning glory. Interestingly, the title makes a connection with some of the most recognized pre-NT material, including the Philippians hymn, the Colossians hymn, and the early material found in Thessalonians 4. In many ways, the בַּר אֱנָשׁ illustrates the understanding of Jesus on how he would usher in the kingdom in the last days.

The Christological Significance of the Son of Man Title

Due to the nature of the כְּבַר אֱנָשׁ title, attention needs to be given to the Christological importance of the title. While this theme will be addressed in the examination of the passages in question, the degree of the Son of Man's importance deserves an excursus to afford sufficient attention to the eschatological and apocalyptic importance of the title. This section will consider the origins of the Son of Man figure in Daniel 7. Additionally, consideration needs to be given to the early understanding of who the Son of Man represented—a heavenly redeemer or the people of Israel. Finally, the excursus will eventually lead to a defense that the Son of Man sayings indeed represents an early pre-Easter tradition rather than a post-Easter tradition. Even though a post-Easter understanding does not remove the sayings from the lips of Jesus, it does tend to place more emphasis on the interpretation of the church than is

---

[631] In most cases, the Aramaic בַּר אֱנָשׁ will be used in place of the English Son of Man title.

necessarily warranted.[632] Thus, it shall be argued that the Son of Man traditions derived from a pre-Easter understanding but was most assuredly given further interpretation from the early church.

Origins of the Son of Man Title

The name כְּבַר אֱנָשׁ is steeply rooted in the eschatological and apocalyptic imagery of Daniel 7 and throughout the book of Ezekiel. The seventh chapter is found in the Aramaic portion of Daniel.[633] The chapter features a series of night visions that Daniel had while in the first year of King Belshazzar's reign (Dan. 7:1). In the visions, Daniel witnessed four beasts rising from the sea—the first was like a lion, but had eagle's wings (Heb., כְאַרְיֵ֔ה; Dan. 7:4); the second was like a bear (Heb., לְדֹ֔ב; Dan. 7:5); the third was like a leopard (Heb., כִּנְמַ֔ר; Dan. 7:6); and the fourth was an unnamed beast which was far different and more ferocious than the previous three, and boasted ten horns with an additional little horn (Dan. 7:7). After the presentation of the four beasts and noting the foul-mouthed nature of the fourth beast, Daniel then sees the throne of the Ancient of Days (Heb., וְעַתִּ֥יק יוֹמִ֖ין; Dan. 7:9) sitting upon his throne.[634]

Concluding the depiction of the throne room, Daniel continues by noting the arrogant, haughty nature of the fourth beast before proclaiming the appearance of a new entrant into this compelling sequence. Abruptly, the כְּבַר אֱנָשׁ (i.e., "one like a son of man) appears with the clouds of heaven (Heb., עִם־עֲנָנֵ֣י שְׁמַיָּ֔א). The כְּבַר אֱנָשׁ approaches the וְעַתִּ֥יק יוֹמִ֖ין (i.e., "Ancient of Days") and was escorted before him (Dan. 7:13). The כְּבַר אֱנָשׁ was then given an everlasting dominion and kingdom so that all people would serve him (Dan. 7:13–14).

---

632 This is not to say that some interpretation was not used by the church even with pre-Easter sayings. However, pre-Easter traditions are even earlier than post-Easter sayings. The evidence, as shall be argued, suggests that these sayings were not picked up by the early church, but were primarily focused on the canonical Gospels.

633 The book of Daniel is composed in Aramaic in 2:4–7:28 and in Hebrew for the remaining passages of the text.

634 The וְעַתִּ֥יק יוֹמִ֖ין is a title given to the Almighty God. The antiquity of God's being does not necessarily indicate that God is an old man sitting in heaven, as often depicted in medieval art. But rather, it more likely speaks to the eternal nature of God. His hair, flames, and brilliancy speak to God's power and holiness. Stephen R. Miller, *Daniel,* New American Commentary, vol. 18, E. Ray Clendenen, ed (Nashville, TN: B&H, 1994), 204–205; John E. Goldingay, *Daniel,* Word Biblical Commentary, vol. 30, Bruce M. Metzger, David A. Hubbard, and Glenn W. Barker, eds (Dallas, TX: Word, 1989), 165.

Thus, from the text, one finds that the כְּבַר אֱנָשׁ holds a more-than-humanness due to a couple of reasons. First, the כְּבַר אֱנָשׁ was able to approach the Ancient One without perishing. This was something unheard of in OT theology. Unless one was granted permission and went through the process of purification, no one was allowed to enter God's presence without severe consequences. For instance, consider that when Aaron's sons Nadab and Abihu took their own firepans and offered incense to the Lord in an inappropriate fashion, "fire came from the LORD and consumed them (Lev. 10:2). Even for those who were permitted access to God's presence, they were still unable to see God's face and life (Exod. 33:20). Yet one finds this כְּבַר אֱנָשׁ approaching the Ancient One directly without any recourse. Therefore, whoever this כְּבַר אֱנָשׁ may be, he is more than just a regular human being.

Who Does the Son of Man Figure Represent?

But what can be deduced about this mysterious figure? Some scholars, such as N. T. Wright, argue that the בַר אֱנָשׁ represents the nation of Israel rather than a heavenly redeemer.[635] Wright builds his deduction on what he thinks the original hearers would have understood the title to mean, particularly from the focus on the identity of the beasts being linked with enemy pagan nations and from, as he words it, "the extreme probability that those who read this (very popular) chapter in the first century would have seen its meaning first and foremost in terms of the vindication of Israel after her suffering at the hands of the pagans."[636] He references the *Antiquities of the Jews* by Josephus and notes how Josephus understood the Daniel 7 reference to describe how God would fight against enemy nations.[637] The notion that the כְּבַר אֱנָשׁ refers only to the nation of Israel is met with a few problems.

First, the comparison of the כְּבַר אֱנָשׁ with the nation of Israel, while flowing from the overall theme of the book, does not match the content of the specified Danielic pericope. On the one hand, the phrase "son of man" is thoroughly a Semitism pointing to the being's humanity.[638] The Hebrew form of the phrase (בֶן־אָדָם).[639] is found in Numbers 23:19; Job 25:6; Isaiah 56:2; and Ezekiel 2:1, among other passages. In the Hebrew texts, the phrase identifies a normal, mortal human being. On the other hand, the figure in Daniel 7:13–14

---

635 N. T. Wright, *The New Testament and the People of God* (Minneapolis, MN: Fortress, 1992), 291–297.

636 Ibid., 292.

637 Ibid.; Josephus, *Antiquities of the Jews* 10.267.

638 Goldingay, *Daniel,* WBC, 170.

639 That is, "*ben adam.*"

has a more-than-humanness nature in the text. In fact, the Aramaic/Hebrew letter כ complicates the matter, as the writer claims that the heavenly being has the appearance of a human being but is not necessarily of human origin. Just as the beasts had the appearance of a bear, leopard, and so on, the being approaching the Ancient One, in this case, only looked (כ) like a בַר אֱנָשׁ. To reiterate, the being was not a בַר אֱנָשׁ but only looked like one. Thus, the character's more than human nature points to something higher. It could be argued that since Israel communed with God through their temple worship, then the כְּבַר אֱנָשׁ referenced their approach to the Ancient One. However, this being does not only approach the Ancient One, but he also came on the clouds of heaven, indicating a heavenly status.

Second, early Christian and Jewish interpreters understood the כְּבַר אֱנָשׁ to reference a heavenly redeemer. To further complicate the matter, not only did the כְּבַר אֱנָשׁ come on the clouds of heaven to approach the Ancient One, but the כְּבַר אֱנָשׁ was also given an everlasting kingdom, one "that would not pass away" (Dan. 7:14). Does it make sense that the kingdom of Israel would be given a kingdom if it already references a kingdom, per se?

Though the exact identity of the כְּבַר אֱנָשׁ does not hold consensus, Goldingay has noted that a great deal of evidence suggests that both Christian and Jewish writers held that the "humanlike figure to be the hoped-for future king of Israel who would fulfill the hopes of a Davidic redeemer expressed in OT prophecy (the 'messiah')."[640] According to the Jewish rabbinic tradition, the messianic redeemer was believed to either come in the victorious manner described in Daniel 7—riding on the clouds of heaven—or according to the lowly manner described in Zechariah 9:9—riding on a lowly donkey.[641]. The

[640] Ibid.

[641] Sanhedrin 98a, https://www.sefaria.org/Sanhedrin.98a.13?lang=bi.

former would occur if the people merited redemption, whereas the latter would come if the people did not warrant such redemption..[642]

The Christian tradition is more straightforward. Of the 86 occurrences of the title "Son of Man" in the NT, all but four are found in the teachings of Jesus. Of the four extra-Gospel uses of the title, all but one refers to the Son of Man being a heavenly redeemer..[643] At his execution, Stephen sees the heavens opened and "the Son of Man standing at the right hand of God!" (Acts 7:56). The text's link with Daniel 7:13–14 representing a heavenly figure is undeniable. Stephen's speech is eerily reminiscent of Jesus's own proclamation while being tried, saying, "and you will see the Son of Man seated at the right hand of Power and coming with the clouds of heaven" (Mk. 14:60)..[644] Additionally, the ripping of the high priest's robes and his charge that Jesus had blasphemed by identifying himself as the כְּבַר אֱנָשׁ speaks to the priest's understanding of the כְּבַר אֱנָשׁ being a heavenly redeemer.

The other two NT references to the heavenly Son of Man are found in the book of Revelation. Both texts in Revelation also speak to the early church's understanding of the Son of Man being the heavenly messianic redeemer..[645] Thus, the early church understood the title of the Danielic כְּבַר אֱנָשׁ to represent the heavenly redeemer. But the connection made to Jesus being the כְּבַר אֱנָשׁ seems to have arisen from Jesus himself. It is odd that the כְּבַר אֱנָשׁ is rarely used as a title of Jesus in the NT literature, outside of the few references noted, compared to the voluminous occasions that Jesus uses the title for himself. If the title were an early church invention, one would assume

---

642 "Rabbi Alexandri says: Rabbi Yehoshua ben Levi raises a contradiction between two depictions of the coming of the Messiah. It is written: "There came with the clouds of heaven, one like unto a son of man…and there was given him dominion and glory and a kingdom…his dominion is an everlasting dominion" (Daniel 7:13–14). And it is written: "Behold, your king will come to you; he is just and victorious; lowly and riding upon a donkey and upon a colt, the foal of a donkey" (Zechariah 9:9). Rabbi Alexandri explains: If the Jewish people merit redemption, the Messiah will come in a miraculous manner with the clouds of heaven. If they do not merit redemption, the Messiah will come lowly and riding upon a donkey." Sanhedrin 98a, https://www.sefaria.org/Sanhedrin.98a.13?lang=bi.

643 The exception is found in Hebrews 2:6 where the title is used for a human being, as quoted from Psalm 8:4.

644 Matthew's quotation of Jesus is identical with Mark's at this juncture.

645 "…and among the lampstands was one like the Son of Man, dressed in a robe and with a golden sash wrapped around his chest" (Rev. 1:13). The clearest identifier is found in another text in Revelation, which says, "Then I looked, and there was a white cloud, and one like the Son of Man, was seated on the cloud, with a golden crown on his head and a sharp sickle in his hand" (Rev. 14:14).

that the title would be used with far greater frequency in the NT literature than what is found. The data suggests that the connection of Jesus with the כְּבַר אֱנָשׁ must have flowed from Jesus himself. As Jeremias postulates, the title must have been preserved because of being "sacrosanct, and no-one dared to eliminate it."[646]

Does this mean that Israel is completely out of the picture with the כְּבַר אֱנָשׁ imagery? Absolutely not! It may be that the representative in heaven speaks to God's work with the nation of Israel to bring about the security and divine promises given to them. Josephus seems to take this interpretation. While he does not mention the כְּבַר אֱנָשׁ vision, he does mention God's providential work in creation and governing the affairs of the nations. He concludes with the following:

> So that, by the forementioned predictions of Daniel, those men seem to me very much to err from the truth, who determine that God exercises no providence over human affairs; for if that were the case, that the world went on by mechanical necessity, we should not see that all things would come to pass according to his prophecy.[647]

Thus, Josephus views God as the providential ruler bringing about his work to humanity, even governing the direction of the nations. There is no discrepancy between Josephus's view and that the כְּבַר אֱנָשׁ is God's instrument to deliver God's work to the nations. John J. Collins avers that the כְּבַר אֱנָשׁ could be an angelic representative of Israel, as is the apocalyptic understanding found in the *Book of Jubilees* and *1 Enoch*.[648] He deduces that the כְּבַר אֱנָשׁ figure is not the righteous community but is its heavenly *Doppelgänger*.[649] The question remains: Who was this heavenly representative? For the books of *Enoch,* the mysterious OT namesake for whom the books were written was assumed to be the כְּבַר אֱנָשׁ by some early interpreters.[650] In *3 Enoch*, the angelic figure

---

[646] Jeremias also contends, as has been previously noted in this research, but is well worth repeating, that "the apocalyptic Son of Man sayings which we have recognized as the earliest stratum must in essentials go back to Jesus himself." Jeremias, *NT Theology,* 266–267.

[647] Josephus, *Antiquities of the Jews* 10.280, in Josephus and William Whiston, *The Works of Josephus: Complete and Unabridged* (Peabody: Hendrickson, 1987), 285.

[648] John J. Collins, *The Apocalyptic Imagination: An Introduction to Jewish Apocalyptic Literature,* 3rd ed (Grand Rapids, MI: Eerdmans, 2016), 82–83.

[649] Ibid., 231.

[650] Ibid., 234. However, it appears that Enoch was distinguished from the Son of Man in *1 Enoch* 70:1.

Metatron is assumed to be the "Prince of the Divine Presence."[651] In the *Book of Jubilees,* written somewhere between 175 to 167 BC, two classes of angels are noted—the angels of sanctification and the angels of presence.[652] These angels work on behalf of Israel, working to "[sanctify] Israel, that they should be with [God] and His holy angels."[653] Jesus and the NT writers were unique in their interpretation of the כְּבַר אֱנָשׁ, as they viewed Jesus himself as the heavenly redeemer sent to earth to sanctify and bring the saints of God with him to heaven, while also sanctifying and redeeming the people of God. The Sermon on the Mount does not necessarily connect directly with the connection made with the Danielic כְּבַר אֱנָשׁ. Even still, the connection that Jesus makes with him ushering in the kingdom of God to earth is certainly found in the message. Thus, the link that Jesus makes with himself and the mystical כְּבַר אֱנָשׁ figure could very well impact the overall Christological focus of his divine mission and task.

Even while there may be further problems to work through, sufficient evidence has been provided to show that the view of the כְּבַר אֱנָשׁ as a heavenly redeemer finds a home in early NT interpretation along with the Jewish insight of the time. The insight that Jesus had of his ministry was largely impacted by the way he viewed his connection with the כְּבַר אֱנָשׁ figure. The notion that the כְּבַר אֱנָשׁ referred to the community of Israel alone simply does not find a home with the apocalyptic understanding of the time. The biggest question was which historical figure represented the כְּבַר אֱנָשׁ. For the earliest church, there was no doubt that Jesus of Nazareth assumed that role.

Argument for the Pre-Easter Nature of the Son of Man Sayings

Can it be said that the כְּבַר אֱנָשׁ sayings represent pre-Easter sayings—that is, sayings that occurred during the teaching ministry of Jesus—or post-Easter sayings—that is, sayings that occurred after the resurrection of Jesus of Nazareth? As previously noted, Joachim Jeremias, who is far from an ultra-conservative interpreter, has argued that the Son of Man sayings finds a home in the Jesuanic didactic.[654] Before leaving this section and evaluating the early nature of the Son of Man sayings in Matthew's Gospel, an argument will be offered to show why it is believed that the Son of Man sayings represents early

---

651 Ibid.; *3 Enoch* 12:5.

652 *Book of Jubilees* 2.2; 2.18; and 15.26–27.

653 *Book of Jubilees* 15:27.

654 Jeremias, *NT Theology,* 266–267.

pre-Easter traditions, which by default would date the Son of Man sayings earlier than post-Easter traditions.

1. Either the Son of Man sayings stem from pre-Easter or post-Easter traditions.
2. Pre-Easter traditions are less likely to reference the resurrection of Jesus.
3. Post-Easter traditions are more likely to reference the resurrection of Jesus.
4. Apocalyptic and eschatological concepts are not necessarily linked with the resurrection of Jesus but are focused more on the eschaton.
5. The Son of Man sayings are largely apocalyptic and eschatological in nature.
6. Therefore, the Son of Man sayings are not necessarily linked with the resurrection of Jesus.
7. Therefore, the Son of Man sayings most likely stem from pre-Easter traditions.

Even though it is not necessary to hold that the Son of Man sayings are pre-Easter traditions to hold their value to early Semitic traditions, it does contend that the assessment of Jeremias holds merit, as he links the Son of Man sayings to the very self-assessment of Jesus himself. If the sayings are pre-Easter, then it can be said that the כְּבַר אֱנָשׁ helped formulate early understandings of the messianic work in both the kingdom of heaven that had come to earth through Jesus, the future eschatological blessings to come, and would help assuage any fears that the people may have had when dealing with persecution from pagan nations, something to which Daniel speaks heavily. One of the things that the exploration of the Son of Man sayings will want to consider is whether the resurrection plays a major role in the teachings. If it does, then the presented argument holds less impact than it would if they do not.

Now that the exploration of the Son of Man's significance to Christology has concluded, the research will explore the early nature of two *logia* of Matthean material. The first section will analyze the view that Jesus held concerning exorcism and the unpardonable sin. The second section will examine the more eschatological pericope of the two, as Jesus portrays the return of the כְּבַר אֱנָשׁ. Both *logia* illustrate the connection that Jesus made between the Son of Man figure and his role as the *Shaliach* of God, in addition to the strong relationship he holds to the power of YHWH to bring about his kingdom to earth in an already-not-yet fashion.

Exorcism and the Unpardonable Sin (Matt. 12:22-40)

The first passage to be examined with a בַּר אֱנָשׁ reference is found in the interaction that Jesus held with the Pharisees after healing a demon-possessed individual. The young man was described as one who was blind and unable to speak (12:22). Jesus healed the man of his possession and, thereby, his infirmities which drew the astonishment of the crowds (12:23). They asked one another, "Could this be the Son of David?" (12:23). The text notes the supernatural knowledge of Jesus, as he knew the thoughts of the Pharisees (12:24). The Pharisees had been attributing the power of Jesus to Beelzebub, the prince of demons (12:24). Jesus confronted their accusation with a profound diatribe. He first argued that Satan could not drive out Satan, as such actions would cause his house to be divided (12:26). Jesus said, "Every kingdom divided against itself is headed for destruction, and no city or house divided against itself will stand" (12:25).[655] After affording a brief illustration on the needed stealth of one to rob the possessions of a strong man's house, Jesus then grants his teaching on the unforgivable sin, saying,

> Therefore, I tell you, people will be forgiven every sin and blasphemy, but the blasphemy against the Spirit will not be forgiven. Whoever speaks a word against the Son of Man, it will be forgiven him; but whoever speaks against the Holy Spirit, it will not be forgiven him, either in this age or in the one to come (12:31–32).

As was noted earlier in this chapter, it will be interesting to see whether the בַּר אֱנָשׁ sayings speak to the resurrection of Jesus.[656] If they did, then one would think that they would stem from a post-Easter interpretation more than

[655] This line has been used by many throughout the ages, including President Abraham Lincoln when speaking on the state of the divided country during the days of the American Civil War.

[656] An exception to this is found in the connection that Jesus made with Jonah in the belly of the fish with the temporary burial of the בַּר אֱנָשׁ before his bodily resurrection (Matt. 12:38–40).

a pre-Easter teaching of Jesus.[657]

Jesus does not seem to connect the בַּר אֱנָשׁ teaching with his own personal resurrection in this account, but rather connects his ministry to the direction of the Spirit of God in bringing forth the kingdom of heaven to earth. Prior to this transaction, Jesus connects his ministry with the Servant of the YHWH motif found in the book of Isaiah. Quoting Isaiah 42:1–4, he directs the people not to make his name known, so that the prophecy of Isaiah could be fulfilled according to the plan of the Father.[658] Thus, the blasphemy against the Holy Spirit most likely refers to the rejection of the advances of the Spirit in one's life, especially as it pertains to the Spirit's ministry in the life of Jesus the Son of Man.[659] Such an interpretation correlates with other biblical teachings on the issue, including Hebrews 6:4–6,[660] 1 John 5:16,[661] and Acts 4:12.[662]

The Jesus Seminar affords a fairly high ranking to much of this passage. The Seminar lists verses 25–26 in gray, indicating that the ideas relate to

---

657 Riesner finds a great deal of agreement with the Scandinavian school of oral traditions (i.e., Riesenfeld and Gerhardsson) than the formal historical school. He argues that many of the sayings of Jesus in the Synoptic Gospels are pre-Easter in origin. "Da ein vorosterlicher Beginn der Jesus-Uberlieferung aus mehreren Gruden naheliegt, darf man mit Riesenfeld und Gerhardsson ein grosseres Vertrauen in die Zuverlassigkiet der 'formgeschichtlichen Schule' her moglich ist." Rainer Riesner, "Judische Elementarbildung und Evangelienuberlieferung," *Gospel Perspectives,* France and Wenham, eds, 220.

658 "Here is my servant whom I have chosen, my beloved in whom I delight; I will put my Spirit on him, and he will proclaim justice to the nations. He will not argue or shout, and now one will hear his voice in the streets. He will not break a bruised reed, and he will not put out a smoldering wick, until he has led justice to victory. The nations will put their hope in his name" (Isa. 42:1–4, quoted in Matt. 12:18–21).

659 Blomberg, *Matthew,* NAC, 204.

660 "For it is impossible to renew to repentance those who were once enlightened, who tasted the heavenly gift, who shared in the Holy Spirit, who tasted God's good word and the powers of the coming age, and who have fallen away. This is because, to their own harm, they are recrucifying the Son of God and holding him up to contempt" (Heb. 6:4–6).

661 "If anyone sees a fellow believer committing a sin that doesn't lead to death, he should ask, and God will give life to him—to those who commit sin that doesn't lead to death. There is sin that leads to death. I am not saying he should pray about that" (1 John 5:16).

662 "There is salvation in no one else, for there is no other name under heaven given to people by which we must be saved" (Acts 4:12).

something Jesus said. The Seminar lists verses 27–29 at an elevated level, listing them as pink—something that Jesus probably said. Oddly, the remainder of the teaching is listed as black—something that was the evangelist's invention. But with that said, it is now time to investigate how the text coheres with the tests prescribed in this study, first beginning with unique rabbinic concepts. It will be argued that the passage finds a greater level of confidence than what the Seminar asserted.

Unique Rabbinic Concepts

When investigating the correlation between rabbinic concepts and the truths found in Matthew 12:22–40, a few areas of research rise to the surface. The first issue concerns exorcisms in general. Did rabbis perform exorcisms or hold to their viability? Obviously, the camp of the Sadducees would not be included, as they did not believe in an afterlife, a soul, spiritual beings (such as angels and demons), or even divine interaction in the course of humanity.[663] But did the Pharisees? It is quite interesting to note that the rabbinical teachers did believe in exorcisms, indeed. However, rabbis called for the exorcist to use certain rituals, specific prayers, and invoke "power-authority"[664] to claim power over the demon being exorcized. The *Testament of Solomon* was not a rabbinical writing but was rather a pseudepigraphal possibly written around AD 100.[665] However, Josephus knew the content of the document.[666] Thus, this

[663] (16) But the doctrine of the Sadducees is this: That souls die with the bodies; nor do they regard the observation of anything besides what the law enjoins them; for they think it an instance of virtue to dispute with those teachers of philosophy whom they frequent; (17) but this doctrine is received but by a few, yet by those still of the greatest dignity; but they are able to do almost nothing of themselves; for when they become magistrates, as they are unwillingly and by force sometimes obliged to be, they addict themselves to the notions of the Pharisees, because the multitude would not otherwise bear them." Josephus, in Josephus and Whiston, *Works of Josephus: Complete and Unabridged*, 477–537. See also Matt. 22:23.

[664] Graham H. Twelftree, *Jesus the Exorcist: A Contribution to the Study of the Historical Jesus* (Eugene, OR: Wipf & Stock, 2011), 23.

[665] Jolley sets a range of AD 100–300. Marc A. Jolley, "Solomon, Testament of," *Eerdmans Dictionary of the Bible,* David Noel Freedman, Allen C. Myers, and Astrid B. Beck, eds (Grand Rapids, MI: W.B. Eerdmans, 2000), 1240.

[666] Josephus, *Antiquities of the Jews* 8.2.5.

indicates that either the document was earlier than projected by Jolley, or it represents an oral tradition that was known in the first century.

The *Testament* mentions a list of incantations that Solomon purportedly conducted over various demons to help him build the Second Temple..[667] The document grants one a glimpse of how first-century Jews believed that one could exorcise demons. As Twelftree notes, this process included five steps. First, the exorcist must confront the demon..[668] Second, the exorcist must address and/or abuse the demon..[669] Third, the exorcist must have some form of power-authority to convince the demon to flee..[670] Fourth, the exorcist must converse with the demon. Finally, the exorcist must convince the victim to turn to God..[671] An example of this practice is found in the rabbinical writings, except the story does not pertain to Solomon. The Talmud contains a story of a rabbi named Rabbi Shimon ben Yohai who cast out a demon named Ben Temalyon from the young daughter of an Emperor. The story reads, "When Rabbi Shimon ben Yohai arrived there, the emperor's palace, he said: 'Ben Temalyon, emerge! Ben Temalyon, emerge! And once Rabbi Shimon called to him, Ben Temalyon emerged and left the emperor's daughter, and she was cured.".[672] The rabbi followed a similar practice as spelled out in the *Testament of Solomon.* He called the demon's name and cast him out. While Jesus sometimes used a method comparable to the one prescribed in Jewish tradition, he often exorcised the demon by his power alone without any prescribed ritualistic methods. Such seems to be the case in the story presented in Matthew 12. Even more compelling, however, is that rabbinical tradition held that it was virtually impossible to cast out a demon that caused one to go mute..[673] Since it was held that the exorcist must communicate with the demon inside the victim, and the person must be able to talk for the demon to speak through the victim, then it stands to reason that mutism created a major barrier to any kind of success. As such, mutism created a condition in which exorcism proved

---

[667] The *Testament of Solomon* 35–43 lists a number of demons that Solomon purportedly cast out. See *Testament of Solomon,* http://www.esotericarchives.com/solomon/testamen.htm.

[668] Twelftree, *Jesus the Exorcist,* 23.

[669] Ibid.

[670] Ibid.

[671] Ibid.

[672] *b. Me'il* 17b.

[673] Fruchtenbaum, *Yeshua,* vol. 2, 368–370; Twelftree, *Jesus the Exorcist,* 25–27, 50–52.

impossible.[674] Matthew indicates that the formerly demon-possessed individual had been both blind and unable to speak (12:22). Perhaps this may account for the response of the people standing nearby, who said, "Could this be the Son of David?" (12:23).

Second, the Pharisees accused Jesus of driving out demons by the power of Beelzebul (12:24). This brings up two questions that must be considered. First, did the rabbinic teachings ever mention Beelzebul? *Beelzebul* was a Hebrew pun on the Philistine god known as *Baal-zebub* (2 Kings 1:2–3, 6, 16).[675] The original Philistine name *Baal-zebub* originally mean the "Lord of heaven."[676] However, Jews corrupted the name to say *Baal-zebul,* meaning the "lord of dung"[677] or "the lord of the flies."[678] The rabbis did indeed mention a derivation of the Palestinian god. Rabbi Ahadvoi ben Ami is accredited as saying, "And they made *Baal-berith* their God: this refers to the fly-god of Baal Ekron. It teaches that everyone made a likeness of his idol and put it in his bag: whenever he thought of it he took it out of his bag and embraced and kissed it."[679] In other parts of the Talmud, *Ba'al ob* is linked with the "offering of incense to the Prince of the Demons."[680] Second, did the rabbinic teachers later suggest that Jesus used his power for malevolent reasons? Indeed, they did. According to Lachs, a Baraitha notes, "Yeshu [of Nazareth] practiced sorcery and led Israel astray."[681] The name "Ben Stada" is often used for Jesus in rabbinic material.[682] In one instance, Jesus is said to have carved the name of Yahweh on his body as he brought witchcraft to Israel from Egypt.[683] Thus, the polemical tradition that was preserved in the Talmud extends back to the time of Jesus.

---

[674] "And, finally the success … of these particular healers is reflected in their names being used in 'incantational' exorcisms." Twelftree, *Jesus the Exorcist,* 52.

[675] Morris, *Matthew,* PNTC, 259.

[676] Fruchtenbaum, *Yeshua,* vol. 2, 372.

[677] Morris, *Matthew,* PNTC, 259.

[678] Ibid.

[679] *b. Shabbath* 83b, https://www.sefaria.org/Shabbat.83b.3?lang=bi.

[680] *b. Kerithoth* 3b.

[681] Samuel Tobias Lachs, *A Rabbinic Commentary on the New Testament* (Hoboken, NJ: KTAV, 1987), 211; *b. Sanhedrin* 107b; *b. Sot.* 47a; and *TJ Hag.* 2.2, 77d.

[682] Fruchtenbaum, *Yeshua,* vol. 2, 374.

[683] *b. Shabbath* 104b; Fruchtenbaum, *Yeshua,* vol. 2, 374–375.

The exorcism that Jesus performed in Matthew 12:22–32 and the response of the Pharisees find unique but strong parallels to the concepts of rabbinic tradition. For that reason, this passage passes the first test with great ease. Much more could be said to link the text to rabbinic traditions, but the data presented must suffice for now.[684] Passing the first test, add 2 points to the passage's score.

Early Christological Concepts

The passage at hand demonstrates strong Christological concepts. While Jesus did not claim sonship, as such, he did communicate that he was connected to and empowered by the Holy Spirit. Jesus conveys that his ministry is derived from the divine Spirit of God, rather than the Pharisees' accusation that his miracles were driven by Beelzebul (12:24). The Spirit's work is shown to usher in the kingdom of God through the ministry of Jesus (12:28).[685] Two areas particularly demonstrate the belief that Jesus was ushering in the kingdom of God by the Spirit's power—the finger of God motif and the unpardonable sin.

First, one finds the finger of God motif in the teaching of Jesus in this particular passage. While it is not explicitly said, the finger of God is found in Matthew's Lukan parallel. Matthew 12:28 reads, "If I drive out demons by the Spirit of God, then the kingdom of God has come upon you" (12:28). The Lukan parallel says, "If I drive out demons by the finger of God, then the kingdom of God has come upon you" (Luke 11:20). In both Gospels, the reference is that the power to perform miracles comes from the Spirit of God (or, ἐν πνεύματι θεοῦ).[686] Jesus appears to be directing his hearers to the advent of the kingdom. Rather than relying on incantations and the persona so implacably vital in Jewish exorcisms, Jesus is relying solely on the power of God and his mission to usher in the dawning of God's eschatological kingdom.[687] The finger of God peers back to the power of God exhibited in full display in the exodus.[688] The magicians said to Pharaoh, "This is the finger of God"

---

[684] This is an area that deserves further exploration beyond the scope of this research.

[685] The current project is replete with examples of the Christological focus of the kingdom of God. For more information on this aspect of Jesus's teaching, see especially Chapter 1. Since the project has mentioned the kingdom of God already, there seems little reason to rehash the material again. Yet, one should note that this is a strike in favor of the current passage's Christological concept.

[686] Morris, *Matthew,* PNTC, 316.

[687] Hagner, *Matthew 1–13,* WBC, vol. 33a, 343.

[688] Bock and Simpson, *Jesus According to the Scripture,* 351.

(Exod. 8:19) when speaking of the plagues that Yahweh had brought upon the land. It is in this passage that Jesus makes the clearest of all declarations that the miracles he performed were signposts to show the inauguration of the kingdom of God and the arrival of the Messiah.[689] Because of the link between Jesus's ministry and the Spirit of God, one should not be surprised by the next Christological aspect of the passage—that is, what constitutes as the unpardonable sin.[690]

Second, a major Christological focus is found in the description of the so-called unpardonable sin. Jesus said, "Therefore, I tell you, people will be forgiven every sin and blasphemy, but the blasphemy against the Spirit will not be forgiven. Whoever speaks a word against the Son of Man, it will be forgiven him; but whoever speaks against the Holy Spirit, it will not be forgiven him, either in this age or in the one to come" (12:31–32). The terms "Spirit" and the "kingdom of God" are rarely found together in the NT, particularly in the Gospels.[691] Jesus already noted that it was ἐν πνεύματι θεοῦ[692] that he cast out demons. Thus, if one were to ascribe the work that had been done to Beelzebul, then it stands to reason that such skeptics are speaking against the divine Spirit of God. As Hagner avers, "To blaspheme against the Spirit was in this case to attribute the work of God's Spirit to Satan and so in the most fundamental way to undercut the very possibility of experiencing the reality of God's salvation."[693] Jesus could have implied, or at least had in mind, the writings of Isaiah, who said, "But they rebelled and grieved the Holy Spirit. So he became their enemy and fought against them" (Isa. 63:10). By the usage of βλασφημία—a term that indicates a deliberate refusal to acknowledge God's power[694]—Jesus contends that the major problem behind the Pharisees' refusal to acknowledge the miracles that had been performed was found in their ultimate

---

[689] Blomberg, *The Historical Reliability of the New Testament,* 121.

[690] Twelftree affords four defenses for the authenticity of the "finger of God" statements. "1) The 'kingdom' was a central theme of the public ministry of Jesus. 2) The fact that the kingdom of God is said to have *already* come … suggests that the saying arose in Jesus'[s] own ministry. 3) Also, the verse is part of an antithetic parallelism—a characteristic of Jesus'[s] speech. 4) The early Church did not associate the dawning of salvation with Jesus'[s] exorcisms." Twelftree, *Jesus the Exorcist,* 110.

[691] Although, many parallels are often found between the two. Bauckham, *The Christian World Around the NT,* 475.

[692] I.e., "by the Spirit of God."

[693] Hagner, *Matthew 1–13,* WBC, vol. 33a, 347.

[694] France, *Matthew,* TNTC, 214.

rebellion against the workings of God's Spirit. Thus, since the power to perform miracles came from the Spirit, and the kingdom of God was being ushered in by the Spirit through Jesus; then when one rejects the Spirit's work, they are rejecting the salvific plan of God. If they reject God's salvific plan, then they are, in essence, denying their chance for salvation, leading them to eternal condemnation.

At first glance, one may be inclined to hold that Jesus presented a tripartite view of the Godhead, which was formulated later in the church..[695] However, this need not be the case. Jesus shows the divine connection he has with the Father through the Spirit. Essentially, he uses the same already-not-yet kingdom language so frequently in his messages, by noting his power to bring about the kingdom comes from God. The phrase "finger of God" (Luke 11:20)/ "ἐν πνεύματι θεοῦ" (Matt. 12:28) explicitly demonstrates this connection between Jesus and the Father. With the kingdom language and the conjunction of the Father's plan and Jesus's mission, a case can be made that the *logia* show signs of early Christological concepts, thereby, permitting the passage to clear the second test, thus, scoring 5 points.

Theological Terminology Relating to Early Christological Concepts

When looking at the theological terminology in Matthew 12:22–40, two Christological titles come to mind—one explicit and the other implicit. First, the more explicit name is obvious considering the title of the present chapter. Here, of course, the name "Son of Man" is considered. Due to the emphasis already given to the title, there is little need to overly expand on the concept. However, for the purposes of this study, one would need to see whether the Son of Man title finds root in a pre-Easter tradition in this passage. In verse 32, Jesus connects the power of the Spirit to the kingdom being ushered in by the בַּר אֱנָשׁ. The בַּר אֱנָשׁ title was a way in which Jesus referred to his messianic function from his interpretation of the role, and not by the popular notion of the people..[696] In the present usage of the title, the imagery is not connected to the resurrection. Rather, it is connected to the imagery of God's defeat over the power of Satan and the powers of darkness (12:29–30). Thus, at face value, the usage of the בַּר אֱנָשׁ title does not appear to dictate the

---

[695] This is not to say that Trinitarian language was not found in the NT. Rather, it merely points to the earlier bipartite language that serves as an earmark for early Christological concepts and language.

[696] Morris, *Matthew,* PNTC, 319.

necessity of a post-Easter tradition. If anything, the emphasis is placed on the Spirit's work in the kingdom of God even over that of the בַּר אֱנָשׁ.

The Servant of Yahweh is an implicit title found in the passage. The Servant motif is found throughout the book of Isaiah, but especially in 40–55.[697] In verse 18, the evangelist connects the ministry of Jesus to the Servant of Yahweh in Isaiah 42:1–4. The entire *logia* are encapsulated around the Servant motif. Thus, the humility expressed by Jesus in his servitude to the movement of the Spirit, as flowing from the Father's command, exhibits his self-understanding of his messianic role as the Servant of Yahweh, its fulfillment of what he sees as a messianic prophecy in the book of Isaiah, and his self-understanding of assuming the messianic role.[698] As such, his servitude to the Spirit of God is connected to a previous statement, where Jesus encourages individuals, saying, "Take up my yoke and learn from me, because I am lowly and humble in heart, and you will find rest for your souls" (Matt. 11:29). The Servant of Yahweh was viewed not only as a human figure, but as the unique God in both his humiliation and exaltation.[699] This is especially in view, as noted by Richard Bauckham, in Philippians 2:6–11, the book of Revelation, and throughout the Gospel of John.[700]

The בַּר אֱנָשׁ and Servant of Yahweh titles are entrenched in steep Christology. Because both titles are either found or implied in the text, then one can safely deduce that this passage holds all that is necessary to permit it to pass the third test. Therefore, the text scores an additional 4 points. It was also determined that the usage of בַּר אֱנָשׁ in this passage was not linked to a proposition concerning the resurrection, but rather to the understanding that Jesus held of the inauguration of a Spirit-led eschatological kingdom. Thus far, this passage has handsomely passed the first three criteria.

Mnemonic & Rhythmic Patterns

The text struggles to meet the criteria of the fourth test. Verse 28 shows traits of antithetic parallelism which has been shown to be a regular characteristic of the teaching style of Jesus.[701] The emphasized point is primarily Christological in that the kingdom has partially come, but the coming

---

[697] The Servant of Yahweh is especially viewed in 42:1–4; 49:1–6; 50:4–9; and 52:13–53:12.

[698] Hagner, *Matthew 1–13,* WBC, 348.

[699] Bauckham, *Jesus and the God of Israel,* 36–37.

[700] Ibid, 37.

[701] Twelftree, *Jesus the Exorcist,* 110; Jeremias, *NT Theology,* 14.

of the kingdom points to God's final eschatological victory over evil.[702] Concerning the present test, even though verse 28 shows signs of a rhythmic pattern, the rest of the teaching does not. The parabolic teaching of the strong man (12:29) could show some signs of mnemonic patterns, but not enough to warrant support. Thus, the final conclusion is that while the passage shows some signs of mnemonic and rhythmic patterns, sufficient evidence does not exist to claim that the majority of the text meets the standards of the present test. Verse 28 could be the sole exception. Therefore, the passage tentatively fails the fourth test.

Aramaic/Hebraic Literary Characteristics

Matthew 12:22–40 holds numerous Aramaic characteristics that would qualify it to pass the fifth test. First, the text shows signs of *casus pendens* in Matthew 12:32.[703] As it was noted, *casus pendens* is understood as a grammatical structure in which the initial noun has been displaced. *Casus pendens* is not exclusively found in Semitic languages. However, it is much more common in Hebrew and Aramaic than it is in Koine Greek.[704]

Second, Aramaic scholars contend that φθάνω may be a translation of the Aramaic term *m*ᵉ*ta* as found in Daniel 4:21, just as a parallel usage of *peplerontai* may be a translation of *malkuth* ᵉ*laha* or *q*ᵉ*rabhath,* meaning "The Kingdom of God has come."[705] Not only does the term hold an Aramaism, but it also finds a home in the book of Daniel which has proven to revolve around the בַר אֱנָשׁ motif, along with adhering to the common theme of an eschatological already-not-yet kingdom.

Third, verse 32 appears again on the list of Semitic characteristics. The term ἀφεθήσεται, meaning "it will be forgiven him," is a Semitism and has parallels with the same phrase in Daniel 7:25, *millin l*ᵉ*sadh mallel,* noting a person speaking against God Almighty.[706] The expression has connotations to the Hebrew term בָּרַךְ (*bārak*). The term בָּרַךְ is unique in the sense that it is normally

---

[702] Hagner, *Matthew 1–13,* WBC, 344.

[703] Black, *Aramaic Approach to the Gospels and Acts,* 53.

[704] Ibid., 51.

[705] Ibid., 211; C. H. Dodd, "The Fall of Jerusalem and the 'Abomination of Desolation,'" *Journal of Roman Studies,* 37 (1947): 47–54.

[706] Meaning "to speak words against the Almighty." In the Greek LXX, the phrase is rendered *Kai logous pros ton hupsiston lalesei.*

used to describe a blessing.[707] However, in rare instances (e.g., 1 Kings 21:13, Job 1:11, and Job 2:9), the term can be used as a euphemism to express the false charge of cursing.[708]

Fourth and finally, Maurice Casey avers that the term Βεελζεβοὺλ is so deeply rooted in the Semitic culture of the time that he places the entire *logia* within the confines of the theoretical Q, thus making it among the earliest texts of the NT.[709] The more popular term for the devil at the time was oJ Satana:V. According to Casey, Βεελζεβοὺλ holds a stronger tie to the Aramaic understanding of the devil over that of Hellenistic theology.[710] Even while holding to the antiquity of the text, he still suggests that Matthew most likely edited the material substantially to "intensify Jesus'[s] achievement, and to ensure that his readers would regard it as miraculous."[711]

From the previous four points, one will note that Matthew 12:22–32 displays numerous affinities to the Aramaic language. Casey's attribution of the pericope with Q speaks of the heavily induced Semitic characteristics of the text at hand. Therefore, it can be said with a good deal of confidence that Matthew 12:22–32 passes the fifth test, thereby leaving the current passage's score at 4 and 1, while also adding another 5 points to its weighted score. Because of the text's strong standing thus far, it has already secured a home in the yellow zone of certitude.

Semitic Cultural Concepts of First-Century Israel

Because of the text's performance with the fifth test, it should come as no surprise that the passage excels with the sixth test. As already noted, the use of Βεελζεβοὺλ by Jesus and the Pharisees speaks to the cultural understanding of the demonic term as particularly found in Semitic backgrounds. Thus, this is a strike in favor of the text's link with the culture of the day.

Second, Jesus recognizes the practices of exorcism in his day that are directly associated with the understood Jewish practices of the day.[712] Exorcism was not something that the Pharisees engaged in too frequently.

---

[707] Joshua G. Mathews, "Cursing," *Lexham Theological Wordbook*, Lexham Bible Reference Series, ed. Douglas Mangum et al., (Bellingham, WA: Lexham Press, 2014), Logos Bible Software.

[708] Ibid.

[709] Maurice Casey, *An Aramaic Approach to Q*, 165.

[710] Ibid., 162–163.

[711] Ibid., 156.

[712] See the first test for more information on Jewish exorcist practices.

However, it does appear that the scribes in Jerusalem of the time did perform exorcisms and used the term Βεελζεβοὺλ..[713] From the text, it does not appear that Jesus is disparaging the Jewish exorcisms that had been performed. Rather, he is pointing out that such works point to the divine moving of God's Spirit. For his work, he is directly corresponding to the Spirit's ushering in the kingdom of heaven. Holding to the ancient interpretation of the identification of the ancient exorcists, Shirock deduces that the usage of the phrase οιJ υιοἰ ὑμων was Jesus's "olive branch, one of the last, held out by Christ to those who despised him.".[714]

From the two points mentioned and many others that could be added, it has been sufficiently shown that the passage relates to early known cultural issues of the time. The text does not show signs of a later invention, but rather fits well within the timeframe of Jesus and the early church. Thus far, the passage has passed 5 of the first 6 tests. Since it passed the sixth test, 4 more points are added to the weighted score, already placing it in the green zone with both tests. The final test will gauge whether the text finds itself even more embedded within the green layer of certitude.

Similarities to NT Creeds, Summaries, and Early Literature

For the final test, the text matches two of the five themes listed by Cullmann as complementary to early credal material..[715] The first matching theme is exorcism, which is quite obvious. The entire passage deals with the exorcism performed by Jesus (12:22), the crowd's response to said exorcism (12:23), the Pharisee's criticism (12:24), and the response given by Jesus to the Pharisee's criticism of his exorcism (12:25–32). As noted throughout this section, Jewish forms of exorcism may be alluded to or implicated by Jesus's teaching. Thus, if exorcism is a theme related to material identified as early, then it stands to reason that this passage finds a home within the confines of the exorcism theme.

Second, the teaching of Jesus is quite polemical against what one would call a heresy. Heresy is understood as a rejection of an understood, accepted truth. The Pharisees and scribes did not deny the practice of exorcism. Jewish

---

713 Casey, *Aramaic Approach to Q*, 165; Robert Shirock, "Whose Exorcists Are They? The References of οι υιοἰ ὑμων at Matthew 12.27/Luke 11:19," *Journal for the Study of the New Testament* 46 (1992):14–51.

714 Shirock, "Whose Exorcists Are They? The References of οι υιοἰ ὑμων at Matthew 12.27/Luke 11:19," *JSNT* 46: 51.

715 As a reminder, the five themes are 1) baptism and catuchemenisms, 2) worship, 3) exorcism, 4) encouragements against persecution, and 5) polemics against heresies. Cullmann, *Earliest Christian Confessions,* 18.

charismatic leaders such as Hanina ben Dosa, who was not identified with any particular sect of Judaism, was considered by the people of his day to a righteous Jew.[716] Thus, exorcism was not the problem. Rather, Jesus called them to recognize that it was the Spirit of God that permitted these exorcisms to occur, and not by one's own power. To deny the Spirit's involvement was to commit the most heinous and unforgivable of sins. The equivocation of Jesus's power to that of Satan denied the Spirit, thereby leading the Jewish leaders of the day into heresy.

While the text does not necessarily find a home in the credal types of materials—it is not being contended that the passage is a creed—the passage does gravitate toward two of the five themes presented by Cullmann. As such, it is contended that the text at hand matches the basic criteria of the final test and scores 5 additional points. Thus, the passage passes all but one of the seven tests.

Conclusion and Color Assignment

As a review, Matthew 12:22–32 passed the first rabbinical test. It was observed that Jewish exorcisms were performed by those in the Pharisaical party, moreso by those who were scribes. Additionally, the term *Beelzebul* matched the Talmudic usage of the phrase. Both speak in favor of the unique rabbinical context of the passage. Second, it was noted that the passage passed the second test, as well. The passage emphasizes Christ's ushering in of the kingdom of God—a Christological theme that is proclaimed and recognized in early credal material such as the Philippians hymn (Phil. 2:5–11) and the Colossians creed (Col. 1:15–20). Third, the passage also passed the theological terminology test as the passage bolstered such Christological titles as the בַּר אֱנָשׁ and the Servant of Yahweh—a title thoroughly found in the book of Isaiah. Thus, the text strongly casts Jesus in a similar kind of Christology that is found in the earliest church.[717] The passage did not pass the fourth test as no rhythmic patterns could be found except for a possible exception in 12:28. The text passed the fifth test because of four traits that exhibited Semitic characteristics. As it was noted, the passage of Scripture is strong in this area. The use of the name *Beelzebul* and a possible olive branch extended by Jesus, by a possible nod to the scribal exorcists of the day, illustrated but a few of the numerous cultural

---

[716] Blomberg, *Matthew,* NAC, 202; Geza Vermes, *Jesus the Jew* (Philadelphia, PA: Fortress, 1973), 63–68; A. E. Harvey, *Jesus and the Constraints of History* (Philadelphia, PA: Westminster, 1982), 98–119.

[717] Bauckham, *Jesus and the God of Israel,* x, 235.

traits of the Scripture. Finally, it was noted that the passage affords a teaching on exorcism and a polemic that is notable in early material.

Altogether, Matthew 12:22–32 passes six of the seven tests placed before it. Given the test that it fulfilled, Matthew 12:22–32 scores a whopping 25 points on the weighted scale, placing it firmly within the green zone of certitude in both tests.

Another facet that favors the early nature of the text is the recognized position that the passage holds within the theoretical Q material.[718] Because of the text's overlap with Mark, some scholars have even argued that this passage may precede Mark's work.[719] Whether this is true or not, such discussion extends beyond the scope of the present research. However, that such a discussion is held about this text speaks favorably for its early nature.

Coming of the Son of Man (Matt. 24:27, 30-44)

The second passage of Scripture in this chapter comes from a portion of the message of Jesus popularly known as the Olivet Discourse. The Olivet Discourse (24:1–25:46) is the last of the major Jesuan discourses recorded in the Gospel of Matthew.[720] The discourse is so named because of Jesus's location, sitting on the Mount of Olives when delivering the message (24:3). The central theme of the passages is judgment.[721] Jesus discusses the judgment on Jerusalem (24:1–35); judgment coinciding with the parousia (24:36–51); two parables concerning judgment (25:1–30); and the eschatological judgment at the end of time (25:31–46). The Olivet Discourse poses many interesting issues for the interpreter. One of the issues involves the connection between the destruction of the Temple of Jerusalem and the Second Coming of Jesus in the eschaton.[722]

As interesting as the aforementioned issues may be, this chapter will focus on the Semitic nature of the passage, particularly those related to the בַּר אֱנָשׁ sayings. Of the 30 בַּר אֱנָשׁ sayings in Matthew, 6 of them occur in the passage being reviewed. Thus, 20 percent of the בַּר אֱנָשׁ sayings are found in Matthew 24:27–44. The major focal point of the text is on alertness and preparedness for the imminent return of the בַּר אֱנָשׁ. The message begins by noting the speed by which the Son of Man would come, comparing it to the speed of lightning streaking across the sky (24:27). Then, the signs are described

---

718 Casey, *Aramaic Approach to Q*, 146–147.

719 Ibid., 147.

720 Morris, *Matthew,* PNTC, 593.

721 France, *Matthew,* TNTC, 336.

722 Ibid., 337.

that will accompany the Son of Man's return, including the sound of the trumpet and the angels gathering the elect from the four winds (24:29–31). Additionally, Jesus gives the Parable of the Fig Tree, where he avers that just as one can tell see the signs of summer from a fig tree, so can one see the signs of his return (24:32–35). Finally, the return of the Son of Man at the eschaton is likened to the days of Noah (24:36–44). The case for the text is quite compelling as Jeremias even argues that parts of the passage, particularly Matthew 24:27, show signs of belonging to the earliest material.[723]

In contrast, the Jesus Seminar lists the majority of the pericope in black except for a few verses listed in gray. The gray passages include verses 27, 32–33, 36, and 40–42. Oddly, none of the בַר אֱנָשׁ sayings are listed in anything other than black. The members of the Seminar argue that the בַר אֱנָשׁ describes the people of Israel rather than the apocalyptic heavenly figure.[724] However, as was previously shown, this does not take into consideration the total usage of the motif. It is ironic that while the Seminar recognizes the early nature of the בַר אֱנָשׁ sayings in this passage as they link it with Q, they could not ascribe them to Jesus because of the strong apocalyptic context.[725] Yet it is precisely the strong apocalyptic content that is a sign of Jesuan authenticity for so many others.[726] This will prove to be a most interesting exploration.

Unique Rabbinic Concepts

The rabbinic material on eschatology is quite massive and impressive.[727] While distinct in various areas, the rabbis coincided with the eschatological teachings of Jesus in a couple of areas. First, like Jesus, the rabbis used the blossoming fig tree to gauge the impending implementation of God's kingdom in the end times. Jesus issued the parable of the fig tree to note the coming of the kingdom. He said, "As soon as [the fig tree's] branch becomes tender and sprouts leaves, you know that summer is near. In the same way, when you see all these things, recognize that he is near—at the door" (Matt. 24:33). In the Talmud, Rabbi Levi uses Song of Songs 2:13 to show that the blossoming fig tree indicates a time when the glory of God's house will be built,

---

723 Jeremias, *NT Theology,* 263.

724 Funk, Hoover, and the Jesus Seminar, *The Five Gospels,* 251.

725 Ibid., 252.

726 E.g., Jeremias, *NT Theology,* 263.

727 Arnold Fruchtenbaum furnishes a voluminous supply of rabbinic citations from the Talmud that addresses the end-times and what was anticipated with the advent of the eschaton. See Fructenbaum, *Yeshua,* vol. 3, 367, fn 74; 475–483.

and "this last House shall be greater than the first one."[728] While the rabbinic teaching is much later than that of Jesus, it is still of interest that the fig tree is used in both Jewish and early Christian thought.

Second, like Jesus, rabbinic teaching also includes an eternal dichotomy between an eternal heaven and eternal hell.[729] According to *Midrash Rabbah,* God is said to have given three gifts—the Torah, the land, and the "Life to Come."[730] The "Life to Come" was held to be the messianic age in which God would bring judgment to sinners and the light of his grace to believing Israel.[731] The thought continues by pointing to a time when the Messiah would establish people for believing Israel and would allow them to "eat in Paradise."[732] The one deemed righteous to enter this future celestial Land to Come would be one who was "meek, humble, stooping on entering and on going out, and a constant student of the Torah without claiming merit thereof."[733] It is also of great interest to note that two words reference the afterlife in Jewish theology: *Olam-haba*—referring to the world of the resurrection, and *Gan-Eden*—that is, Paradise, which refers to the spiritual abode of the departed that awaits the final resurrection.[734]

But what of those who are not deemed righteous? Unfortunately for the Gentiles, most of them were deemed as not taking a part in either *Gan-Eden* or the *Olam-haba.*[735] Partially, the Gentiles may not have been included because of the necessity of studying the Torah. For many rabbis, the study of the Torah granted one complete access to the World to Come.[736] The fate of the unrighteous was sealed in a place known as Gehenna—a place seen as one where the souls of sinners would burn for all eternity. It is unclear whether it was held that the bodies of the unrighteous were burned, or if they only implied

---

728 *Shir HaShirim Rabbah* 2:13, https://www.sefaria.org/Shir_HaShirim_Rabbah.2.13.3?ven=Rabbi_Mike_Feuer,_Jerusalem_Anthology&vhe=Midrash_Rabbah_--_TE&lang=bi.

729 In this sense, the term *Gehenna* is often used.

730 *Midrash Rabbah:* Exodus 1:1; Fruchtenbaum, *Yeshua,* vol. 3, 329.

731 Ibid., 15.3.

732 Ibid., 24.4.

733 *b. Sanhedrin* 88b, Fruchtenbaum, *Yeshua,* vol. 3, 329.

734 Rabbi Abraham Stone, "The World-to-Come," *The Jewish Press, Expounding the Torah* (May 2, 1986), 28; Fruchtenbaum, *Yeshua,* vol. 3, 330.

735 *Midrash Rabbah: Leviticus* 13.2.

736 "You lay up for Me Torah and precepts in this world, and I will lay pup for you a good reward for the World to Come." *Midrash Rabbah: Deuteronomy* 7.9.

that the souls of the unrighteous would burn.[737] Since children were sacrificed to Moloch in the valley of the son of Hinnom, in southern Jerusalem, the valley was held to be accursed. Therefore, the valley served as an analogy for hell and was said to be governed by a demon who desired multiple victims.[738]

Rabbinical literature placed a high value on eschatology as did Jesus. However, in contrast with rabbinic literature, Jesus did not claim that one's heritage with Israel would be what allowed one to enter the eschatological kingdom of heaven. The absence of any mention of Israel being taken and the Gentiles being left behind is quite startling given the attention that the Talmud and Mishnah place on Israel. Rather, Jesus avows that the Son of Man will come in a moment that no one anticipates. At that time, "two men will be in the field; one will be taken and one left" (24:40). The "elect" (Gk: *eklektos*) is the only term that Jesus uses to describe those who would be taken (24:31). Therefore, one can postulate that Jesus finds a parallel to the rabbinic thought process, but he was quite unique in his interpretation. The rabbis voluminously wrote on the topic of the eschatological ushering in God's kingdom.[739] However, their focus was on Torah reading and being part of national and ceremonial Israel to find a place in either the *Gan-Eden* or *Olam-haba.* Jesus only points to the importance of being part of the kingdom of heaven in which he was being used to bring forth. It would have been nice to have found more distinct parallels in the passage. Nevertheless, it is contended that sufficient evidence has been provided that allows the passage to pass the first test, granting it two points on the weighted scale.

Early Christological Concepts

The recognized early creeds often portrayed Jesus coming back to redeem his people and to victoriously rule over the powers of darkness. The Philippians hymn is one such passage that relates to the Matthean passage at hand. Scholars are nearly universal in their consensus that Philippians 2:5–11

---

[737] "The censers of these sinners against their own souls, implying that their souls were burned, but their bodies were unharmed. And the other? He maintains that they were literally burnt … and what is the meaning of against their souls? That they incurred the punishment of fire because of [the pollution] of their souls." *b. Sanhedrin* 52a.

[738] *b. Sanhedrin* 52a.

[739] See also *m. Avoth* 4.17, 6.4; *y. Shabbat* 16.1; *y. Yebamot* 8.3, 15.2; *y. Nedarim* 3.8; *y. Maaserot* 3.10; *y. Sanhedrin* 6.3, 10.1–10.5; and *b. Sanhedrin* 91b, 107a, 110b–111b.

contains a “beautiful example of a very early hymn of the Christian church.”[740] The Philippians hymn provides insight into the Christological thinking of the earliest church. Christ was viewed as not only “existing in the form of God” (Phil. 2:5) but was also noted to hold an eschatological victory over the worldly powers, to the point that “every knee will bow—in heaven and on earth and under the earth—and every tongue will confess that Jesus Christ is Lord, to the glory of God the Father” (Phil. 2:10–11). Additionally, Paul most likely quotes from a pre-NT creed in 1 Thessalonians 4:13–17.[741] This creed notes the swift arrival of the Lord, arriving with the trumpet of God (1 Thess. 4:16), and the saints of God—both deceased and alive—to be “caught up together with them in the clouds to meet the Lord in the air” (1 Thess. 4:17). Taking the Philippians hymn and the 1 Thessalonians creed together, one sees a similar picture as is drawn from the Jesus tradition of Matthew 24:27, 30–44. The Jesuan teaching of the Olivet Discourse paints a comparable portrait to that of the early creeds. Both describe the swift appearance of the Lord. Both indicate that the redeemed of God will be swept up to meet the Lord in the air. Both describe the victory of Jesus over the powers of the world. Furthermore, both call for readiness and preparedness by the people of God.

Additionally, the passage shows a bipartite connection between the Father and Son, though it may be more implicit. Matthew 24:29–31 is distinctively taken from the בַּר אֱנָשׁ motif of Daniel 7:13–14 among other passages, such as Zechariah 2:6; 12:12; Isaiah 27:13; and Ezekiel 32:7. Nonetheless, Jesus identifies himself with the בַּר אֱנָשׁ coming on the “clouds of heaven with power and great glory” (24:30). Given the connection the Jesus tradition holds with the early creeds, and the early Christology found in Jesus’s bipartite relationship with the Father and the ushering in of the kingdom at the

---

[740] Gerald F. Hawthorne, *Philippians,* Word Biblical Commentary (Dallas, TX: Thomas Nelson, 1983), 76; G. Walter Hansen, *The Letter to the Philippians,* Pillar New Testament Commentary (Grand Rapids, MI; Cambridge, UK: Eerdmans, 2009), 122.

[741] Drawing from many of the traits sought after in this study, Green deduces the following concerning 1 Thessalonians 4:13–17: “These characteristics suggest that the apostle appeals to a pre-Pauline creed that had been handed over to the church and that both the apostolic company and the Thessalonians confessed.” Gene L. Green, *The Letters to the Thessalonians*, The Pillar New Testament Commentary (Grand Rapids, MI; Leicester, England: W.B. Eerdmans Pub.; Apollos, 2002), 220.

eschaton, one discovers good reasons to suggest that the passage passes the second test, granting it 5 extra points.

Theological Terminology Relating to Early Christological Concepts

Matthew 24:27, 30–44 exhibits signs of early theological terminology concerning eschatology. Due to the text's connection with the present chapter, Jesus's use of בַּר אֱנָשׁ title presents a case for early Christological terminology. Maurice Casey makes the case for a community interpretation, noting that the "'son of man', is a pure symbol of the Saints of the Most High, a description of the people of Israel."[742] However, as Morna Hooker argues, as does Jeremias—as noted previously, "the phrase was *understood* as a title: but there is no indication that it became a 'major Christological title', or that this was 'needed' by the Christian community."[743] What can the text itself tell us about Jesus's understanding of the בַּר אֱנָשׁ?

In verses 29–31, Jesus exhibits an understanding that the בַּר אֱנָשׁ was an individual, rather than a community, as he connects the title with Daniel 7:13–14 and other apocalyptic passages. This is seen in a few ways. First, the arrival of the בַּר אֱנָשׁ in the eschaton is accompanied by signs and wonders. Drawing from the apocalyptic literature of Isaiah 13:10,[744] Joel 2:10,[745] 4:15,[746] and Isaiah 34:4;[747] the בַּר אֱנָשׁ would bring about apocalyptic judgment as evidenced by the complemented celestial and terrestrial phenomena. As noted by the scenes in the OT passages noted above, the imagery used by Jesus matched the sort of portrayal commonly given in apocalyptic literature.[748] Wright argues along with Casey in that the text speaks of the victory that the

---

[742] Maurice Casey, *The Solution to the 'Son of Man' Problem* (New York, NY: T&T Clark International, 2009), 126–127.

[743] Morna D. Hooker, "The Solution to the 'Son of Man' Problem." *The Journal of Theological Studies* 60, 2 (2009): 643.

[744] "Indeed, the stars of the sky and its constellations will not give their light. The sun will be dark when it rises, and the moon will not shine" (Isa. 13:10).

[745] "The earth quakes before them; the sky shakes. The sun and moon grow dark, and the stars cease their shining" (Joel 2:10).

[746] "The sun and moon will grow dark, and the stars will cease their shining" (Joel 4:15).

[747] "All the stars in the sky will dissolve. The sky will roll up like a scroll, and its stars will all wither as leaves wither on the vine, and foliage on the fig tree" (Isa. 34:4).

[748] Hagner, *Matthew 14–28,* WBC, 713.

people of God would have over the enemy forces..[749] In contrast with the community interpretation, the phrase "the sign of the Son of Man will appear in the sky" (24:29) uses the singular tense indicating an individual. There is no indication from the text itself that Jesus understands the בַּר אֱנָשׁ to be the people of God. The focus of the passage is on the preparation of the people of God for the imminent appearance of the בַּר אֱנָשׁ. In Jesus's portrayal of the Parousia, some people would be taken while others would be left behind (24:39–41). Therefore, alertness is key.

Second, the language of verse 30 is extremely similar to the passage in Daniel 7:13–14. The בַּר אֱנָשׁ will "appear in the sky" (24:30) and the "peoples of the earth will mourn" (24:30) as they see the בַּר אֱנָשׁ "coming on the clouds of heaven with power and great glory" (24:30)..[750] Jesus contrasts the majestic appearance of the בַּר אֱנָשׁ at the eschaton with his lowly appearance during his first advent..[751] Due to the parallels of Daniel 7:13–14, some have held that the passage may not be genuine..[752] However, due to the Pauline interpretation of the בַּר אֱנָשׁ as simply the ὁ ἄνθρωπος (Rom. 5:15; 1 Cor. 15:27; Phil. 3:21; and Eph. 1:22) and the absence of the early church's use of the title proper, the evidence seems to point to the Jesuan teaching being pre-Pauline..[753]

Lastly, the בַּר אֱנָשׁ is shown to be in charge of the angels of heaven. As noted in the previous section, this matches the language of 1 Thessalonians 4:16, which is held to be an early creed. The בַּר אֱנָשׁ sends out his angels to gather "his elect from the four winds" (24:30). As such, the angels of God will gather the saints of God by the command of the בַּר אֱנָשׁ. The בַּר אֱנָשׁ cannot be identified as the saints of God seeing that the saints of God would be gathered from creation at the command of a heavenly ruler who had authority over the angels of God.

This exercise indicates Jesus's interpretation of the בַּר אֱנָשׁ being a heavenly being rather than the community of God. As such, the title matches a messianic understanding that is foreign to the rendering given by Casey and Wright. If the offered assessment holds, then it can be contended that the usage

---

[749] Wright, *Jesus and the Victory of God,* 361–363.

[750] There is considerable debate over what constitutes the sign of the Son of Man in verse 30. The literature from the early church identified the cross as the sign of the Son of Man. See *Apocalypse of Peter* 1 and *Epistula Apostolorum* 16. See also G. Kittel and G. Friedrich, eds, *Theological Dictionary of the New Testament,* ET (Grand Rapids, MI: Eerdmans, 1964), 236–238.

[751] Morris, *Matthew,* PNTC, 610.

[752] Jeremias, *NT Theology,* 264.

[753] Ibid., 265.

of the בַר אֱנָשׁ title offers a Christological and theological title that would permit this passage to pass the third test, clinching 4 points. Furthermore, as Cullmann contends, "Anyone who accepts these sayings as genuine but tries to explain them by the theory that Jesus designates someone other than himself as the coming Son of Man, raises more problems than he solves."[754]

Mnemonic & Rhythmic Patterns

Unfortunately, while the passage does show signs of Aramaisms, as will be shown in the next section, no mnemonic or rhythmic patterns could be detected in the text at hand. The Parable of the Fig Tree from verses 32–36 does find a strong parallel in Mark 13:28–32 and Luke 21:19–33 pointing it back to a common tradition. It could be argued that the strong parallels show evidence of a mnemonic pattern of some sort. However, this does not constitute the data sought after in the test at hand. Therefore, the passage of Scripture fails the fourth test, leaving the text at 3-1.

Aramaic/Hebraic Literary Characteristics

The passage under examination shows a few Aramaic literary characteristics. First, Matthew 24:31 and 38 exhibit signs of parataxis.[755] The parataxis is found in verse 31 at the point where the comma separates μεγάλης and καὶ ἐπισυνάξουσιν.[756] Thus, the parataxis connects the verbs ἀποστελεῖ and ἐπισυνάξουσιν with the term καὶ.[757] In this case, the text uses a hypotactic participle.[758] The verse shows signs of drawing from Isaiah 27:13, Deuteronomy 30:4, and Zechariah 2:6 (LXX), as well as from a Jesus tradition. Perhaps this was due to Jesus's own use of the texts. Nonetheless, there is some evidence of an Aramaism at this juncture. In like manner, verse 38 also shows signs of an Aramaic parataxis in both Matthew's text and the Lukan parallel

---

[754] Cullmann, *Christology of the NT,* 136.

[755] Black notes that the "most characteristic kind of Aramaic parataxis occurs when two indicatives are set down side by side without any connecting particle, a construction limited in Greek to rhetorical statements or to explanatory clauses following *touto.*" Black, *An Aramaic Approach to the Gospels and Acts,* 65.

[756] The full verse in Greek reads as follows in Matthew 24:31: "καὶ ἀποστελεῖ τοὺς ἀγγέλους αὐτοῦ μετὰ σάλπιγγος μεγάλης, καὶ ἐπισυνάξουσιν τοὺς ἐκλεκτοὺς αὐτοῦ ἐκ τῶν τεσσάρων ἀνέμων ἀπ' ἄκρων οὐρανῶν ἕως τῶν ἄκρων αὐτῶν." Or "And he will send out his angels with a loud trumpet and they will gather his elect from the four winds of the end of heaven to other" [author's translation].

[757] Black, *An Aramaic Approach to the Gospels and Acts,* 65.

[758] Ibid.

(Luke 17:28). Like verse 31, verse 38 separates two clauses with the term καὶ.[759] Where Matthew uses "τρώγοντες καὶ πίνοντες, γαμοῦντες καὶ γαμίζοντες" (Matt. 24:38),[760] Luke uses "ἤσθιον, ἔπινον, ἠγόραζον, ἐπώλουν, ἐφύτευον, ᾠκοδόμουν" (Luke 17:28).[761] Matthew separates the comparisons with καὶ while Luke only uses a comma. Nonetheless, both texts show signs of an Aramaic parataxis, a sign of a possible earlier Aramaic influence.

Second, Matthew 24:40–41 contains a partitive *apo/ek* formulation that is indicative of an Aramaic background. The first, found in verse 40, is found in the phrase "εἷς παραλαμβάνεται καὶ εἷς ἀφίεται" (24:40)[762] and the second, in verse 41, is in "μία παραλαμβάνεται καὶ μία ἀφίεται" (24:41).[763] In both cases, the εἷς-to-εἷς connection is a recognized NT Semitism.[764] Additionally, Black sees evidence of an impersonal plural in Matthew 24:30 which adds to the Aramaic characteristics of the text.[765]

Sufficient evidence has been provided to show that elements of the teaching at hand indeed show signs of Aramaic characteristics that may point to an earlier Jesus tradition. Thus, there is no reason to deny at least Matthew 24:30–44 clearance to pass the fifth test, thereby earning 5 points. Like the Sermon on the Mount, it could be that certain texts are part of the early Jesus tradition, whereas the evangelist, using redactionary skills, pieced them together to further flesh out the meaning, while remaining true to the original message. This follows Kenneth Bailey's informal controlled model, but it also coheres with Gerhardsson's model, as well, since Matthew meticulously preserved the traditions. Hence, something comparable to a semiformal controlled method is at play. Nonetheless, Matthew 24:30–44 now stands at 4-1.

Semitic Cultural Concepts of First-Century Israel

Some of the issues discussed do not necessarily match the time of Jesus, especially the destruction of the Temple (AD 70) and future eschatological events. At first glance, one might envision that no cultural concepts could be found in such an eschatologically minded passage. For instance, in his book *Jesus Through Middle Eastern Eyes,* Kenneth Bailey never

---

759 Ibid.

760 Translated as "to eat and to drink, to marry and to give in marriage."

761 Translated as "to eat, to drink, to buy, to sell, to plant, to harvest."

762 Translated, "one taken and one left."

763 Translated, "one taken and one left."

764 Black, *An Aramaic Approach to the Gospels and Acts,* 108.

765 Ibid., 126–127.

references Matthew 24:27, 30–44. Nevertheless, a few elements of the passage do relate to the cultural concepts of early first-century Israel. First, the image of the householder (24:43–44) most assuredly fits the context of early first-century Israel. Unfortunately for the people in more urban areas of Israel,[766] burglary was common.[767]

Though stealth is often a common tactic used by burglars, it is suggested that in first-century Israel that thieves may have broken into homes in other ways than just simply knocking through the door. For instance, many thieves may have dug through the house—that is, invading the house in a variety of ways—particularly with homes made with mudbrick walls.[768] With homes made of limestone, the thieves may have dug under the house for entry.[769] Most assuredly, such an invasion would not have been a quiet process. Just as in modern times, homeowners will take every precaution to ensure that his or her home is secured from the possibility of burglary. A church where this writer formerly served as pastor went so far as to obtain the services from the county sheriff to ensure the safety of the facility. The sheriff observed any weak points in the facility that needed to be bolstered for security.

Likewise, the allegory that Jesus conveys in one's preparedness for the appointed time of divine judgment[770] coinciding with home security is one found in the context of understanding within first-century Israel.[771] Taking the cultural milieu of Jesus's sayings and the fact that the evidence suggests that the words from Christian prophets were separated from the *logia* of Jesus (ex. Rev.

---

[766] This includes communities and outposts, such as Nazareth and Capernaum (Jesus's headquarters).

[767] Keener, *GMSRC*, 592.

[768] Ibid.; T. W. Manson, *The Sayings of Jesus* (London, UK: SCM, 1979), 116; Robert H. Gundry, *Matthew: A Commentary on His Literary and Theological Art* (Grand Rapids, MI: Eerdmans, 1982), 495.

[769] Keener, *GMSRC,* 592.

[770] For divine judgment being likened to a nighttime thief, see Jer. 49:9, Obadiah 4–6, and Joel 2:9.

[771] While the crime reports are not as abundant in first-century Israel as they are in other locales, it is well documented that Egyptian villages faced severe problems with burglary. Naphtali Lewis, *Life in Egypt under Roman Rule* (Oxford, UK: Clarendon, 1983), 77, 123.

16:15), even more critically-minded scholars have accepted Matthew 24:43 as authentic and pre-Matthean.[772]

Second, some have argued that the expression of Jesus in that the angels would gather the elect "from one end of the sky to the other" (24:31) matches the vernacular of the day. The phrase "from one end of heaven to the other" figuratively points to the totality of the whole in first-century understanding (i.e., Mk. 13:27; Isa. 11:12).[773] The earth was believed to have been surrounded by the dome of heaven.[774] Even the gathering of Israel has a connection with the Jewish eschatology of the time, emphasizing the calling out of the people of God from the earth.[775] A few examples of this are found in Isaiah 11:12,[776] Isaiah 43:5,[777] and the apocryphal work *2 Esdras* 13.[778] Even the sounding of the trumpets shows a cultural familiarity that points to a pre-Matthean context as it is quoted by Paul in a pre-NT text.[779] While the trumpet blast may alert people for war or attack,[780] it could also signal the advance of a conquering warrior, such as in Zechariah, which says, "Then the LORD will appear over them, and his arrow will fly like lightning. The Lord GOD will sound the ram's horn and advance with the southern storms" (Zech. 9:14). The tenth benediction of the Shemoneh Esreh exhibits the same theme. It says,

---

[772] Pace, Bultmann, and Taylor contend that as late as the writing of Rev. 16:15 that Christian prophets distinguished the words of Jesus from their own. Vincent Taylor, *The Formation of the Gospel Tradition,* 2nd ed (London, UK: Macmillan & Company, 1935), 108.

[773] Keener, *GMSRC,* 586.

[774] Gundry, *Matthew:CLTA,* 489.

[775] Keener, *GMSRC,* 586–587.

[776] "He will lift up a banner for the nations and gather the dispersed of Israel; he will collect the scattered of Judah from the four corners of the earth" (Isa. 11:12).

[777] "Do not fear, for I am with you; I will bring your descendants from the east, and gather you from the west" (Isa. 43:5).

[778] "And as for your seeing him gather to himself another multitude that was peaceable, these are the nine tribes that were taken away from their own land into exile in the days of King Hoshea, whom Shalmaneser, king of the Assyrians, made captives; he took them across the river, and they were taken into another land" (*2 Esdras* 13:39–40).

[779] "Then we who are still alive, who are left, will be caught up together with them in the clouds to meet the Lord in the air, and so we will always be with the Lord" (1 Thess. 4:17).

[780] Keener, *GMSRC,* 587.

"Sound the great shofar for our freedom and raise a banner to gather our exiles and unite us together from the four corners of the earth.[781] Blessed are you, LORD, who regathers the scattered of his people Israel."[782] Thus, the entire eschatological imagery of the passage, though unique to the Jesuan didactic in certain points particularly in the focus on the elect of God rather than nationalism, holds a distinctive root in the Jewish theology of the day.

Other parallels can be drawn from the text that links the passage with early cultural beliefs. Nonetheless, sufficient evidence has been provided to illustrate why this passage should be granted a passing grade for the sixth test. Given the passing grade, the passage can safely add 4 more points to its weighted score. As such, the passage stands at a record of 5-1 at this juncture. The final test will determine whether the text enters the green zone of certainty or remains in the yellow with the cumulative test. Already, the text has earned a green light for the weighted scale.

Similarities to NT Creeds, Summaries, and Early Literature

The passage only fits one of the thematic criteria for pre-NT material. It does not match themes of baptism, worship, exorcisms, or polemics since the passage is eschatologically focused.[783] However, it does seem to fit Cullmann's fourth theme, being an encouragement against persecution.[784] The passage finds a home in a larger warning issued by Jesus about the coming destruction of Jerusalem (24:15–22). But then he switches focus from Jerusalem to the end of time (24:23–51). Jesus seems to be saying that the destruction of Jerusalem is but a sign of the coming destruction at the end of the age. In a sense, the destruction of Jerusalem is a typology for what would be to come in the eschaton.[785] Thus, Jesus prepares his listeners for the persecution to come. Yet he also encourages them to be prepared and endure

---

[781] W. D. Davies, *Paul and Rabbinic Judaism: Some Rabbinic Elements in Pauline Theology,* 4th ed (Philadelphia, PA: Fortress, 1980), 82.

[782] "Kibbutz Galuyot," *Hebrew4Christians.com, https://www.hebrew4christians.com/Prayers/Daily_Prayers/Shemoneh_Esrei/Kibbutz_Galuyot/kibbutz_galuyot.html,* accessed on March 11, 2022.

[783] Cullmann, *Earliest Christian Confessions,* 18.

[784] Ibid.

[785] Bock holds this view as well. He postulates that Luke illuminates Jesus's teaching in such a way that the destruction of Jerusalem Temple is a "'pattern' type of the end," which Matthew and Mark also pattern. Bock, *Jesus According to Scripture,* 445.

in their faith as the בַּר אֱנָשׁ would come at a time when no one expects (24:36–44). As such, the text fits well within the scope of Cullmann's fourth theme.

The text also seems to match certain criteria of the formulaic prose so readily found in pre-NT material. One of the most fascinating aspects of the passage is found in 24:42, where Jesus says, "Therefore be alert, since you don't know what day your Lord is coming" (24:42). The term κύριος ("Lord") relates to Christ is extremely important. Κύριος can be used for a master or a form of address, but it can also be used as an "honorific title for God".[786] or a title indicating the divine authority of Jesus..[787] While other people may use the term κύριος for Jesus in a polite form of address (8:2–4; 8:5–13; 15:21–28, etc.), the disciples used the term in reference to Jesus's divine authority. Longenecker argues that in such cases the usage of κύριος "reflects something of a confessional stance.".[788] Matthew 24:42; 25:37, 44 all use κύριος to convey Jesus as the eschatological ruler come comes in the power of God. This is a powerful piece of evidence in favor of an early Jesus tradition predating the time in which the Gospel was written.

From the two lines of evidence presented, one finds a strong connection to early pre-NT material. It could be asserted that the evidence for this passage is even more compelling than others that have been favored by the seventh test. Be that as it may, one can find adequate evidence to support the passage passing the seventh and final test, securing a final 5 points. Therefore, the passage finds itself with a final record of 6-1, faring quite well.

Conclusion and Color Assignment

This examination has been quite fascinating. Matthew 24:27, 30–44 has fared well according to the test formed for this project. The text passed the first test as it related to the rabbinic use of the blossoming fig tree when foreseeing divine judgment. Also, like Jewish rabbinic theologians, Jesus exhibited a dichotomy between an eternal heaven and hell. As it was noted, Jewish rabbis noted the existence of an *olam-haba* (a hellish Gehenna) and a *Gan-Eden* (Paradise). The teachings of Jesus find a unique place in the rabbinic teaching.

The text passed the second test as the passage conveyed a similar Christological focus as did two recognized early credal passages in Philippians 2:10–11 and 1 Thessalonians 4:13–17. Also, a bipartite connection that is

---

[786] Longenecker, *New Wine Into Fresh Wineskins,* 83.

[787] Ibid.

[788] Ibid., 84.

prominently found in early Christological literature is found in the passage at hand.

Due to the usage of the בַר אֱנָשׁ title and its association with the current chapter, one would already assume that the text would pass the third test. Jesus's usage of the בַר אֱנָשׁ motif was shown to match the individual heavenly redeemer position rather than that of a corporate group of people. The use of signs and wonders, coming with the clouds of glory, and having oversight over the angels of heaven all attests to Jesus's understanding of the בַר אֱנָשׁ depicting an eschatological heavenly redeemer. Because of this usage of the בַר אֱנָשׁ title, the text is validated and confirmed to pass the third test.

No rhythmic pattern or mnemonic device could be found in the text. Therefore, the passage failed the fourth test. However, it fared well with the fifth test. There are reasons to believe that the text shows Aramaic characteristics, particularly with its use of a parataxis and partitive apo/ek indicative—both having a strong connection to Aramaic usage.

The text passed the final two tests. The mention of a householder and preparedness against theft speaks to the high burglary rate in early first-century Israel. Burglars were noted to dig through the walls of mudbrick houses and under the floor of limestone houses. Neither would have been performed if the homeowner was in the house. Also, the mention of the angels gathering the elect from one end of heaven to the other speaks to the cultural understanding of a heavenly dome over the earth. Both speak to the connection that the passage holds with the cultural understandings of the time. The seventh test was quite compelling. As was noted, the text fits Cullmann's fourth recognized theme of early material, as Jesus provided encouragement against persecution. The additional use of *kurios* as a title for divine authority speaks strongly to its connection with early pre-NT material.

After all was completed, the passage scored a total score of 6-1. This is enough to place the text in the green zone of probability. Given that the text scored 25 of 30 points and scored 6 of 7 points in the cumulative tally, Jesus's teaching on the coming of the Son of Man scores extremely high. Thus, it can be said that Matthew 24:27, 30–44 shows strong signs that at least parts of the text stemmed from early Jesus traditions that predate the composition of Matthew's Gospel. Addedly, we can safely assert that Jesus proclaimed his divine status, predicted his resurrection, and foresaw his ascension well before the events of the Passion Week ever took place.

Conclusion

This chapter has examined the בַר אֱנָשׁ sayings throughout the Gospel of Matthew. Most assuredly, there are many other בַר אֱנָשׁ sayings in Matthew's Gospel that were unaddressed. Both Matthew 12:22–32 and Matthew 24:27, 30–44 fared very well with the tests afforded in this study. Both texts scored a

6-1 record which landed them in the green zone of probability. The biggest factor concerning the בַּר אֱנָשׁ motif involves its usage. While the earlier part of the chapter defended the belief that Jesus used the title to convey an eschatological heavenly redeemer rather than a community of individuals, his focus on the kingdom of God would have included the righteous saints of God. Much more work needs to be done in this area. While critical scholars such as N. T. Wright and Maurice Casey have claimed that the בַּר אֱנָשׁ only speaks to Israel and the righteous saints of God,.[789] it is not at all clear that Jesus held the same belief concerning the figure. For this researcher, it would seem that the link Jesus makes back to Daniel 7:13–14 shows an individual heavenly redeemer who conquers enemy nations and redeems a select group of people for God's glory. Thus, the saints of God are involved in the work of the בַּר אֱנָשׁ, but they are not necessarily the primary focus. Regardless of whether one adheres to the conclusion this research defends concerning the בַּר אֱנָשׁ, the texts surrounding the בַּר אֱנָשׁ motifs do show signs of an early pre-Matthean tradition that predates the Gospel writing.

---

[789] Wright, *The New Testament and the People of God*, 291–297; Casey, *The Solution to the 'Son of Man' Problem*, 126–127.

CHAPTER FIVE
THE INTERACTIONS OF JESUS

Thus far, the project has examined the specific teachings of Jesus. The Sermon on the Mount, the Parables, and the Son of Man sayings all constitute aspects of the overall theological and ethical ethos of Jesus's didactical system. The previous chapters allow one to peer inside the core belief system of Jesus of Nazareth. And, as it pertains to the primary focus of the project at hand, the majority of these teachings have fared well, except for the parables.[790] However, a good deal of the Gospel narratives depict the interactions that Jesus had with other people. From the very beginning, the Gospel of Matthew shows how Jesus engaged John the Baptist (Matt. 3:13–17) and even his dealings with Satan's temptations (Matt. 4:1–11). The Gospel of Matthew concludes with the interactions the risen Jesus had with the disciples on a mountain in Galilee (Matt. 28:16–20). Could this be the same mountain from which he delivered the messages that constituted the Sermon on the Mount?[791] Regardless, the density of material relating to the relationships between Jesus and others is quite telling.[792]

Though many passages could be chosen for review in this final chapter, two stand out as excellent candidates to mine for Semitic residue—that is, signs of early Jesus traditions. The first passage involves a personal interaction between Jesus and Simon Peter, one of his inner circle disciples in Matthew

---

[790] As it was noted by Kenneth Bailey's informal controlled model, Middle Eastern culture afforded greater flexibility to the transmission of parables. It is highly probable that this flexibility may account for the parables' less than favorable outcome when tested by the more controlled criteria of this project.

[791] From the outset, it appears that it could be. Keener notes that "The 'mountain' (28:16) recalls the other sites of revelation in the Gospels (5:1; 17:1), and various other features indicate that Matthew has heavily reworked the tradition behind the closing scene of his Gospel to conclude with an important theological message." Keener, *GMSRC,* 715. Remember, the informal controlled model allows for some reworking, so long as the essentials of the data are not changed. Thus, in this case, the mountain and the essentials of the message would be true even if Matthew reworked certain details. Keener continues by saying, "Certainly the Lukan, Johannine, and Matthean commissions, as well as the missionary spirit of Pauline and Markan Christianity, leave little evidence of a Christianity *without* missionary impetus; that Christianity's unanimous urge for missions derives from its founder seems inherently likely. And the different forms of the commission suggest its essential accuracy by multiple attestation." Ibid.

[792] This is telling in the sense that relationships between God and humanity, Jesus and humanity, and the disciples and humanity play an important role in the overall gospel message.

16:13–23. Jesus first asks his disciples who people think him to be (16:13). The disciples respond by saying that people think him to be John the Baptist, Elijah, Jeremiah, or another one of the prophets (16:14). Then, Jesus reformats the question to make it more personal, asking, "who do you say that I am?" (16:15). Though Simon Peter's self-impulsive lack of restraint often causes him complications, it is here that his forwardness is rewarded, when Jesus says, "You are the Messiah, the Son of the living God" (16:16). Jesus then calls Peter the rock upon which he will build his church (16:18–19). Finally, in a unique twist, Peter's compulsiveness causes him issues yet again. He tells Jesus that he would defend him when Jesus revealed that would be killed and raised from the dead (16:21–22). Jesus called out Satan, who was stirring up evil behind Peter's good intentions (16:23).

The second passage to be studied comes from the interaction that Jesus has with the disciples of John the Baptist in Matthew 11:2–19. Jesus had been baptized by John the Baptist early in his ministry (3:13–17). Some have claimed that Jesus may have been John the Baptist's disciple before beginning his ministry..[793] Nevertheless, John the Baptist was imprisoned at this moment in his life. Realizing that his life was most likely to soon end, he sent his disciples to Jesus to inquire whether he was truly the Anointed One or if they should expect someone else (11:3). Perhaps the messianic secret used by Jesus caused John to stop and take pause. Regardless, Jesus performed miracles in their sight.[794] and told them to "Go and report to John what you hear and see: The blind receive their sight, the lame walk, those with leprosy are cleansed, the deaf hear, the dead are raised, and the poor are told the good news, and blessed is the one who isn't offended by me" (11:4b–6). Jesus then grants a message

---

[793] Bruce Chilton avers that Jesus was a rebellious and venturesome soul, who desired to become John's *talmid* to learn a *halakhah* from John. As such, Chilton sees John the Baptist as crucial for understanding the early Jesus. "Jesus learned from John, disputed with him, and developed the ideas that would change his own life and the course of religious history. John led Jesus on the path that made an alienated *mamzer* and starving, wayward pilgrim into an apprentice in the subtleties of Judaic practice, and later into an acknowledged rabbi with a charismatic personality and a distinctive path to God that was all his own." Chilton, *Rabbi Jesus,* 33–34. However, one should note that the Gospel of John implies that the Baptist did not officially know Jesus before baptizing him (John 1:33). While this topic is beyond the scope of the present research, it is something that deserves further attention.

[794] The miracles are implied in Matthew's Gospel but are directly shown in Luke's Gospel. Luke writes, "At that time Jesus healed many people of diseases, afflictions, and evil spirits, and he granted sight to many blind people" (Luke 7:21).

explaining the greatness of John the Baptist and the distinctions between the two ministries.

Both texts show promise for holding Semitic residue. The former holds a confession by Peter, whereas the latter holds a Son of Man title and multiple attestation. But the question is, to what level and degree do these interactions hold? Just from gauging what has been revealed in the previous chapters, one would assume that at least portions of the teachings of Jesus link back to a pre-NT Jesus tradition. This chapter holds great intrigue, as it could hold clues to see how one could gauge the narratives of the Gospels in future studies with the given tests in this project.

Jesus's Question & Peter's Confession (Matt. 16:13–23)

Since Matthew 16:13–23 deals with an interaction between Jesus and Peter, it will be important to deem what the most pressing issues are found in the passage. First and most apparent, Jesus invites the disciples to enter the realm of messianic expectation and identity. Even though Jesus never directly calls himself the Messiah, he accepted the messianic ascription that Peter placed on him. Notice that he did not deny the title. Rather, he said that Peter was blessed because the Father had revealed this insight to him (16:17). Thus, the issue of messianic anticipation finds a place in this text.

Additionally, the concept of the church is a topic that will need to be addressed. Was the concept of the church something that Jesus attached to his kingdom teachings, or is this simply a redaction of the material from a post-Easter understanding?.[795] Granted, the latter would appear to be the case, at least from a precursory reading. The teaching of Jesus here could be something rooted in an early tradition but was further explained by a later evangelist. However, if enough Semitic residue is found, then one may be inclined to warrant a connection to earlier material. This will be an interesting issue to consider moving forward.

Finally, the notion of the suffering and rising Servant of the Lord is found in 16:21–23. The direct mention of Jesus dying and rising could be very early, as it is a concept found in the early pre-NT material. However, is there sufficient evidence to mark this as pre-Easter? Deciphering between pre-and post-Easter understandings may prove difficult, if not impossible, seeing that early credal material also held these concepts. Nevertheless, if enough

[795] Some scholars deny even the remotest possibility that Jesus could have spoken of the church. Rather it is held that the church was a concept developed by the followers of Jesus after his ascension. M. Eugene Boring, *Sayings of the Risen Jesus: Christian Prophecy in the Synoptic Tradition,* Society for New Testament Studies Monograph (Cambridge, UK: Cambridge University Press, 1982), 213–214.

connections are made to early Jesus traditions, then it at least leaves the door open that Jesus himself held this understanding.

The Jesus Seminar was not overly fond of Matthew 16:13–23. The entire chapter was labeled in black,[796] except for verses 25–26[797] which are labeled in gray.[798] The Seminar believed that the words were not associated with early Jesus traditions for two reasons. First, they held that the early church created scenes like these—using *Thomas* 13:1–8; John 1:35–42; 6:66–69; and 11:25–27 as examples—to promote confessional statements from the apostles rather than emphasizing the words of Jesus.[799] However, their assessment seems to be a bit of a misnomer, if not a categorical mistake. 1 Corinthians 15:3–9 is held to be an early NT formulation.[800] 1 Corinthians 15 lists the different people that the risen Jesus approached. Other credal materials address the early confessions of the church (e.g., Rom. 10:9). If these encounters and confessions date to such an early time, it is not a far stretch to accept the possibility that Jesus had such an encounter with Simon Peter. Quite honestly, as Gary Habermas notes, the crucifixion and resurrection of Jesus was an "indispensable part of the gospel (Rom. 10:9; 1 Cor. 15:1–5) and the heart of early preaching (Acts 4:2; 4:33). It was the impetus for evangelism (Matt. 28:18–20; Luke 24:45–48) and the chief message in Paul's church planting methods (Acts 17:1–4).[801]

Second, the Seminar denied the possibility that Jesus held any foreknowledge as to what would occur in the Passion Story.[802] As such, they held that 16:21–23 was a complete invention of the church. However, the historical criteria of authenticity include multiple attestations, dissimilarity, coherence, Aramaic substratum, embarrassment, cultural appropriateness,

---

[796] As a reminder, the Jesus Seminar used black type to indicate content of a later tradition and not associated with Jesus. Funk, Hoover, and the Jesus Seminar, *The Five Gospels,* 36.

[797] "For whoever wants to save his life will lose it, but whoever loses his life because of me will find it. For what will it benefit someone if he gains the whole world yet loses his life? Or what will anyone give in exchange for his life?" (Matt. 16:25–26).

[798] Funk, Hoover, and the Jesus Seminar, *The Five Gospels,* 206–208.

[799] Ibid., 207.

[800] Even Bart Ehrman concedes that the traditions that Paul inherited "were older … and so must date to just a couple of years or so after Jesus's death." Ehrman, *Did Jesus Exist?,* 131.

[801] Habermas, *The Historical Jesus,* 133.

[802] Funk, Hoover, and the Jesus Seminar, *The Five Gospels,* 208.

and/or historical plausibility.[803] The principle of embarrassment seems appropriate for this passage of Scripture, which casts the Seminar's conclusions about this text as a bit suspicious. Be that as it may, the text will now be placed under the scrutiny of this research's seven tests. It will be interesting to see whether the text fares better than it did in the test conducted by the Jesus Seminar.

Unique Rabbinic Concepts

With his interaction with Simon Peter and the disciples, Jesus brought up two theological concepts that could be compared with rabbinic theology. The first is the anticipation of the Messiah and the kingdom of God. Previous chapters have already covered these areas in great length. However, it should be noted that *Sanhedrin* 98a–99a discusses messianic expectations in great detail, some going against the perspective of Jesus to a degree. In *Sanhedrin* 98a, Rabbi Hama bar Hanina (c. AD 250–290) argued that the "Son of David will not come until the contemptuous kingdom of Rome [ceases] from the Jewish people."[804] If Rabbi Hanina's belief dated back to the time of Jesus, which appears that it did, then this posed problems for Jesus's followers since it was evident that the Romans had not left Israel.[805] Additionally, Rabbi Hanina interpreted Zephaniah 3:11 to say that the Messiah would not come until the arrogant had been flushed out of Israel. Again, this was something that had not happened in Israel at the time of Jesus. Jewish literature also anticipated that certain prophets would precede the coming of the Messiah.[806] With all the theories pertaining to the Messiah and who might precede him (and how many), it only stands to reason that Jesus asked the disciples who people claimed him to be. Additionally, it also makes sense as to why Jesus wanted the disciples'

---

[803] Darrell L. Bock, "Historical Jesus," *The Historical Jesus: Five Views,* James K. Beilby and Paul R. Eddy, eds (Downers Grove, IL: IVP Academic, 2009), 252.

[804] *Sanhedrin* 98a, https://www.sefaria.org/Sanhedrin.98a.7?ven=William_Davidson_Edition_-_English&vhe=Wikisource_Talmud_Bavli&lang=bi.

[805] Perhaps this was behind the disciples' motivation in asking Jesus before his ascension, "Lord, are you restoring the kingdom to Israel at this time?" (Acts 1:6).

[806] Some texts argued that Enoch and Elijah would appear again before the coming of the Messiah. *1 Enoch* 90.31. Other texts held that Moses and Elijah would precede the Messiah's appearance. "God said to Moses: 'When I send the prophet Elijah, both of you shall go together.'" *Midrash Deuteronomy* 3.10.1. See also Cullmann, *Christology of the NT,* 18. It is interesting that Moses and Elijah appeared with Jesus on the Mount of Transfiguration just one chapter later, perhaps serving as a confirmation to the disciples that Jesus was the Messiah (Matt. 17:1–13). In this text, Jesus affirms that John the Baptist was the Elijah who preceded his appearance.

personal perspectives concerning his identity. The blessing that Jesus gives to Simon Peter for correctly pinpointing his identity is also something found in Jewish backdrops.[807]

Second, the issue of the church is another theological concept that needs to be reviewed according to a Jewish backdrop. As previously noted, the Jesus Seminar attacked the mention of the church as unrealistic and most assuredly pointing to a late invention rather than an early Jesus tradition. But is there merit behind such a charge from a Jewish perspective? Probably not as much as one might think. Jewish teachers of antiquity often created communities to advance their theological teachings.[808] Even if Jesus and the early community anticipated an expedient return,[809] a community would still have developed to advocate a sense of holiness and separation from the world,[810] if not for anything else than for practical and organizational principles.[811] Moreover, the Qumran community, who held that God would bring an expedient eschatological end, formed a separatist community to await the advance of God's kingdom.[812] Therefore, Jesus's establishment of the Church does not pose as much of a threat to the text's Semitic residue as the Jesus Seminar first proposed.

Since messianic theology is found in rabbinic theology and early Jewish sects developed communities comparable to the later Christian Church, then there is no reason why the text cannot pass the first test and earning 2 points for our weighted scale. The unique nature of the Jesuan message was that he

---

[807] Keener, *GMSRC,* 426; Brad H. Young, *Jesus the Jewish Theologian* (Peabody, MA: Hendrickson, 1995), 199.

[808] R. Alan Culpepper, *The Johannine School: An Evaluation of the Johannine-School Hypothesis Based on an Investigation of the Nature of Ancient Schools,* Society of Biblical Literature Dissertation Series 26 (Missoula, MT: Scholars Press, 1975), 123.

[809] The data suggesting that Jesus held to an expedient return is scant in this writer's opinion. It is not at all clear that Jesus held such a view.

[810] David Flusser, *Judaism and the Origins of Christianity,* Brad Young, ed (Jerusalem, IL: Hebrew University Press, 1988), 35.

[811] James Philips Hyatt, "The Dead Sea Discoveries, *Journal of Biblical Literature* 76 (1956): 8.

[812] "The early Church in Jerusalem was evidently organized as a separate Jewish sect, but the ideological basis for the concept of the Church was laid down, as far as we can see, in the later stratum of Christianity which we call Pre-Pauline, under the influence of ideas which led to similar consequences among the Qumran covenanters." Flusser, *Judaism and the Origins of Christianity,* 35. Kohler holds that the concept of the Church may have originated from *1 Enoch.* W. Kohler, *Dogmengeschichte,* vol. 1 (Zurich, CH; Cambridge, UK: Cambridge University Press, 1951), 232, 234.

served the role of the prophesied Messiah—though he never promoted the concept—and that his early followers would develop a community to advocate his already-not-yet kingdom. His community of disciples, known as the ἐκκλησία, would serve as a righteous remnant, continuing the lineage of the covenant community from Old Testament times,[813] and would be known for their faithful love of God and humanity (John 13:35).[814]

Early Christological Concepts

Matthew 16:13–23 most assuredly holds early Christological concepts as it aligns with a messianic understanding of Jesus. The entire pericope is illuminated with early Christological beams of light. Jesus inquires into the Christological belief systems of the disciples. They answer with the understanding of others before Jesus presses them, gently yet directly, to present their own beliefs. The passage exhibits an early Christology in two areas. First, the more obvious of the two is the focus on the lordship of Christ. As will be shown in the next section, the Son of God title, an early Christological title, takes center stage in this passage, co-starring with the Anointed One title. Peter's confession in verse 16 shows the clearest connection to the early *kerygmatic* material of the early church. Confessions as the one Peter provides were used in early baptisms, worship, and teaching.[815] Additionally, the construction of Peter's confession (Σὺ εἶ χριστὸς ὁ υἱὸς τοῦ θεοῦ τοῦ ζῶντος).[816] aligns well with other Christological confessions that are part of the earliest *homologia*.[817] The messianic connection with the lordship of Jesus is quite intriguing. Some have maintained that the Son of God title is something new introduced to the messianic concept of the time.[818] However, it is possible that the disciples made the connection between the Messiah and his lordship from their messianic interpretations of the royal psalms and the

---

813 Keener, *GMSRC,* 428.

814 Oh, that the modern church would rekindle that vision!

815 Vernon H. Neufeld, *The Earliest Christian Confessions* (Leiden, NL: Brill, 1963), 63.

816 The emphasis being on Σὺ εἶ.

817 Other constructions include ejgwv eijmi, aujtovV ejstin, and aujto;n eij:nai. Neufeld, *Earliest Christian Confessions,* 111.

818 W. Michaelis, *Zur Engelchristologie im Urchristentum* (Berlin, DE: HMV, 1942), 10.

Jewish expectation of a king.[819] It is possible that they could have obtained this connection from Jesus himself.

One may ask whether such a divine understanding of Jesus goes against the early Jewish understanding of God and the Messiah. Early Jewish literature understood God to be the universal ruler over all things.[820] The high priest also connects the messianic title with Son of God in Matthew 26:63. If Jesus was understood to be the instrument to bring about God's eschatological kingdom in the earliest church (as exemplified in Phil. 2:5–11), then it is no stretch to hold that Peter confessed that Jesus was both Messiah and the Son of God. Peter's confession fits well within the parameters of the theology of Second Temple Judaism.[821] Additionally, the worship of Jesus was not a late invention, but rather a practice that dates to no later than the first decade of the church.[822]

The second early Christological theme is on the already-not-yet eschatological kingdom (16:17b–19). Peter's confession shows the early understanding that Jesus was the fulfillment of Yahweh's promise in 2 Samuel 7:4–16 in that David's "house and kingdom [would] endure before me forever, and your throne will be established forever" (2 Sam. 7:16). The Messiah was shown to be more than just a human agent to bring the eternal kingdom to pass; he somehow participated in God's being and served as a manifestation of God.[823] As such, the bipartite language of early Christology is implied. An extra third theme could be the messianic secret of verse 20, a trait found prominently in the Gospel of Mark.

However, the question is whether the tradition shows a pre- or post-Easter tradition. Though the text provides the missional view of Jesus in that he would suffer, die, and rise from the dead—earmarks of post-Easter sayings, the confessional aspect of the text at hand exhibits what one finds from early

---

[819] Cullmann, *Christology of the NT,* 274. The royal psalms generally include Psalm 2, 18, 20–21, 45, 72, 101, 110, 132, and 144.

[820] Examples include Psa. 47:3; 83:19; 97:9; *Sir.* 50:15; Dan. 4:14; and *1Qap Gen.* 20:12–13. See Bauckham, *Jesus and the God of Israel,* 116 for a full list.

[821] Bauckham writes, "When New Testament Christology is read within the context of the understanding of Second Temple Jewish monotheism we have sketched, it can readily be seen that early Christians applied to Jesus all the well-established and well-recognized characteristics of the unique divine identity in order, quite clearly and precisely, to include Jesus in the unique identity of the one God of Israel." Bauckham, *Jesus and the God of Israel,* 172.

[822] Larry W. Hurtado, *One God, One Lord: Early Christian Devotion and Ancient Jewish Monotheism,* 3rd ed (London, UK: Bloomsbury, 2015), 5.

[823] Hagner, *Matthew 14–28,* WBC, 468.

primitive Christianity. Even critical scholars admit as much.[824] It may be impossible to determine whether the tradition stemmed from a pre-Easter occurrence with any degree of certainty. Nonetheless, given the rich saturation of Son of God teachings found throughout the Synoptic Gospels, one could say that it is most probable that the occurrence finds a home within early Christological concepts. As such, the text passes the second test, resulting in a 2-0 standing thus far, and earning an additional 5 points.

Theological Terminology Relating to Early Christological Concepts

Matthew 16:13–23 is rich with theological terminology. In fact, the text holds more theological titles than any other passage that has been investigated in this project. At least four titles are found in the text. First, the Messiah is the most obvious title. Peter directly calls Jesus the Messiah after being asked who he thought Jesus to have been (16:16). The number of implications of the title is legion for the early church. The title *Christos* originated with, as Cullmann notes, "the Jewish hope for the future."[825] Peter's confession is formulaic and was even repeated by the demons during Jesus's lifetime (Mark 3:11; 5:7).[826] Nevertheless, the messianic hope was something that certainly preceded the time of Jesus and the early disciples.

Second, Jesus uses the title בַר אֱנָשׁ in verse 13. It is of interest to note that the בַר אֱנָשׁ is the only title that Jesus uses for himself. Even when asking about the perceptions of others, he uses the title בַר אֱנָשׁ. The last chapter thoroughly noted the ramifications of the title. Therefore, there is no need to regurgitate the material once more. Nevertheless, the inclusion of the title is but one more Christological title referenced in the passage. However, it should be noted that Jesus does not necessarily use the title בַר אֱנָשׁ pointing to Daniel 7 in this passage. Rather, he uses the title more as an idiom referring to himself.

---

824 "The story of Peter's confession of Jesus (Matt. 16:13–20; Mark 8:27–30; Luke 9:18–21) is a classic of primitive Christology. The Petrine account has Jesus ask who people say that he is. Common identifications are given (John the Baptist, Elijah, one of the prophets). Jesus then asks who the disciples say that he is, and Peter answers that he is the Christ. The direction of the questioning leads away from the notion that a prophetic Christology is adequate; the disciples are implicitly encouraged by Jesus to try another category, which is precisely what Peter attempts. The response of Peter occasions a signal variation within the Synoptic tradition." Bruce D. Chilton and Jacob Neuser, *Classical Christianity and Rabbinic Judaism: Comparing Theologies* (Eugene, OR: Wipf & Stock, 2004), 205.

825 Cullmann, *Christology of the NT,* 111.

826 However, the demonic confession only notes to Jesus being the Son of God and not the Messiah.

While this lessens the impact of the title's use, the importance of the title remains of considerable interest.

Third, the title Son of God (ὁ υἱὸς τοῦ θεοῦ) is part of Peter's confession. While the title was not often linked with messianic connotations, it was a common title used in mythology and even used by those who were held to be great men.[827] Julius Caesar was deified as the "divine Julius" or *divi filius* after his death.[828] Other emperors of the first century were deified, including Tiberius, Claudius, Vespasian, Titus, and Nerva.[829] Some Jewish texts speak of a son of God. Scroll 4Q246 spoke of a messianic figure who would be called the Son of God and the son of the Most High.[830] Scrolls 1Q28a and 1QSa also address a messianic figure who holds a prominent role in bringing forth eschatological events.[831] In the case of Peter, he connects Jesus's identity with the Father, as his son and divine agent. While such a concept may sound foreign to ancient Judaism, nothing could be farther from the case. The writer of *1 Enoch* 46[832] viewed the Son of Man in Daniel 7:13–14 as the Chosen One, one who God would use as his representative, and the one who would usher in the eschatological kingdom.[833] It is most probable that Hurtado is correct when saying, "Even if this tradition is no earlier than the late first century C.E. … the description of Enoch as God's chief agent is an example of the ability of ancient Judaism to accommodate this or that figure in a position in God's rule like that

---

[827] Morris, *Gospel according to Matthew,* PNTC, 209.

[828] Robert L. Mowery, "Son of God in Roman Imperial Titles and Matthew," *Biblica* 83 (2002): 101.

[829] Neil Elliott and Mark Reasoner, *Documents and Images for the Study of Paul* (Minneapolis, MN: Fortress, 2011), 141.

[830] Marcus Bockmuehl, James Carleton Paget, eds, *Redemption and Resistance: The Messianic Hopes of Jews and Christians in Antiquity* (London, UK: T&T Clark, 2007), 27–28.

[831] David Seal, "Son of God," *Lexham Bible Dictionary* (Bellingham, WA: Lexham Press, 2016), Logos Bible Software.

[832] *1 Enoch* 46 holds some interesting parallels to the portrayal of Jesus in the book of Revelation. *1 Enoch* states, "And there I saw One who had a head of days, and His head was white like wool, and with Him was another being whose countenance had the appearance of a man, and his face was full of graciousness, like one of the holy angels." *1 Enoch* 46.1, https://www.ccel.org/c/charles/otpseudepig/enoch/ENOCH_2.HTM, accessed March 20, 2022.

[833] Hurtado, *One God, One Lord,* 56.

of a vizier of the royal court."[834] But for Peter's confession, Jesus is more than just a representative or vizier, rather he is part of God's being in some sense.[835] Thus, the bipartite connection between Father and Son is something visible in Peter's confession, a trait that is found in the early pre-NT material.[836]

Fourth, the Servant of YHWH is an implicit title found in the prophetic foretelling of Jesus's passion in the latter verses of the pericope. After Jesus praised Peter for his wise observation of the identity of Jesus, Matthew notes that Jesus instructed them on the necessity for him to go to Jerusalem and be killed and raised from the dead on the third day (16:21). Some have postulated that it would have been impossible for Jesus to have predicted his death.[837] But even on a human level, this is absurd. Many individuals throughout the ages have had premonitions concerning their impending death.[838] The sentence exhibits an early Aramaic construction, which speaks of its early nature.[839] Furthermore, the pattern shows an acknowledgment of the Suffering Servant of YHWH as shown through the Servant Songs in the book of Isaiah.[840]

From the four messianic titles either observed or implied in Matthew 16:13–23, it is no stretch to say that the passage comfortably passes the third test. It is quite fascinating to consider that this passage has manifested more

---

[834] Ibid., 57.

[835] Hagner, *Matthew 14–28,* WBC, 468; W. D. Davies and Dale C. Allison, *A Critical and Exegetical Commentary on The Gospel According to Saint Matthew* (Edinburgh, UK: T&T Clark, 2001), 2:603, Logos Bible Software.

[836] Hurtado presents a convincing case for the high level of devotion that Q gives to Jesus. Examining Q, Hurtado deduces that the Q community understood Jesus to function in a divinelike role (Q 13:34–35) and his divine sonship in relation to the Father. While he does not necessarily draw upon Peter's confession, he states that the striking Christological declaration in Q 10:21–22 emphatically "confirms both that Jesus'[s] divine sonship is an important theme in Q and that it connotes a transcendent status." Larry W. Hurtado, *Lord Jesus Christ: Devotion to Jesus in Earliest Christianity* (Grand Rapids, MI: Eerdmans, 2003), 252–253.

[837] William Wrede, *The Messianic Secret,* J. C. G. Greig, trans (Cambridge, UK: James Clarke & Company, 1971), 82–92.

[838] This writer worked as a hospice chaplain while writing this dissertation. Numerous accounts have been observed where a person held a premonition of their demise, only to find that their premonitions proved true. If such events can happen with normal people, then why could it have not also arisen with Jesus?

[839] Keener, *GMSRC,* 432. This will be further addressed in the section concerning Aramaic/Hebraic Literary Characteristics.

[840] Isaiah 42:1–9; 49:1–13; 50:4–11; and 52:13–53:12.

early Christological titles than any passage yet investigated. A fifth title may also be found. Peter calls Jesus κύριοV in 16:22. Nevertheless, his use of the title may be more of a salutation in this instance than an official Christological title. The text stands at a record of 3-0 from the testing thus far, placing it at the precipice of entering the yellow zone of probability and earning an additional 4 points.

Mnemonic & Rhythmic Patterns

With as strong of a showing that the passage had with the last test, it is somewhat a surprise that the text lacks in the next area of examination. From what can be observed in the text, no mnemonic or rhythmic patterns are found. Certainly, the passage shows patterns of early material. The construction of Jesus's prediction of his death, burial, and resurrection shows some patterns that resemble early materials as found in 1 Corinthians 15:3–9 and holds traits of an early Aramaic nature.[841] A divine passive is found in 16:21,[842] yet this form of language is more indicative of an Aramaism than a mnemonic device or rhythmic pattern. As noted with the divine passive, those traits that come close to this category fit more in the fifth test than the present one. Because of this issue, nothing of particular substance stands out in the text showing a relationship to the rhythmic patterns and mnemonic devices as was found in the Sermon on the Mount or in some of the parables. As it stands at this juncture, the passage does not show the characteristics that are needed to pass the fourth test. Therefore, the text stands at a record of 3-1.

Aramaic/Hebraic Literary Characteristics

When it comes to the fifth test, Matthew 16:13–23 is rich with possibilities. Not only does one find Aramaic traits in the sayings of Jesus, but one also finds Aramaisms in the sayings of Peter and even in the name that Peter is called. Whereas the passage failed the last test miserably, it appears to pass the fifth test comfortably. Matthew 16:13–23 shows at least five Semitic literary characteristics.

First, as noted in the last section, Matthew 16:21 uses a divine passive. Verse 21 reads, "From then on Jesus began to point out to his disciples that he needed to go to Jerusalem and suffer many things from the elders, chief priests,

---

[841] Keener, *GMSRC,* 432.

[842] A divine passive is the use of passive voice when God is the subject implied. The divine passive is used to avoid the name of God. Jeremias, *NT Theology,* 12–13.

and scribes, be killed, and be raised on the third day" (Matt. 16:21).[843] The divine passive is found in the latter part of the passage which reads, "καὶ τῇ τρίτῃ ἡμέρᾳ ἐγερθῆναι."[844] The text does not say who would raise Jesus from the dead. However, it was implied that God would be the one who performed the resurrection. The general restraint in using the divine name is clearly an Aramaic and Hebraic practice over its Grecian counterpart.[845] The divine passive was particularly used by the LXX (i.e., ἐλογίσθη in Gen. 15:5, LXX) as well as in the apocalyptic literature of the time.[846] Thus, two observations can be made: 1) The evangelist uses a divine passive to reference God's activity in Christ's resurrection, and 2) there may be an apocalyptic hint in the passion story.[847] Nonetheless, the divine passive shows evidence of a Semitic literary characteristic.

Second, the title bar-Jonah (Gk., Βαριωνά) is an Aramaic name. A great deal of discussion has gone into discovering why Jesus used bar-Jonah rather than bar-Yôḥānān[848] as is found in John 1:42 and 21:15. Some have claimed that Jesus may have used bar-Jonah as an ominous warning of martyrdom along with a promise of resurrection since Jesus connected his resurrection with the story of Jonah (Matt. 12:40).[849] Perhaps the better alternative is that the name bar-John was changed to bar-Jonah to elevate Peter's status.[850] Whatever his intention, the usage of the title shows an Aramaic trait since the Aramaic term for son *bar* was used instead of the Hebraic *ben.*

Third, Matthew 16:13 employs the use of an Aramaic indefinite anqropoV as an idiom. Here, Jesus inquires, "Who do people say that the Son of Man is?" (Matt. 16:13). As noted previously, the title בַר אֱנָשׁ was not used as

---

843 Ἀπὸ τότε ἤρξατο ὁ Ἰησοῦς δεικνύειν τοῖς μαθηταῖς αὐτοῦ ὅτι δεῖ αὐτὸν εἰς Ἱεροσόλυμα ἀπελθεῖν καὶ πολλὰ παθεῖν ἀπὸ τῶν πρεσβυτέρων καὶ ἀρχιερέων καὶ γραμματέων καὶ ἀποκτανθῆναι καὶ τῇ τρίτῃ ἡμέρᾳ ἐγερθῆναι.

844 I.e., "and be raised on the third day."

845 Jeremias, *NT Theology,* 12.

846 Ibid., 13.

847 The project cannot dig into this area. Nonetheless, the apocalyptic connotations are only listed as an observation and as a potential for future study.

848 Hagner, *Matthew 14–28,* WBC, 469.

849 Robert H. Gundry, *Matthew: A Commentary on His Literary and Theological Art* (Grand Rapids, MI: Eerdmans, 1982), Kindle.

850 Hagner, *Matthew 14–28,* WBC, 469; W. D. Davies and Dale C. Allison, *Matthew,* International Critical Commentary Series, vol. 2 (Edinburgh, UK: T&T Clark, 1991), 2.622.

a title connecting back with Daniel 7 as much as it was intended to be used as another word for "I." Black also contends that Jesus uses the Son of Man in this case as a circumlocutionary idiom for "I."[851] This idiom was used during and prior to the time of Jesus in such a manner in some cases.[852] However, the circumlocutionary use of Son of Man is not found in post-classical Hebrew and is exclusively found in the Palestinian-Galilean dialect.[853] The use of the Son of Man in this text fits within the timeframe of Jesus and, thereby, serves as a fascinating Aramaism in favor of the question coming from early Jesuan traditions.

Fourth, the use of an asyndeton is found in Peter's declaration in Matthew 16:16. The asyndeton, which has been previously observed in numerous texts, is yet another trait that Peter's confession stems from an underlying tradition originating in Aramaic. As previously noted, asyndetons are traits often found in Aramaic literature. Peter's confession is one of at least 60 examples of asyndetons found in the Synoptic Gospels.[854] Thus, Matthew 16:16 finds yet another trait that points to an earlier underlying tradition.

The fifth and final Aramaic characteristic is found in yet another aspect of Peter's confession. Peter concludes his proclamation by saying that Jesus was the ὁ υἱὸς τοῦ θεοῦ τοῦ ζῶντος.[855] The Aramaic trait is found in Peter's use of the term ζῶντος. In some ancient MS, the term ζῶντος is used, whereas the term swvζῶντος is used in the D-text. Black avers that the variants ζῶντος and swvζῶντος both stem from the Aramaic adjective חַיי as opposed to the Hebrew verb חָיָה.[856] חָיָה means "to live."[857] Benjamin Davis adds, "Some grammatical forms of *ḥāyâ* can mean "to keep alive" and "let live": Noah was to bring animals into the ark to keep them alive (*ḥāyâ*; Gen 6:19–20)."[858] The Aramaic חַיי is used as an adjective describing something that has the state of

---

[851] Black, *An Aramaic Approach to the Gospels and Acts,* 326.

[852] This most certainly does not indicate that the title was always used in this manner. Context is key when deciphering how the title was conveyed.

[853] Ibid., 327.

[854] Ibid., 58–59.

[855] I.e., "the Son of the Living God."

[856] Black, *An Aramaic Approach to the Gospels and Acts,* 245.

[857] Ibid.

[858] Benjamin S. Davis, "Life," *Lexham Theological Wordbook*, Logos Bible Software.

life, a span of life, and/or describing something as being alive.[859] חיי was often read as "who saves" from the Aphel participle.[860] To word it another way, the key distinction is that the Hebrew verb חָיָה was used to describe the action of preserving life. In contrast, the Aramaic adjective חיי described a living state of being. Both variants—ζῶντος and swvζῶντος—appear to flow from the Aramaic participle rather than the Hebrew verb. Thus, Peter acknowledges that Jesus was the Son of God who was in a perpetual state of living existence. For the purposes of the present exploration, the vernacular used in both variants exhibits a connection with an Aramaic layer which provides additional Semitic residue.

From the five points previously given, one is warranted to permit the present text to pass the fifth test. The question that Jesus poses and the divine passive in the implied forecast that Jesus gives concerning his resurrection speaks strongly to an earlier Aramaic tradition. However, it is Peter's confession that conveys the strongest signs of Aramaic influence. The text comfortably passes the fifth test, leaving it with a record of 4-1 and earning 5 more points.

Semitic Cultural Concepts of First-Century Israel

When considering the Semitic cultural concepts of Matthew 16:13–23, the passage also excels for a few reasons. Davies and Allison accept the authenticity of the text due to the identification of the cultural setting due to its geographical setting, along with the Semitisms of the passage, and the criterion of dissimilarity among other things.[861] The text matches the cultural concepts of the pagan area in at least three potential ways.

First, the reference to the "gates of Hades" (16:18) parallels the setting of the text in Caesarea Philippi (16:13). Caesarea Philippi was a largely pagan territory located around twenty-five miles north of the Sea of Galilee and was found at the foot of the massive Mount Hermon,[862] which stands at around 9,200 feet.[863] The city had undergone a few name changes later in the first-century. Agrippa II's attempt to rename the city Neronias, to pay homage to

---

[859] Ibid.

[860] Black, *An Aramaic Approach to the Gospels and Acts,* 245.

[861] The full list of reasons includes 1) the evidence in Gal. 1:11–21, 2) Semitisms, 3) indicators of Palestinian provenance when compared with the Dead Sea Scrolls, 4) criterion of consistency, 5) criterion of dissimilarity, 6) the geographical setting, and 7) the weakness of objections against the text being authentic. Davies and Allison, *Matthew,* ICC, vol. 2, 609–615. See also Keener, *GMSRC,* 423–424; and Bauckham, *Christian World Around the New Testament,* 462.

[862] Morris, *Gospel According to Matthew,* PNTC, 419.

[863] Brian Algie, "Caesarea Philippi," *LBD,* Logos Bible Software.

Nero, did not last and was quickly changed back to Caesarea Philippi after Nero's death in AD 68.[864] Nonetheless, Agrippa II rebuilt the city and named it Neronias in AD 60.[865] Because of the reference to the name Caesarea Philippi (16:13), the tradition dates to a time earlier than AD 60. During the time of Alexander the Great (c. 4th century BC), a shrine was erected in honor of the god Pan—a Greek god of forests, deserted places, flocks, and shepherds.[866] A cave, popularly called the Gates of Hell, was an extremely deep cavern in which water flowed. It was believed that this cave led into the underworld. Niches were often carved into the wall surrounding the cave.[867] Caesarea Philippi was a battleground for spiritual combat due to the conflict between paganism and Judaism. This served as a perfect place for Jesus to accept the messianic label that Peter ascribed to him and to declare war on the spiritual powers of darkness.

Second, the Roman road system allowed extensive traveling capabilities possible. It may initially appear odd that Jesus and the disciples would have visited the pagan city of Caesarea Philippi. However, as Bauckham has noted, the Roman roads of the first-century were well constructed and permitted extensive traveling ability for itinerant preachers like Jesus and others whose business required one to move about the area.[868] Pagan worship flourished in the area until a later Christian demonstrated that Jesus was more powerful than Pan in a miraculous demonstration.[869] According to Eusebius, a Christian named Astyrius prayed that the delusional work of the demon in the area would come to an end. After his prayer, the pagan's sacrifice floated on the surface of the fountain and never sank, bringing an end to pagan worship in the area.[870] Going back to the passage, the ease by which Jesus and his disciples could travel to the Caesarea Philippi matches the road system and the *Pax Romana* established in early first-century Israel. While this may not be the

---

[864] See Josephus, *Antiquities of the Jews* 20.9.4, 214; Josephus, *Jewish Wars* 3.10.7, 514.

[865] Lamoine F. DeVries, "Caesarea Philippi," *Eerdmans Dictionary of the Bible,* Allen C. Myers, Astrid B. Beck, and David Noel Freedman, eds (Grand Rapids, MI: Eerdmans, 2000), 208.

[866] John Francis Wilson, *Caesarea Philippi: Banias, the Lost City of Pan* (New York, NY: I. B. Tauris, 2004), 2; Algie, "Caesarea Philippi," *LBD,* Logos Bible Software; and Keener, *GMSRC,* 424.

[867] DeVries, "Caesarea Philippi," *EDB,* 208.

[868] Bauckham, *The Christian World Around the New Testament,* 26.

[869] Keener, *GMSRC,* 424.

[870] Eusebius, *Ecclesiastical History* 7.17.1., 304.

strongest connection among those mentioned in this section, it is still worth considering.

Third, even though Jesus's use of the term ἐκκλησία has brought considerable scrutiny,[871] the community that Jesus establishes through the testimony of Peter matches what ancient teachers would have done in his time.[872] Teachers often developed communities to learn, organize, and further their teachings.[873] Many scholars have recognized that it would have been inconceivable to have a "Messiah without a Messianic Community"[874] within the confines of ancient Judaism. Furthermore, Jewish teachers would have afforded blessings to those who correctly answered their questions as seen with Jesus verses 17–19.[875] The book of Acts preserves a sermon summary from Gamaliel, a respected leader of the Sanhedrin (Acts 5:35–39). Gamaliel mentions two false teachers—Theudas and Judas the Galilean—who claimed to be the Messiah. Both Theudas and Judas developed a small community of followers (Acts 5:36, 37). Even though Jesus may have anticipated the eschatological end within a few generations,[876] the literature in Qumran and their Teacher of Righteousness, who expected the end to come in his lifetime, also developed a community.[877] The Essenes described themselves as the קָהָל

---

[871] M. Eugene Boring, *Sayings of the Risen Jesus: Christian Prophecy in the Synoptic Tradition,* Society for New Testament Studies Monograph 46 (Cambridge, UK: Cambridge University Press, 1982), 213–214.

[872] This was discussed in the first test. Whereas the first text examined the community in the sense of rabbinic understanding, the sixth test peers into the way the culture viewed the community of God. Even though there may be some overlap, the focal points are different.

[873] Culpepper, *Johannine School,* 123.

[874] William Foxwell Albright and C. S. Mann, *Matthew,* Anchor Bible (Garden City, NY: Doubleday, 1971), 195; Archibald M. Hunter, *The Message of the New Testament* (Philadelphia, PA: Westminster, 1944), 53.

[875] Keener, *The Historical Jesus of the Gospels,* 248; Brad H. Young, *Jesus the Jewish Theologian* (Peabody, MA: Hendrickson, 1995), 199.

[876] This writer is not wholeheartedly convinced that he did. In the Olivet Discourse, one finds a few reasons to believe that he may have expected a span of time between his resurrection and the end of the world.

[877] The *Damascus Document* describes the Teacher of Righteousness more than any other text in the DSS. See also Keener, *GMSRC,* 428.

(Hebrew word for a congregation) of God.[878] Jesus similarly uses the term ἐκκλησία.

For the three reasons given above, the text matches the cultural themes of Jesus's day. Some of the parallels are beyond the scope of what was anticipated. The cultural connection between Jesus's use of the ἐκκλησία with the understanding of a godly קָהָל is especially telling. The parallel between his understanding of the community with the Jewish teachers of his time strengthens confidence in the text's authenticity and bolsters the probability that the text bears Semitic residue of underlying early Jesus traditions. Because of the text passing the sixth test, the passage now stands at an amazing record of 5-1 and an additional 4 points.

Similarities to NT Creeds, Summaries, and Early Literature

Due to the structure of Peter's confession, it is unsurprising that Matthew 16:13–23 passes the seventh and final test. The text shows signs of containing both thematic and structural patterns that match what one would hope to find in *kerygmatic* passages that contain the common *homologiai* of the early church. First, one will need to consider the matching theme(s) that the passage holds with early pre-NT material. Second, one will need to focus on the structural patterns that match early confessions and creeds.

Due to how the passage is built around the confession of Peter, the text meets the theme of baptism and catechumenisms.[879] Granted, one may ask how this text fits a baptismal confession. Baptismal confessions are not necessarily used at baptismal services. Rather, they show the fixed ways of communicating one's faith, especially when gathering with a community of faith, something of a community formula.[880] Peter's declaration most assuredly meets the bill. Since the questioning of Jesus precipitates this confession (16:13–15) and the subsequent blessing reinforces the same (16:17–20), then the conversation fits within the context of the confessional statement.

Concerning the structure of the passage, it undeniably meets the criteria of the single-statement affirmation, so much so that Longenecker lists Matthew 16:16 as one of the many examples in Scripture.[881] The text certainly matches the verbal structure of a kerygmatic and confessional nature as Peter

---

[878] Keener, *GMSRC,* 228; Albright and Mann, *Matthew,* Anchor Bible, 121; Raymond E. Brown, Karl P. Donfried, and John Reumann, eds, *Peter in the New Testament* (New York, NY: Paramus, 1973), 92.

[879] Cullmann, *Earliest Christian Confessions,* 18.

[880] Ibid., 20–21.

[881] Longenecker, *New Wine Into Fresh Wineskins,* 22.

confesses his faith in the messianic identity of Jesus.[882] Paul appears to continue the nature of confessional material with his documentation of the credal material in his epistles, such as Philippians 2:8. Additionally, Galatians 4:4–5 picks up on the sonship of Jesus as identified by Peter. Peter said, "You are the Messiah, the Son of the living God" (Matt. 16:16), whereas Paul wrote, "When the time came to completion, God sent his Son, born of a woman, born under the law, to redeem those under the law, so that we might receive adoption as sons" (Gal. 4:4–5). The idea of Christ's sonship may have first stemmed from Peter's confession.[883]

Matthew 16:13–23 strongly matches the criteria established for the seventh test. It contains a single-statement confession and also matches the baptismal and catechetical format set forth by early pre-NT material. The text matches so well that Matthew 16:16 is even listed as an example of *homologia* in the Gospels. Therefore, the text passes the seventh test and finds itself with a final record of 6-1 and acquires 5 more points.

Conclusion and Color Assignment

The present passage of Scripture has fared quite well with the present test. Matthew 16:13–23 passed the first test. The teachings of Jesus concerning the anticipation of the Messiah and the kingdom of God were comparable to the rabbinic teachings of the day, although his understanding was considerably different. Additionally, the community of saints taught by the rabbinic corpus was similar to the teachings of Jesus regarding the ἐκκλησία.

The text comfortably passed the second test as the text's focus on the Lordship of Christ and the already-not-yet eschatological kingdom matched the early Christological concepts of the early church. The passage excelled at the third test. It was noted that at least four Christological titles were employed in the text—Messiah, בַּר אֱנָשׁ, Son of God, and the Servant of YHWH. The title Lord could serve as a fifth potential title. But, as was noted, the term was used more as a salutation than an official title.

Even though the passage surpassed expectations for the first three tests, nothing by way of mnemonic and rhythmic patterns could be found in the text. Therefore, the passage failed the fourth. The study has grown accustomed to the fourth test serving as a sticking point for many Scriptural texts in this study. This text could not escape its clutches.

The passage continued to do well with the final three tests. The text contained five Aramaic literary characteristics which exhibit signs of early material, including the use of a divine passive, the title bar-Jonah for Peter, an

---

[882] Ibid., 21.

[883] Ibid., 38.

Aramaic indefinite used as an idiom (noted to have been detected in the Palestinian-Galilean of Aramaic), an asyndeton in Matt. 16:16, and the indication that the variants *zontos* and *so' zontos* were taken from the Aramaic adjective חַיי rather than the Hebrew verb חָיָה. The text passed the sixth test with the cultural similarities found with the gates of Hades in Caesarea Philippi (16:18), the freedom to travel along with the well-designed Roman road systems and the *Pax Romana,* and the way in which Jesus's comprehension of community matched those in Qumran and surrounding areas. Lastly, the text passed the seventh test as it matches the theme of baptisms and catechumenisms of the early church, as well as the structural design of single-statement affirmations.

Matthew 16:13–23 passed 6 of the 7 tests and scored 25 of 30 points on the weighted scale. This places the passage of Scripture within the green realm of certainty. Therefore, it can be said that the passage strongly expresses signs that point to early Jesus traditions underlying the text. While some have contended that the use of ἐκκλησία points to a late post-Easter saying, the connections to the community in early first-century Israel diminishes any arguments to the contrary. Thus, one holds strong reasons for believing that Matthew accurately documents the key details of Peter's interaction with Jesus and that the reader has a glimpse into an authentic Jesus tradition that predates the Gospel's composition.

Jesus & John the Baptist (Matt. 11:2–19)

Alas, the research now reaches the final passage of Scripture to be reviewed. The text describes the interaction between Jesus and the disciples of John the Baptist. John had been imprisoned at this time (11:2). Perhaps needing further settling on Jesus's messianic identification due to the secrecy that Jesus maintained concerning said identity, John sent his disciples to Jesus to ask whether he was indeed the "one who is to come" or if they should anticipate someone else. Matthew implies that Jesus performed some work before the disciples before telling them, "Go and report to John what you hear and see: The blind receive their sight, the lame walk, those with leprosy are cleansed, the deaf hear, the dead are raised, and the poor are told the good news, and blessed is the one who isn't offended by me" (11:4–6). Jesus then provides a diatribe against the accusations that many of his critics afforded against him, particularly trying to find fault with both of them, saying, "For John came neither eating nor drinking, and they say, 'He has a demon!' The Son of Man came eating and drinking, and they say, 'Look, a glutton and a drunkard, a friend of tax collectors and sinners!' Yet wisdom is vindicated by her deeds" (11:18–19).

This passage holds great apologetic value. On the one hand, the interactions of Jesus with the disciples of John the Baptist shows his compassion in helping those who doubt. He neither condemns John nor his disciples for holding the questions they present. Rather, Jesus later praises John to such a high degree that he avers that no one born was greater than the imprisoned prophet (Matt. 11:11). On the other hand, the evidential value of Jesus's miracles speaks volumes about the validity of his ministry. While Matthew alludes to the performance of miracles in front of the disciples of John (Matt. 11:4–6), Luke more explicitly spells out that "Jesus healed many people of diseases, afflictions, and evil spirits, and he granted sight to many people (Luke 7:21) before uttering his reply to the disciples of John, the words that are nearly identical to what Matthew preserves in his Gospel (Matt. 11:4–6; Luke 7:22–23). Despite the ideal value the text imparts to the modern apologist, one must inquire whether the text is based on early Jesus traditions. Or, as this research has asked, does the text hold Semitic residue?

Before applying the tests to the text, consider the assessment that the Jesus Seminar grants to the text at hand. Oddly, the Jesus Seminar lists the Scripture reference from Isaiah in verses 4–6 as an invention of the evangelist. The Seminar sees the mention of the blind, deaf, and lame as a direct reference in Isa. 35:5–6; deaf and blind in Isa. 29:18–19; the raising of the dead in Isa. 26:19; and the proclamation of the gospel to the poor in Isa. 61:1.[884] However, their assessment is suspect since Jesus would have most assuredly incorporated his mission from his understanding of Isaiah and the OT. Even if the text did not originate with Jesus as it has been preserved, it would seem that the core contents would stem back to Jesus, especially since the vernacular is almost identical in both Matthew and Luke.[885] As has been noted by other scholars, "Jesus lived in the Old Testament. His sayings are incomprehensible unless we recognize this."[886]

Verses 7–8 are held to a higher degree of authenticity by the Seminar. They give this section the pink label. The praise that Jesus gives to John the Baptist is unique in the minds of the group. They note that "Jesus is probably the only speaker in Christian sources who would have called John the Baptist

---

[884] Funk, Hoover, and Jesus Seminar, *Five Gospels,* 177.

[885] It is possible that Luke could have copied from Matthew. But it is also possible that both Matthew's Gospel and Luke derived this material from an earlier tradition. In either sense, there is no reason to think that the link back to Isaiah did not originate from Jesus himself.

[886] Jeremias goes on to say, "[Jesus's] last word, according to Mark, was the beginning of Psalm 22, prayed in his Aramaic mother tongue (Mark 15:34)." Jeremias, *NT Theology,* 205. The fact that the Jesus Seminar ignores the Aramaism, and other unique features, of the utterance of Jesus in the Markan text from the cross further casts doubt of the integrity of their collaborative assessment, at least in this researcher's mind.

the greatest among all human beings."[887] Despite the Seminar's elevation of the saying ascribing the Baptist as the greatest prophet and their note that Jesus would have been the only one to have made this kind of comment, it is quite bizarre that the Seminar grants the lowest rank to the connection made with Malachi 3:1.[888] One almost begins to wonder whether the Seminar viewed Jesus as completely illiterate, even in the functional capacity, and was incapable of making connections to the OT.[889] The concluding comments of John, who was deemed lesser than the least in the kingdom of heaven, are cast in the gray tier of authenticity.[890]

The remaining section of the pericope, outside of verses 14 and 19, is labeled in gray. The connection Jesus makes with John being Elijah was unanimously labeled as black by the Seminar's community.[891] The primary reason for its rejection was that it is only found in the Q text and no other. That is, it holds no other independent source outside of Q.[892] Oddly, the Seminar labeled the proverb at the end of the text as black.[893] They reasoned that the proverb could have been uttered by any sage and does not distinctively hold a Jesuan flavor.[894]

The Seminar's assessment of this pericope is suspect for various reasons, many of which have been noted in the previous footnotes. However, it will be interesting to see how the text fits within the context of the tests prescribed in this research. It is estimated that the text will most likely score far higher on the Jesuan scale of authenticity than what the Seminar permitted.

---

[887] Funk, Hoover, and the Jesus Seminar, *Five Gospels,* 179.

[888] Ibid., 178.

[889] Here again, Jeremias shines a luminous light of authenticity that contrasts the darkness of the Seminar's skepticism.

[890] There is another oddity in the Seminar's assessment. The Seminar elevates the *Gospel of Thomas* in their research. Yet it is a bit strange that they do not grant a higher ranking (red) to the text since it is found in both Q and *Thomas.* Stranger still is their refusal to acknowledge Jesus's connection with the OT, as previously mentioned.

[891] Funk, Hoover, and the Jesus Seminar, *Five Gospels,* 179.

[892] Ibid.

[893] Ibid., 180.

[894] Ibid.

Without further ado, it is time to assess the passage, first beginning with its connection with rabbinic material.

Unique Rabbinic Concepts

Since Jesus speaks more of John the Baptist than he does of himself, discovering parallels between the theology of Jesus and the rabbinic writings poses a bit more daunting task. It is not enough to say that no connection exists. But rather the scope of focus must be directed toward a couple of particular aspects of the pericope. First, one must consider the understanding of the observance of Jesus, seeing in himself the fulfillment of messianic prophecy from the sphere of his miracle-working and evangelistic capacities, in addition to his relationship with similar Jewish understandings of the same. As was noted before, many scholars believe that the quotation of Isaiah in verses 4–6 is a later Christian invention.[895] However, the belief that these traits (i.e., healing and preaching) indicated the coming of a messianic kingdom is not unique to Jesus. Jesus connects the Hebrew verb לבשר with εὐαγγελίζεσθαι, which is almost always translated as such in the LXX.[896]

Additionally, others saw themselves as bringing fulfillment to the Isaianic foretellings of a messianic kingdom. An example is found in the author of the Thanksgiving Scroll.[897] The author believed that his message brought about the good tidings mentioned in Isaiah 61:1–2 and 52:7. The author of the scroll particularly related himself to the illumination of the Holy Spirit, as with Isaiah 61, and those who were blinded by false teachers receiving the light of God.[898] Interestingly, Jesus alludes to Isaiah 61 in Matthew 5:3–5, part of the Beatitudes. In that passage, the Jesus Seminar warrants a pink rating, except for verse 5. But concerning the rabbinic understanding of the advent of Messiah, most rabbis held that peace and prosperity would accompany the Messiah's

---

[895] Funk, Hoover, and the Jesus Seminar, *Five Gospels,* 177.

[896] Flusser, *Judaism and the Origins of Christianity,* 111.

[897] Ibid.

[898] "Your holy spirit [sic] illuminates the dark places of the heart of your servant, with light from the sun. I look to the covenants made by men, worthless. Only your truth shines, and those who love it are wise and walk in the glow of your light. From darkness you raise hearts. Let light shine on your servants. Your light is everlasting." *Thanksgiving Psalm* 23, Dead Sea Scrolls Texts, *Gnostic.org,* www.gnosis.org/library/psalm.htm, accessed April 2, 2022.

coming.[899] *Sanhedrin* 98a:3 held that when no wages were necessary for work and no rent was to be paid, then the Messiah would come.[900] While the understanding of the messianic kingdom was different in the mind of Jesus as compared to other rabbinic teachers, both held similarities in the sense that they anticipated a great move of the Holy Spirit to reveal the truth and to provide peace. Nonetheless, Jesus held a greater comparison with the Qumranic author of the *Thanksgiving Scroll* than necessarily the rabbinic understanding of the messianic kingdom. Matthew 11:5–6 is held in such confidence that even Bultmann and most modern scholars accept it as authentic.[901]

Second, another aspect to consider is the understanding of John serving in the capacity of the Elijah that was to come. Jesus said of John, "This is the one about whom it is written: 'See, I am sending my messenger ahead of you; he will prepare your way before you'" (11:10). Jesus then said, "And if you are willing to accept it, he is the Elijah who is to come" (11:14). Although Jewish people often thought that the age of prophecy ended with Malachi,[902] Jesus conveys that the prophetic line continued and ended with John the Baptist. *Eruvin* 43b:5 notes that Elijah would not come on the eve of Shabbat or the eve of a festival.[903] Even though the passage describes the times that Elijah would not come, it still implies that an eschatological Elijah would come. Other Talmudic passages indicate that Elijah would come to "declare unclean or clean, to distance or draw near."[904] Further association with the Elijah to come and the Messiah is found in other passages.[905] Jesus may have held a different interpretation than the rabbinics—as is not unusual from what this research has already shown; nonetheless, it cannot be said that the connection between

---

[899] *Mishneh Torah, Kings and Wars* 12.5, *sefaria.org*, https://www.sefaria.org/Mishneh_Torah%2C_Kings_and_Wars.12.5?ven=Yad-Hachazakah,_edited_by_Elias_Soloweyczik%3B_London,_1863&vhe=Torat_Emet_363&lang=bi, accessed April 2, 2022.

[900] *Sanhedrin* 98a:3, *sefaria.org*, https://www.sefaria.org/Sanhedrin.98a.3?ven=William_Davidson_Edition_-_English&vhe=Wikisource_Talmud_Bavli&lang=bi, accessed April 2, 2022.

[901] Keener, *GMSRC,* 333; Davies and Allison, *Matthew,* ICCS, 244.

[902] Craig S. Keener, "The Function of Johannine Pneumatology in the Context of Late First-Century Judaism." Ph.D. dissertation, Duke University Graduate School, Durham, NC, 1991, 77–91; Keener, *GMSRC,* 338.

[903] *Eruvin* 43b.5, *Sefaria.org.*

[904] *Kiddushin* 71a.8, *Sefaria.org.*

[905] *Eruvin* 43b.7, *Sefaria.org.*

the eschatological prophet and Messiah does not find any root in rabbinic traditions.

More could be said concerning the link between the rabbinical understandings of the rabbinics and Jesus within this pericope. For instance, the understanding that the law and the prophets pointed to the Jewish recognition of the messianic era finds a home in Jewish literature.[906] Nonetheless, sufficient evidence has been shown to connect the passage to the criteria needed to pass the first test and earning the 2 points assigned for the initial test. This researcher estimates that further investigation would show further ties if space permitted.

Early Christological Concepts

Like many of the passages this research has studied, Matthew 11:2–19 connects with early Christological concepts grounded in early credal material and the early *kerygmatic* proclamation. The text exhibits the bipartite link between Father and Son in the sense that Jesus viewed himself as the *Shaliach*[907] (שָׁלִיחַ) (i.e., the divine agent of God).[908] The שָׁלִיחַ was more than just a מַלְאָךְ,[909] the שָׁלִיחַ was endowed with the authority and power of the one who sent him, and held the authority to act on the sender's behalf.[910] The link that Jesus finds in himself with the *Shaliach* of God is seen in two examples in the pericope.

First, Jesus understands that the works and wonders accomplished through his ministry are indicative of his role as the divine agent of God (11:4–6). Though the Jesus Seminar doubted the validity of these verses, even Rudolf Bultmann accepted verses 5–6 as authentic,[911] even though he was reserved about the setting behind the statements.[912] However, there exist good reasons for holding to the validity of the statements and setting. First, the connection with Isaiah 61 is made in other instances by Jesus. For instance, the first three

---

[906] *b. Berakot* 34b; *Sanhedrin* 99a; and *Shabbot* 63a.

[907] Hebrew for messenger or emissary.

[908] Witherington, III, *Christology of Jesus*, 51.

[909] Hebrew, *mal'ak*. The term מַלְאָךְ, often used for divine beings (i.e., angels), indicates one who is simply a messenger.

[910] Carl F. H. Henry, ed, *Revelation and the Bible: Contemporary Evangelical Thought* (Grand Rapids, MI: Baker, 1958), 192; Witherington, *Christology of Jesus,* 51. The highest form of the שָׁלִיחַ was the λόγος, who was held as God's chief agent, especially in the works of Philo. See Hurtado, *One God, One Lord,* 50–51.

[911] Keener, *GMSRC,* 333; Davies and Allison, *Matthew,* ICCS, 244.

[912] Rudolf Bultmann, *History of the Synoptic Tradition,* J. Marsh, trans (Oxford, UK: Blackwell, 1963), 22, 115, 135; Witherington, III, *Christology of Jesus,* 42.

Beatitudes depend on Isaiah 61.[913] The blessings ascribed to those who are poor in spirit, those who mourn, and the humble (5:3–5) only make sense with the understanding that in the eschatological kingdom Yahweh would use his *Shaliach* to "bring good news to the poor … heal the brokenhearted, to proclaim liberty to the captives, and freedom to the prisoners; to proclaim the year of the LORD'S favor, and the day of our God's vengeance" (Isa. 61:1–2). Another independent source shows Jesus reading Isaiah 61:1–2 at a synagogue in Nazareth (Luke 4:16–19). Additionally, the blessing ascribed to the one who is not offended by the speaker in verse 6 only makes sense when considering the one who was the proclaimer.[914] Jesus uses the term σκανδαλισθῇ in the blessing formula in Luke 17:2; Mark 4:17; 6:3; 9:42–47; and 14:27, 29.[915] Thus, four independent sources (Matthew, Mark, Luke, and possibly Q) all lend to the notion that the blessing is genuine, which also points to the legitimacy of the ministry of Jesus with Isaiah 61. Finally, the unique nature of the eschatological kingdom found in Jesus's teaching is not something that was rampant but found in Philo, Daniel, and the books of Enoch.[916]

Second, the way Jesus contrasts his ministry with the ministry of John the Baptist speaks to his self-identification as the *Shaliach* of God (11:7–19). Jesus distinguishes his ministry from that of the Baptist. As evidenced in the Pseudo-Clementine writings, the disciples of John the Baptist believed that John was the final prophet of God who ushered in the kingdom.[917] In other words, the revelation of God ended with John, thereby leaving a Messiah unnecessary. However, Jesus showed that John the Baptist was the last in the prophetic lineage, even combatting the Jewish notion that Malachi was the final prophet before the advent of the messianic age.[918] In a manner of speaking, Jesus viewed himself as the final prophet, serving as the *Shaliach* of Yahweh, who initiated the arrival of the kingdom of heaven on earth. Jesus identifies John's prophetic ministry as the final מַלְאָךְ in verses 7–10. But starting in verse 11, Jesus develops the distinction between the מַלְאָךְ of God and the שָׁלִיחַ. Even though John's ministry was great, the least in the kingdom would be greater than him because of the establishment of the messianic age (11:11). Furthermore, John abstained from normal food and drink, whereas Jesus ate and drank with those deemed less than ideal (11:18–19). This could possibly

913 Flusser, *Judaism and the Origins of Christianity,* 110.

914 Dunn, *Jesus Remembered,* 695.

915 Witherington, *Christology of Jesus,* 44.

916 Cullmann, *Christology of the NT,* 159.

917 Ibid., 26.

918 Ibid.

speak of the invitation that Jesus brought to the people of the world to join the kingdom.[919]

Because of the connection Jesus draws of himself serving as the *Shaliach*/שָׁלִיחַ of Yahweh, he affords a bipartite connection between the Father and himself while also exhibiting the same eschatological traits that have flourished in this research's examination of the passages under review. Thus, it can be said that sufficient evidence can be shown to connect the passage to early Christological concepts found in the *kerygma* of the church and the early pre-Pauline creeds. Therefore, this passage passes the second test and now stands at a record of 2-0 and secures 5 points.

Theological Terminology Relating to Early Christological Concepts

Matthew 11:2–19 holds one explicit theological title that relates to Christological concepts. That title, which has been influential in this work, is Son of Man. However, it is questionable whether Son of Man is used as much as a title in this passage as much as an idiom referring to the self. It may be that Jesus uses the title in its official sense to show that the people rejected his office as the heavenly *Shaliach* of Yahweh. But he does not connect the title with a heavenly motif of him coming on the clouds of heaven as seen in other uses.[920] In this case, he more likely uses the term to identify himself,[921] saying, "For John came neither eating nor drinking, and they say, 'He has a demon!' The Son of Man came eating and drinking, and they say, 'Look, a glutton and a drunkard, a friend of tax collectors and sinners!' Yet wisdom is vindicated by her deeds" (11:18–19). Thus, the explicit use of Son of Man is of no benefit for the present test.

Before anyone discounts any connection in the text, consider the relationship between the *Shaliach* of Yahweh and the Servant of Yahweh. While the Servant of Yahweh (עֶבֶד יהוה) is often portrayed within the Suffering Servant motif, the healing ministry and the proclamation of the gospel are often

[919] A good parallel is found in the Parable of the Wedding Feast in Matt. 22:1–14. In the story, those who were invited to the wedding feast gave excuses and did not attend. Therefore, the king sent out his servants to the streets to invite everyone to the wedding feast. One person, perhaps one previously invited, was found in the banquet, but he was not properly attired. Thus, he was cast out of the wedding banquet. More than just a few parallels are found between this parable and the distinction Jesus makes between John's ministry and his own. Be that as it may, the key message is that people rejected John for his asceticism while rejecting Jesus for living within the community.

[920] See Chapter 4 for some of the connections Jesus makes between the Son of Man and the heavenly eschatological ambassador of God.

[921] Hagner, *Matthew 1–13,* WBC, 310.

associated with the prophet Isaiah and his view of the Servant of Yahweh. Consider the evangelist's remarks in Matthew 8:16–17 and his association with Jesus's healing ministry and proclamation of the gospel with Isaiah's Suffering Servant. After Jesus healed Peter's mother-in-law, people brought many sick and afflicted to Jesus for healing. Matthew writes, "When evening came, they brought to him many who were demon-possessed. He drove out the spirits with a word and healed all who were sick, so that what was spoken through the prophet Isaiah might be fulfilled: He himself took our weaknesses and carried our diseases" (8:16–17). The healing ministry was viewed as part of the ministry of the Servant of Yahweh. Most interestingly, Cullmann notes that Jesus's consciousness of the Servant of Yahweh and the titular function originates with Jesus himself just as much as the concept of the Son of Man.[922]

Also, it is undeniable that Jesus connects himself to the role of prophet. The comparison he makes between John's ministry and his own in 11:18–19 speaks to his association with a similar prophetic function to that of John's. However, as it has already been noted, Jesus sees a great deal of difference between John's role as a messenger of God and his role as God's emissary. Nonetheless, the titular role of a prophet is evident in the text. Cullmann brings up an interesting point to consider. Even though the Synoptic writers did not make use of the title of the eschatological prophet when speaking of Jesus, the texts suggest that at least some people viewed him in such a manner (i.e., Matt. 16:13–23).[923] As far as Jesus goes, he saw himself as a prophet of sorts. However, to borrow the words of James D. G. Dunn, the eschatological significance of his ministry "transcended the older prophetic categories."[924]

Given the emphasis on the Son of Man title in this work, this passage leaves the current quest for signs of ancient oral traditions in a unique position. The only explicit title in the passage is used as an idiom rather than a title, forfeiting its use as an early Christological title. However, the implied roles of the Servant of Yahweh and eschatological prophet bolster confidence that this passage includes some early Christological titular roles. Therefore, the implied titles save the passage from failure and grant it a passing grade with 4 points. This leaves the current text at 3-0.

Mnemonic & Rhythmic Patterns

The fourth test has been quite a sticking point for many passages in this study. However, certain parts of Matthew 11:2–19. Verses 4–6 especially

---

922 Cullmann, *Christology of the NT,* 68–69.

923 Ibid., 35.

924 Dunn, *Jesus Remembered,* 666.

hold quite an interest when it comes to mnemonic and rhythmic patterns. C. F. Burney and Joachim Jeremias have detected a 4+4+2 pattern, which they call a four-beat pattern,[925] in verses 4–6.[926] The four-beat pattern is also found in Matthew 6:9–13; 6:24; 10:16; 10:24–27; 13:52; 16:17–19; Mark 13:9–13; Luke 6:27–29; 6:36–38; 10:16; 11:9; 12:32–37; and 12:42.[927] Concerning 11:4–6, the Semitic structural pattern has led even the most skeptical scholars to accept its basic authenticity.[928] While questioning what he considers the secondary nature of the setting, John Meier holds that the structural pattern is so strong that it contends for an early oral tradition or written narrative that provided the framework for these sayings.[929] He goes on to say that Jesus must have worded some of his statements in a rhythmic pattern for the purposes of memorization and transmission while permitting flexibility in how the statements are told.[930] As previously noted, this so happens to be a classic trait of the informal controlled model.[931]

Additionally, the children in the marketplace analogy in 11:16–17 exhibit signs of meter and rhyme when translated back into Aramaic.[932] It is as if the children's response was a "mock funeral dirge."[933] The requiem forms an imitation word-play that is also found in Matthew 7:2; Mark 7:2; and Luke 6:38.[934] The rhythmic text notes the people's refusal for accepting the truth no matter who delivered the message of God—regardless of one's role as a *mal'ak*

---

[925] Jeremias, *NT Theology,* 23.

[926] C. F. Burney, *The Poetry of Our Lord* (Oxford, UK: Clarendon, 1925), 117.

[927] Jeremias, *NT Theology,* 23, fn 2.

[928] Bultmann, *History of the Synoptic Tradition,* 22.

[929] John P. Meier, *A Marginal Jew: Rethinking the Historical Jesus,* vol. 2, Anchor Yale Bible Reference Library (New York, NY: Doubleday, 1994), 130.

[930] Ibid.

[931] Bailey, "Informal Controlled Oral Tradition and the Synoptic Gospels," *Themelios* 20, 2: 7.

[932] Keener, *GMSRC,* 341.

[933] The children's sing-song is transliterated in Aramaic as follows: "*zᵉmárnan lᵉkṓn wᵉlā raqqēdtûn ʿᵃlénan wᵉlā ʾarqēdtûn.*" Jeremias, *NT Theology,* 26.

[934] Ibid.

or *Shaliach*, and no matter whether one is ascetic or a participant of the culture.[935]

Matthew 11:2–19 far exceeded expectations when considering the mnemonic and rhythmic patterns in the text. Witherington goes so far as to claim that everything from the six parallel clauses and a closing remark cast in poetic form speaks strongly to the Aramaic poetry so characteristic of Jesus's teaching style.[936] Therefore, there is no hesitation in ascribing to the text a passing grade for the fourth test, attaining 5 points. The text now stands at a record of 4-0 which permits it to enter the yellow zone of authentic probability.

Aramaic/Hebraic Literary Characteristics

The fourth test indicated the level by which Matthew 11:2–19 exhibits poetic patterns that are indicative of Aramaic literary characteristics. From the degree of material shown, the passage already shows signs that it passes the fifth test. However, other traits of the text also indicate an underlying Aramaic tradition undergirding the written material.

First, Matthew 11:11 typifies the Jewish rhetoric of antiquity. Carl Kraeling notes that in the Mekhilta, "we have statements about both Joseph and Moses that use the same expression … 'there is not among his brethren one greater than he,' and about Moses 'there is not in Israel one greater than he.'"[937] Also, Black made a connection between γεννητοῖς γυναικῶν in 11:11 and the usage of the same phrase in Exodus 14:29 and the poetic *haggada* of the Targum.[938] Thus, the phrase "no one greater than John the Baptist has appeared" (11:11) finds a home in the literary characteristics of Jewish literature.

The following Aramaic attributes of the passage are found in Black's material. Second, the prepositional form διὰ τῶν μαθητῶν αὐτοῦ matches the literary form as found in the Palestinian Talmud, particularly in *Bikkurim* 1.6.64 and *Makkoth* 2.[939] The connection is quite compelling. Third, and most impressively, the phrase καὶ μακάριός ἐστιν ὃς ἐὰν μὴ σκανδαλισθῇ ἐν ἐμοί (11:6) concludes an Aramaic based four-line stanza which connects with Matthew 5:11, Luke 6:22, and Luke 7:22.[940] The Aramaic nature is best seen in

---

[935] Keener, *GMSRC,* 341.

[936] Witherington, III, *Christology of Jesus,* 43.

[937] Carl H. Kraeling, *John the Baptist* (New York, NY: Charles Scribner's Sons, 1951), 139.

[938] Black, *Aramaic Approach to the Gospels and Acts,* 298.

[939] Ibid., 115, 282.

[940] Ibid., 158.

the poetic development that was discussed in the last section. Fourth, the *anthropos tis* idiom is found in verse 8. Black notes that this idiom frequently occurs in the sayings of Jesus, especially in Mark and Q.[941] Fifth, the wordplay in verse 17 matches Aramaic paronomasia and puns found in Semitic literature.[942] The Old Syriac Peshitta shows the structure of verse 17 even better, as it says, "*z*^{e}*marn l*^{e}*khon w*^{e}*la raqqedhton, w*^{e}*lain l*^{e}*khon w*^{e}*la 'arqedhton.*"[943]

Numerous other examples could be given for the Aramaic traits and structure found in Matthew 11:2–19. Quite honestly, this researcher was overwhelmed at the number of characteristics found. The passage firmly passes the fifth test. A great deal of further research should be given to the Semitic patterns found in this passage. Outside of the Beatitudes and Lord's Prayer, no other passage has exhibited as strong a connection with Semitic literary characteristics as this text has. Chaulk up another 5 points for the passage. Thus, Matthew 11:2–19 finds itself not only with a passing grade for the fifth test but also with a current record of 5-0.

Semitic Cultural Concepts of First-Century Israel

Because Jesus's conversation was directed toward the disciples of John and his own disciples concerning the ministry of John the Baptist, the text does not hold as many cultural concepts as some of the other passages studied. However, that is not to say that there are no cultural connections to its first-century setting. A few areas of interest first include the generalized Jewish understanding that the Messiah's ministry would involve healing. Isaiah 61:1–2 leaves the door open for such an interpretation. However, a fragmentary portion of a scroll found in Qumran (4Q521) removes all doubt that such an interpretation was found in the days of Jesus. It states,

> [For the heav]ens and the earth will listen to his anointed one/Messiah … For he will glorify the pious on the throne of an eternal kingdom, liberating captives, restoring sight to the blind, straightening the be[nt] … And the Lord will do glorious things which have never been … he

941 Ibid., 298.

942 Ibid., 161.

943 Ibid.

will heal the wounded and give life to the dead, he will bring good news to the poor.[944]

Casey mentions a possible difficulty with this interpretation because the term אֲדֹנָי (*Adonai*) is used as the subject.[945] However, there is no reason to deny the belief that the Messiah was viewed as accomplishing these things as early Jewish believers would have seen such works being done through the power of the אֲדֹנָי. This understanding matches the interpretation that Jesus held of the prophesied messianic ministry.

Second, the wisdom motif that Jesus uses in verse 19 matches the practice of the first-century. Jesus said, "Yet wisdom is vindicated by her deeds" (11:19).[946] Two things can be said about Jesus's anthropomorphic depiction of wisdom. First, Jesus personifies wisdom (σοφία) in accordance with Proverbs 1:20–33; 8:1–9:12; and 9:1–12. In the book of Proverbs, wisdom is portrayed as a woman who calls out to "make her voice heard" (Prov. 8:2). She "calls out in the street; she makes her voice heard in the public squares" (Prov. 1:20). Later, Lady Wisdom is contrasted with Lady Folly in Proverbs 9. Wisdom's attributes are described in verses 1–12 and Folly's attributes are in verses 13–18. Wisdom is shown to promote faith (9:1, 10),[947] life (9:11, 18), instruction (9:4–9), and decorum (9:2–3). Folly provides the opposite. The writer of Proverbs teaches that wisdom leads to certain deeds, which find a home with the teaching of Jesus in 11:19. Such wisdom motifs represent the *Sitz im Leben* of the time.[948] Additionally, the first-century BC Jewish theologian Philo of Alexandria held a similar view of wisdom, which relates to his view of the *Logos*. Philo believed in two supreme divine powers—goodness and authority.[949] The *Logos*, or reason, brought the two together. The divine powers of God were shown in a form that resembled both Lady Wisdom and Christian literature.[950] Certainly, Philo was not influenced by the Christian tradition, a claim that would be anachronistic. However, his personification of wisdom and the *Logos*

---

[944] 4Q521, in Casey, *Jesus of Nazareth,* 272.

[945] Casey, *Jesus of Nazareth,* 272–273.

[946] καὶ ἐδικαιώθη ἡ σοφία ἀπὸ τῶν ἔργων αὐτῆς.

[947] The notion of pillars possibly refers to the building of the temple.

[948] Witherington, III, *Christology of Jesus,* 223.

[949] Philo of Alexandria, "Cherubim 1.27," *Works of Philo,* Charles Duke Yonge, trans (Peabody, MA: Hendrickson, 1993), 83.

[950] Particularly the introduction of John's Gospel and the Colossians creed (Col. 1:15–20).

principle matches Jesus's statement and the understanding by certain segments of Judaism in the first-century.

Third, Matthew 11:2–19 matches the cultural milieu of the time in the Jewish view.[951] that God determined the role that an individual would play while accepting that the divine decree of God in no way impeded the freedom that each individual held to accept and fulfill that role. Certainly, Jesus held that God called both John and him to the roles they held.[952] But he also pointed to the means by which they lived out their roles—John as an ascetic and Jesus as a person living within the social community (11:18–19). He also pointed to the actions of the violent seeking to dethrone the kingdom (11:12), but their actions fit within the plan of God. Josephus noted that the general Jewish populace held that God determined all things by fate, but that did not remove each person's responsibility from acting as one saw fit.[953]

Other areas of cultural assimilation are found, including Christ's rejection of the kingdom coming by a violent revolution,[954] the debate over John's relationship to the end-times,[955] and the use of hyperbolic and superlative praise for John the Baptist.[956] Nonetheless, for the purpose of the intended sixth test, sufficient evidence has been provided to show that the text connects back to concepts held in the time of early first-century Israel. With that in mind, the passage passes the sixth test, earns 4 points, and maintains a

---

[951] Particularly of the Pharisees.

[952] An example is found in the divine fulfillment in the role that John played as a messenger to the Messiah, in what he viewed as a fulfillment of Malachi 3:1 (11:10).

[953] "They also pay a respect to such as are in years; nor are they so bold as to contradict them in anything which they have introduced; and, when they determine that all things are done by fate, they do not take away the freedom from men of acting as they think fit; since their notion is, that it hath pleased God to make a temperament, whereby what he wills is done, but so that the will of men can act virtuously or viciously." Josephus, *Antiq.* 18.12b–13, *The Works of Josephus,* 477.

[954] Keener, *GMSRC,* 339; Oscar Cullmann, *The State in the New Testament* (New York, NY: Charles Scribner's Sons, 1956), 20–21; Otto Betz, *What Do We Know About Jesus?* (Philadelphia, PA; London, UK: Westminster, SCM, 1968), 53.

[955] Keener, *GMSRC,* 333–334.

[956] "Jesus' contemporaries and successors developed hyperbolic and superlative praise still further: rabbis called Johanan ben Zakkai "the least" of Hillel's eighty disciples not to demean Johanan but to praise Hillel as a teacher (ARN 28, §57B)." Keener, *GMSRC,* 339.

record of 6-0. That's already enough to permit it to pass into the green zone of probability for both tests.

Similarities to NT Creeds, Summaries, and Early Literature

As amazing as this journey has been, it is now time to place the last passage of Scripture in this study under the last test. Looking first at Cullmann's thematic approach to ancient creeds and early apostolic preaching, Matthew 11:2–9 does not necessarily match the criteria for baptisms and catechesis. The text does not appear to hold a baptismal confession of any sense. Such would require a confession that was comparable to Simon Peter's proclamation of Jesus being the Messiah in Matthew 16:16. Additionally, the text does not hold any of the traits that would be necessary for regular worship—liturgy and preaching.[957] No exorcisms are mentioned in the text, so it does not match Cullmann's third theme either.

The text does seem to match the theme of persecution—the fourth theme.[958] For instance, Jesus does speak of the rejection of both John and Jesus's ministry despite their different lifestyles (11:18–19). He also provides a poem that speaks of the people's rejection of God's prophetic ministry through both Jesus and John (11:17). The text also appears to match the fifth theme of polemics even more.[959] As was alluded to in the last test, the early debate over John the Baptist's relationship with Jesus was something that spilled over into later decades. Jesus acknowledged that John was a major prophet who fulfilled Malachi's prophecy of one who announced the advent of the Messiah.[960]

However, the evangelist preserved Jesus's teaching to potentially combat the opinion of the disciples of John. Some considered that it was John the Baptist who was, in fact, the Messiah. Though dated to the fourth-century, the Pseudo-Clementine literature describes the disciples of John the Baptist as holding this view. The text reads, "Yea, some even of the disciples of John, who seemed to be great ones, have separated themselves from the people, and proclaimed their own master as the Christ. But all these schisms have been prepared, that by means of them the faith of Christ and baptism might be

[957] Cullmann, *Earliest Christian Confessions,* 18.

[958] Ibid., 25–30.

[959] Ibid., 30.

[960] Casey, *Jesus of Nazareth,* 354.

hindered."[961] The book of Acts shows the probability that the disciples of John continued their lineage apart from that of Jesus, potentially indicating an early belief that John was the Messiah.[962] Matthew 11 shows the distinction between the camp of John's disciples and Jesus's own. If the movement was early enough, then Matthew may have used this early Jesus tradition about the interaction between Jesus and John as a polemic device.[963] Thus, the text connects with what one would anticipate with early Jesus material and not from later Christian inventions.[964]

Also, as has been previously noted, the text matches the structural patterns of early material. For instance, Matthew 11:4–6 contains rhythmic patterns that match Jewish poetic structures.[965] Verses 4–6 also afford early Christian convictions of the work and ministry of Jesus of Nazareth.[966] Verse 17 also shows signs of similar poetic structures, which provides an interesting case for its connection with the poetic structure of early traditions. As previously noted, the wisdom motif of verse 19 also speaks not only to the text's early Semitic structural patterns but also corroborates with the first-

---

[961] *Recognitions of Clement* 1.54, Pseudo-Clementine Literature, in *Fathers of the Third and Fourth Centuries: The Twelve Patriarchs, Excerpts and Epistles, the Clementina, Apocrypha, Decretals, Memoirs of Edessa and Syriac Documents, Remains of the First Ages*, The Ante-Nicene Fathers, vol. 8, Alexander Roberts, James Donaldson, and A. Cleveland Coxe, eds, M. B. Riddle, trans (Buffalo, NY: Christian Literature Company, 1886), 92.

[962] Speaking of Apollos, it is said that "he had been instructed in the way of the Lord; and being fervent in spirit, he was speaking and teaching accurately about Jesus, although he know only John's baptism" (Acts 18:25). Also, the distinction between John's baptism of water and Jesus's baptism of the Spirit is in view in Acts 19. Paul asked some of the disciples in Ephesus, "'Did you receive the Holy Spirit when you believed?' 'No,' they told him, 'we haven't even heard that there is a Holy Spirit.' 'Into what then were you baptized?' he asked them. 'Into John's baptism,' they replied. Paul said, 'John baptized with a baptism of repentance, telling the people that they should believe in the one who would come after him, that is, in Jesus'" (Acts 19:2–4).

[963] Kloppenborg Verbin avers that Matthew 11:2–19 served a major role in the organization of the Gospel. Many of the stories, he argues, were maneuvered to anticipate the response that Jesus provided to the disciples of John. Kloppenborg Verbin, *Excavating Q*, 72, fn 22.

[964] Keener, *GMSRC*, 334; Witherington adds, "The absence of any concluding response of or reply by the Baptist points to the primitiveness of the narrative." Witherington, III, *Christology of Jesus*, 165; E. P. Sanders, *The Historical Figure of Jesus* (New York, NY: Penguin, 1993), 94.

[965] Longenecker, *New Wine into Fresh Wineskins*, 10.

[966] Ibid., 11.

century understanding of the *Logos/wisdom* principle. Because of the thematic and structural relationships with early *homologia* and credal material, Matthew 11:2–19 fared extremely well with the final test. The pericope earns 5 more points and clinches a perfect score of 30! Therefore, the passage strongly meshes well within the green zone of probability.

Conclusion and Color Assignment

Matthew 11:4–6 and 11:9–13 are generally held to be part of Q. Could this be one of the reasons that the text scored so highly? Possibly. As a recap, the text passed the first test due to the connections made with the rabbinic understanding that the Messiah's ministry would involve healing and those traits described in Isaiah 61:1–2. Also, the eschatological prophet was viewed to be the Elijah who was to come. Both concepts are found in the Matthean text.

The text passed the second test as the concept of the Messiah being the *Shaliach* of God found a relationship with the bipartite descriptions of Father and Son so commonly found in early Christian traditions. Jesus's understanding of him being the *Shaliach*, that is, the divine emissary of God, is found in his understanding of works and wonders accompanying his ministry. Also, his interpretation of the Messiah bringing forth the kingdom of heaven as a divine agent relates directly with his bipartite relationship between Father and Son.

Ironically, the only explicit title mentioned in the text did not permit it to pass the third test. The title Son of Man was used as an idiom rather than an eschatological title in this case. However, two implicit titles allowed the text to pass, including the Suffering Servant motif and Jesus's role as prophet. Both roles are found within the didactic of the earliest church and are connected to the teaching ministry of Jesus himself.

The text passed the fourth test by exhibiting a four-beat pattern in 11:4–6, a pattern that Jesus often used in his teachings. Additionally, 11:16–17 reveals meter and rhyme that indicates a Semitic poetic device. The fifth test closely aligns with the fourth. Numerous areas showed literary characteristics common with Semitic literature. Jewish rhetoric of antiquity was shown in 11:11. Prepositional forms matched early literary structural patterns. A four-line stanza is in 11:5. The Son of Man idiom aligned with the use of idioms in Galilee during Jesus's day. Lastly, the wordplay in the passage was not only indicative of Semitic literary patterns but also relates to the Sermon on the Mount in 5:17.

The text passed the sixth test with its link with Isaiah 61:1–2 as has proven beneficial in other tests. The wisdom motif of 11:19 matches the cultural concepts of the time, particularly with Philo of Alexandria and other early writings of the time. The connection between divine sovereignty and human freedom in the text aligned with the Pharisaical viewpoint on the matter.

Finally, the seventh test was passed due to its thematic alignment with early polemics. Moreover, the patterns of the texts, especially in 11:4–6 and 11:9–19, match the rhythmic patterns and *homologiai* of early Christian material. Having passed all the tests, Matthew 11:2–19 fared extremely well and scores extremely high on the probability that the contents of the passage stem from early Jesus traditions. The connection with Q makes it even more probable that the content is extremely early.

Conclusion

With other passages of this study, it was largely prognosticated quite accurately how the study would unfold. It was anticipated that the Sermon on the Mount and the Son of Man sayings were scored higher than the parables, especially when considering the probability that the informal controlled method of oral traditions was the most accurate. However, the interactions that Jesus held with other individuals were the wild card of the study. There was a bit of fear when approaching these Jesuan interactions. Would these conversations prove the skeptical admonishment of the Jesus Seminar correct? Would one be left without any semblance of connection with early material? If this occurred, the research would not be necessarily dealt a knockout punch, but it would be given a crushing blow. Surprisingly, the interactions of Jesus allowed the research to score a few punishing hooks and connecting uppercuts to the belief that all Gospel traditions are late.

The exchange between Jesus and Peter in Matthew 16:13–23 matched some of the confessional characteristics found in early credal material. While it failed to account for the mnemonic and rhythmic patterns often found in early material, it may have been that this conversation was easily remembered without it. Nonetheless, the passage passed 6 out of 7 tests, granting it a good chance of containing early material. Statistically, the text would score around an 86% probability given the parameters of this study.

The interaction between Jesus and the disciples of John has often been a favorite for this writer. However, it was not expected that it was fare as well as it did. The Jesuanic sayings of the passage found a huge connection with early theological topics of the early first-century, particularly the Messiah's connection with healing and evangelistic proclamation as foretold in Isaiah 61:1–2. Furthermore, the poetic and rhythmic patterns matched the criteria so well that portions of the text were featured as case studies in Longenecker's work..[967] Scoring well in all the tests placed before it, Matthew 11:2–19 can be connected to early Jesus traditions beyond a reasonable doubt. The numerical

[967] See Longenecker, *New Wine into Fresh Wineskins,* 41, 79.

percentage would score in the high 90s. This researcher feels confident to give it a percentage of 95–99% of holding ancient material passed along by oral traditions.

Before fully concluding this research, a few connections need to be made. In the last chapter, a review will be given of all the texts examined in this study. Then, a few concluding points will be made to connect this body of research to some theological and, especially, apologetic points when considering the authenticity and validation of the Jesus traditions undergirding the Gospel texts, especially that of Matthew's Gospel.

CHAPTER SIX
SEMITIC RESIDUE, INERRANCY, AND THE RELIABILITY OF THE GOSPELS

The journey has now come to an end. Nine passages of Scripture were tested through seven parameters. As noted in the first chapter, it has been argued that the Gospel of Matthew contains Semitic residue that points back to earlier Jesus traditions, originally uttered in Aramaic, that predate the finished written text. Each text produced varying results, but the question at hand is whether the texts produced sufficient results to deduce that such traditions exist. Historically speaking, it is difficult to know with absolute certainty that anything happened in the past or that certain strategies were employed. However, the more data that suggests that something happened in the past, the greater confidence one can have that the event transpired. Thus, one cannot claim with absolute certainty that the texts that scored well represent early Jesus traditions. Even still, this research shows that there are good reasons to suggest that at least some of the texts investigated do. After providing the results of the research, this concluding chapter will return to the idea of oral tradition theory and examine whether this research fits one of the three models previously given..[968] Then, the chapter and research will conclude with any theological reflections and apologetic ramifications. Finally, the research will conclude with areas that deserve further exploration.

Research Findings

Nine passages were divided into four chapters. Each text was graded according to the number of tests it passed. Scores of 1 through 3 were assigned the color red, indicating that the text held something along the lines of Semitic residue. However, its connection was possible at best. Scores of 4 and 5 were assigned the color yellow, showing that it was likely that the text held a connection to an early Semitic residue. Scores of 6 and 7 were given the color green which implied that the text held a strong connection to an early Semitic residue.

Chapter 2 featured two texts from the Sermon on the Mount. The Beatitudes (Matt. 5:1–12) were introduced in the first test. The Beatitudes of Jesus performed very well. They passed all seven tests. The research revealed the possibility that the Beatitudes, and even all of the Sermon on the Mount, could have been miniature sermon summaries of various messages that Jesus preached at the location. One can envision the possibility that Jesus may have held a revival or even a series of theological intensives for the disciples

[968] As a recap, the three models include Bultmann's informal uncontrolled model, the Scandinavian formal controlled model, and the mediating view presented by Kenneth Bailey entitled the informal controlled model.

throughout his time at the locale. Like its other Sermon on the Mount counterpart, the Lord's Prayer also performed very well. The Lord's Prayer also scored a perfect seven on the tests. Jesus seemed to exhibit a self-understanding that he fulfilled the role of the *Shaliach* of Yahweh in the prayer. Both passages in the Sermon on the Mount were far more eschatological than previously expected.

Chapter 3 was the largest of all the chapters in this study. It showcased three of the Matthean parables. Unlike the Sermon on the Mount, the parables struggled to perform as well as the first two passages did. The third examined passage was the Parable of the Harvest in Matthew 13:24–30, 36–40. The Parable of the Harvest struggled from the beginning. It was one of the few texts that did not overtly hold any connection to rabbinic material..[969] The Parable of the Harvest did pass the Christological and theological tests. But the only other test it would pass would be the fifth test (Aramaic/Hebraic Literary Structures). The Parable of the Harvest is the only text to have scored in the red in this study. The fourth passage was the Parable of the Compassionate Employer (Matt. 20:1–16). This parable only surpassed the previous passage by one test. The Parable of the Compassionate Employer passed the first, second, fifth, and sixth tests..[970] Due to its 4 for 7 score, the parable found itself in the yellow zone. The final parable, the fifth text overall, was the Parable of the Wise and Foolish Young Women (Matt. 25:1–13)..[971] Of the parables studied, this one fared the best of them all. Remarkably, it passed the first six tests but could not find the connection needed to allow it to pass the final one. The Parable of the Wise and Foolish Young Women was the only parable to make it to the green zone.

Chapter 4 orbited around the Son of Man sayings in Matthew. A project took time to take an excursus to denote the importance and controversy surrounding the Son of Man sayings. The passages in this chapter scored very well. Both the sixth text, Exorcism and the Unpardonable Sin (Matt. 12:22–40), and the seventh text, Coming of the Son of Man (Matt. 24:27, 30–44), passed all but the fourth test. Neither exhibited any evidence of mnemonic and rhythmic patterns. Interestingly, the fourth test has proven to be the most difficult. The third, fourth, sixth, seventh, and eighth passages all failed the

[969] One could argue that this makes it more exclusive to Jesus. Be that as it may, this does not help the cause of the first test as it was to look for unique teachings within a rabbinic understanding.

[970] I.e., Unique Rabbinic Concepts, Early Christological Concepts, Aramaic/Hebraic Literary Characteristics, and Semitic Cultural Concepts.

[971] Also known as the Parable of the Ten Bridesmaids.

fourth test. Both passages in Chapter 4 scored 6 for 7, placing them in the green zone of probability.

Chapter 5, the last major chapter of the work, featured two interactions that Jesus had. The first text, the eighth overall, featured the interaction that Jesus had with Peter and the disciples at Caesarea Philippi (Matt. 16:13–23). As with the Son of Man passages, the interaction between Jesus and Peter passed every test except for the elusive fourth one. The ninth passage of Scripture to be tested was Jesus's interaction with the disciples of John the Baptist (Matt. 11:2–19). The last passage matched the first two in its connection with Semitic residue, because it passed all seven tests, even the pesky test for mnemonic and rhythmic patterns.

Now for the moment of truth. What do these scores tallied together say about the overall probability that the Gospel of Matthew contains early Semitic residue that points to early traditions that predate the text, at least according to the texts that were examined? Taking all the scores together from this research, 1 of the 7 texts was labeled red, 1 of the 7 texts was labeled yellow, and 7 of the 9 texts scored in the green zone of authenticity. Therefore, the overall research found more texts ranked high in the probability that they hold early Jesus traditions, whereas only 2 either likely or possibly held some link to early Jesus traditions. However, when we plug the different texts in a weighted scale, where tests emphasizing connections with the structure of Aramaisms and mnemonic devices, while also comparing the text with the established early Christology of the church, we then find that even the text that scored in the red finds a home in the yellow zone. All being said, we find a strong probability that many of the teachings and deeds of Jesus in the Gospel of Matthew date back to earlier oral traditions that predate the Gospel text. The following charts lay out the data for a better evaluation.

Text	Score	Color Assignment
Beatitudes	7	Green
Lord's Prayer	7	Green
Parable of Harvest	3	Red
Parable of Employer	4	Yellow
Parable of Bridesmaids	6	Green
Exorcism/Unpardoned Sin	6	Green
Coming of Son of Man	6	Green
Jesus and Peter	6	Green
Jesus and John's Disciples	7	Green

Weighted Score			
Scripture	**Results**	**Score**	**Color**
Beatitudes	2-5-4-5-5-4-5	30	Green
Lord's Prayer	2-5-4-5-5-4-5	30	Green
Parable of Harvest	0-5-4-0-5-0-0	14	Yellow
Parable of Employer	2-5-0-0-5-4-0	16	Yellow
Parable of Bridesmaids	2-5-4-5-5-4-0	25	Green
Exorcism/Unpardonable Sin	2-5-4-0-5-4-5	25	Green
Coming of Son of Man	2-5-4-0-5-4-5	25	Green
Jesus & Peter	2-5-4-0-5-4-5	25	Green
Jesus & John's Disciples	2-5-4-5-5-4-5	30	Green

Which Oral Tradition Model Best Fits the Data?

Earlier in this work, I noted five models of oral traditions were mentioned—three universally recognized with two additional models added. The first came from Rudolf Bultmann. Contending that almost nothing could be known about the "life and personality of Jesus".[972] from the early oral traditions, his position is called the informal uncontrolled model..[973] The model contends that the early church did not hold a formalized method of preserving the early traditions of Jesus. Rather, the transmission was uncontrolled without a basis for safekeeping the truths of Jesus of Nazareth..[974] This model can be likened to the telling of a rumor or informal story. Each person and/or community would have been free to tell the story in any style that they chose.

On the opposite end of the spectrum, one finds the formal controlled model..[975] Birger Gerhardsson and the Scandinavian school popularized this position. According to this position, communities would preserve traditions they felt important by transmitting them according to a methodological and educational framework that ensured that the stories were kept true, and the voice of their teachers was held intact..[976] The transmission was formal in the sense that it was kept secure by a group of appointed teachers and it was controlled in the sense that those transmitting the material were not allowed to add or take away from the stories and teachings.

Between the two models is one that blends part of the former and the latter. Kenneth Bailey popularized a model that he called the informal control model..[977] The transmission is informal in the sense that there is no established teacher..[978] However, the community keeps the information controlled as the body of elders upholds and maintains the integrity of the stories..[979] Bailey observed this practice continued in Middle Eastern communities to this day.

---

972 Bultmann, *Jesus and the Word,* 8.

973 Bailey, "Informal Controlled Oral Tradition and the Synoptic Gospels," *Themilios* 20, 2: 4.

974 Ibid., 5.

975 Ibid.

976 Gerhardsson, *Memory and Manuscript,* 76.

977 Bailey, "Informal Controlled Oral Tradition and the Synoptic Gospels," *Themelios* 20, 2: 6.

978 Ibid.

979 Ibid.

These gatherings are called the *haflat samar*.[980] Despite the community's commitment to accurate preservation, some flexibility is granted in cases of parables to allow for an emotional connection to be established with the listeners.[981] However, names, essential details, and the flow of the story could not be changed. Nothing greater than 15 percent could be changed by the storyteller.[982] While some flexibility was allowed with parables and the like, little to no flexibility was permitted with poems, proverbs, and ethical and theological teachings.[983] In a shame-honor culture, a person who erred in their telling of the story was shamed and called out for their mistake, just as happens in Middle Eastern culture to this day.[984]

However, we also acknowledged that Michael Licona's approach with the Gospel texts could indicate the arrival of another model pertaining to the transmission of early Jesus traditions, one that is maintained by a select group of Gospel writers, but is more adaptable and accepting of fallacious material in the preserved traditions. This view is more conservative than Bultmann's but is more flexible than what Bailey would accept. Remember, Bailey did not believe that any major fact was changed in the oral traditions.[985] Rather, only minor details were tweaked to clarify material and for storytelling purposes. Therefore, we donned Licona's approach with the title "formal controlled model."

Lastly, as I have noted throughout this research, I believe that Gerhardsson and Bailey's models can be combined. The two models are not as far apart as one might expect. Thus, this leads us to a model that I will call the semiformal controlled model. Are there reasons for accepting a that a semiformal controlled approach can be undertaken? Yes, if there are some comparable similarities between the two.

Before examining the present research with the aforementioned models, we should examine to see if there are any similarities between the

---

[980] Ibid.

[981] Ibid., 7.

[982] Ibid.

[983] Ibid.

[984] Ibid.

[985] Ibid.

Scandinavian formal controlled model and Bailey's informal controlled model. At least a couple of similarities rise to the surface.

First, Bailey observes that Middle Eastern culture uses both models even now.[986] Thus, both models are more likely to be used than Bultmann's informal uncontrolled method. I took a unit of Clinical Pastoral Education in Psychospiritual Care at Wake Forest School of Medicine after completing my dissertation—the very content on which this book is built. One of the students in class was a Muslim chaplain serving the Islamic students at Wake Forest University. This young woman had lived many years in the Middle East and had loved ones still residing there. I defended my dissertation as I first started the program. After learning about my successful defense and obtaining my Doctor of Philosophy degree, the class asked about my dissertation. After mentioning my dissertation and the method defended by Bailey's informal controlled model and the blend with the formal controlled model, the young Muslim lady smiled and said, "You described exactly how we preserve oral traditions to this day. Someone is responsible for telling the story, and the community ensures that he tells it correctly." Thus, the elders and the community they serve work in harmony to preserve accurate information. They also work to confirm that future generations will hear of the traditions they hold so sacred.

Second, the models of Bailey and the Scandinavians have more in common than one might think. On the one hand, Bailey's description is more formalized than one might envision. For instance, he states that the elders are those telling the stories and the congregation is the one listening.[987] This establishes a teacher-student relationship as mentioned by Gerhardsson and the Scandinavian school.[988] On the other hand, Gerhardsson is more open to flexibility than one might think.

For instance, he argues that the gospel tradition holds more in common with the more flexible haggadic material than the more stringent halakhic material.[989] He accepts that certain variations occurred with the redaction of the evangelists.[990] Even still, the gospel writers "worked on the basis of a fixed, distinct tradition from, and about, Jesus—a tradition which

---

[986] Ibid., 6.

[987] Ibid., 6.

[988] Gerhardsson, *Memory and Manuscript,* 76.

[989] Ibid., 335.

[990] Ibid.

was partly memorized and partly written down in notebooks and private scrolls, but invariably isolated from the teachings of other doctrinal authorities.".[991]

Additionally, from the earliest church, it was noted that Jesus chose Twelve disciples to pass along his teachings. Certainly, these apostles held authority as the safekeepers of Jesus traditions. He also chose 72 more early disciples to spread the gospel message (Lk. 10:1–23). Thus, one would assume that the earliest model was slightly more formal than Bailey concedes but more flexible as both the apostles and communities remembered their interactions with Jesus.

Seeing that Jesus chose the Twelve disciples along with 72 other disciples to preserve his teachings and deeds—as was common in with rabbinic traditions—then we must deduce that something more formal than Bailey's model was at play. However, since even the Twelve and 72 were a community selected to serve as the caretakers of these traditions, we cannot strictly say that a few formalized people oversaw these traditions in the Scandinavian sense. Therefore, I suggest a model that combines Bailey's informal controlled model and the Scandinavian formal controlled model, which I will call the semiformal controlled model. The semiformal controlled model blends the community model of Bailey and the more controlled methodology as was comparable with rabbinic models of the day as posited by Gerhardsson and the Scandinavians. A semiformal model uses the communities of disciples, apostles, and eyewitnesses as the caretakers of the Jesus traditions. We also have evidence to suggest this was the case. For instance, Papias speaks of the importance the second-generation Christians placed on hearing the words of the first-generation disciples, particularly those who had walked with Christ. Papias reflects the following:

> If, then, any one who had attended on the elders came, I asked minutely after their sayings—what Andrew or Peter said, or what was said by Philip, or by Thomas, or by James, or by John, or by Matthew, or by any of the Lord's disciples: which things Aristion and the presbyter John, the disciples of the Lord, say. For I imagined that what was to be got from books was not so profitable to me as what came from the living and abiding voice..[992]

In his fragments, Papias also speaks of unwritten traditions. Eusebius, the one who preserved the fragments of Papias, suggested that some of the

---

[991] Ibid.

[992] Papias, "Fragments of Papias I," *Ante-Nicene Fathers,* vol. 1, Logos; also available at https://www.newadvent.org/fathers/0125.htm.

unwritten traditions seemed a bit bizarre and others a bit fanciful.[993] Granted, one should note that Eusebius was skeptical of Papias's eschatological views, which may in part reflect Eusebius's cynicism. Nonetheless, the fragments of Papias disclose the formal role that the apostles and communities held in preserving accurate information about Jesus's words and deeds and filtering out those traditions that were not strongly tied to Jesus. Thus, a semiformal controlled methodology is both warranted and justified.

This research suggests that while the informal controlled model and the formal controlled model are both detected, the data from the Gospels suggest that something more controlled and formalized is present in the material. Therefore, the informal uncontrolled methodology of Rudolf Bultmann and the German school is invalidated and disproven. The Gospel of Matthew and the Gospel of Luke do cast the Sermon on the Mount with a few differences. Nonetheless, their key data points are the same. The same holds true with the interactions that Jesus had with Peter and the disciples of John, as well as the Son of Man teachings. However, in line with the observation of Bailey's informal controlled model of oral tradition, the parables exercised greater fluidity with far less control points than the other passages. Our proposed semiformal controlled method would also allow for this flexibility in storytelling. This would precisely fall in line with what one would anticipate if one were to adopt the informal controlled model or the semiformal controlled model.

But what does the data in this research indicate? If Bultmann's model is correct, then one might expect to find mainly reds and even perhaps some pericopes that do not even match any of the criteria set in place. If Licona's model is correct as it pertains to the transmission of early traditions, then one might expect to find mainly reds and yellows. If Bailey's model is correct, then we would expect to find mainly yellows with a few greens. If Gerhardsson's model is correct, then we should find nearly all greens. However, if the semiformal controlled model that I suggest is correct, then we should find a blend of mostly greens with some yellows. As you can see from the chart above, the semiformal controlled model makes the best sense of the data at hand. According to the tallied test, 7 of the 9 reviewed texts scored in the green (77 percent). 1 of 9 scored in the red (11 percent), and 1 of 9 scored in the yellow (11 percent). However, when we look at the weighted score, 7 of the 9 scored in the green (77 percent), while 2 of the texts scored in the yellow (22 percent). That is what we would expect to find in a semiformal controlled model.

Does this pose a problem when it comes to biblical inerrancy? This question along with a few others will be addressed in the apologetic portion of

993 Ibid., "Fragments of Papias VI."

this chapter. Nonetheless, this research suggests that Bultmann's theory should be rejected in favor of Bailey and Gerhardsson's.

Theological Discoveries

The research crossed over into several theological areas. Due to the tests conducted and the scope of research, very little space was afforded to discuss any theological discoveries that were made. A couple of personal theological reflections are warranted before concluding the work.

First, the research revealed the focus that Jesus placed on the kingdom of God rather than the political kingdoms of the world. Many of the disciples anticipated a military ruler, as evidenced by Peter's refusal to accept Jesus's sacrifice on the cross (Matt. 15:22). From the Beatitudes to the interactions of Jesus with John's disciples, Jesus placed a greater focus on the kingdom than on political entities. In stark contrast to the Jesus Seminar's assessment, Jesus is far more focused on theological matters than political and socioeconomic matters..[994] For Jesus, the kingdom of God is on earth now through the people of God. He ushered in the kingdom through his messianic ministry. Furthermore, the kingdom will be fully actualized in the eschaton. At that time, God will right all the wrongs of society. While it is not wrong for Christians to be involved in politics, it should not be the primary focus of the child of God. A person who is a citizen of the Kingdom of God will ultimately be victorious over all the evil powers of culture and society. As Augustine of Hippo writes, "And therefore it is that humility is specially recommended to the city of God as it sojourns in this world, and is specially exhibited in the city of God, and in the person of Christ its King; while the contrary vice of pride, according to the testimony of the sacred writings, specially rules his adversary the devil.".[995] Thus, as suggested by Augustine and modeled by Jesus, modern evangelicals would do well to place their primary emphasis on the kingdom of God rather than the kingdoms of the world.

Second, it was fascinating to see the emphasis that Jesus placed on his role as the *Shaliach* of God. Even regarding the unpardonable sin, Jesus emphasized the role of the Holy Spirit moving from the authority of the Father. When Christ performed miracles, it appeared that the Triune God was at work. The miracles were performed by the authority of God, the power of the Spirit, and by the command and operation of Jesus being the emissary, or *Shaliach,* of God. Thus, theologically, the Triune nature of God may have been involved

---

[994] See Funk, Hoover, and the Jesus Seminar, *Five Gospels,* 139.

[995] Augustine of Hippo, "The City of God 14.13.1," in *St. Augustine's City of God and Christian Doctrine*, A Select Library of the Nicene and Post-Nicene Fathers of the Christian Church, First Series, vol. 2, Philip Schaff, ed, Marcus Dods, trans, (Buffalo, NY: Christian Literature Company, 1887), 273–284.

with the signs and wonders that Jesus performed, even though the bipartite relationship between Father and Son was more heavily emphasized by the earliest church. These two reflections are something that joins those issues that deserve further attention in future studies. Nonetheless, Jesus exhibited his humility by conveying his ministry as the *Shaliach* of God rather than the title of the Messiah. Perhaps Jesus's refusal to elevate himself to a high status while also recognizing his divine relationship with the Father is behind the humility communicated of him in the early Philippians hymn (Phil. 2:6–11). It may be impossible to say for sure, but it does cause one to stop and consider the possibility.

Apologetic Ramifications

The present work holds three major apologetic ramifications for those who may doubt the authenticity of the Gospel texts. It can answer three questions that modern skeptics often hold. First, should one be concerned with the differences found in the Gospels? The literary approach to this question has centered around possible sharing among the evangelists.[996] However, the study on oral traditions may furnish alternative ways to approach this issue. For instance, while it could be that Matthew embellished earlier traditions preserved in Luke's Gospel, it is also quite possible that Matthew and Luke conserve two different versions articulated by Jesus. Given that the portions of the Sermon on the Mount could bear summarizations of various messages that Jesus spoke over time, it is probable, if not likely, that Jesus repeated his messages with possible alterations for different audiences. If this is the case, then there would not be necessarily one original tradition, but multiple original traditions.[997]

Considering this point, I would also take issue with some of the methods used by Michael Licona in his recent book *Jesus, Contradicted,* primarily with his rejection of harmonization efforts. Concerning the Sermon on the Mount, Licona seems to posit that Jesus only gave one sermon on a plain and that Matthew placed him on a mountain for dramatic effect. He goes on to say that while we may suggest that Matthew tells of a sermon on a mountain and Luke of a sermon on a plain, such harmonization, Licona states, "seem a bit of a stretch to me."[998] Yet, Licona's assessment seems to be more of a polemic against harmonizers of the Gospels than the data. As this research noted, the

---

[996] See Licona, *Why Are There Differences in the Gospels* and McGrew, *The Mirror or the Mask.*

[997] Werner Kelber makes the same argument. See Werner H. Kelber, *The Oral and the Written Gospel* (Philadelphia, PA: Fortress, 1983), 29.

[998] Michael Licona, *Jesus, Contradicted: Why the Gospels Tell the Same Story Differently* (Grand Rapids, MI: Zondervan Academic, 2024), 74.

Sermon on the Mount may be a collection of numerous messages that Jesus delivered on a hillside. And remember, Jesus was an itinerate preacher, meaning that he likely preached the same message to different people in different places over time, and likely included many variations within his messages..[999] If we concede that the Gospel writers relied on early oral traditions, then what they preserve are eyewitness testimonies—their own and those from other eyewitnesses. While I do not take issue with the use of literary devices as Licona presents,.[1000] Licona's belief that the Evangelists only used literary devices without considering the traditions they preserve suggests that the Evangelists wrote in isolation from their communities. This concept becomes problematic for several reasons.

For one, the informal controlled, formal controlled, and semiformal controlled methodologies include the communities to a much greater degree. Benjamin Laird argues that it is likely that the "in light of what may be determined about the manner in which ancient writings were composed and how authors acquired relevant information, it is plausible that many of the biblical writers consulted with those who could provide eyewitness testimony of certain events or insight related to recent developments or subjects that need to be addressed." Given Laird's research, the inclusion of a writer and community in the composition of the Gospels finds a home with the

[999] Serving as a minister myself, I have used the same message in different locations and have tweaked the message each time that I have delivered it. If someone were documenting my message in these different locations, similar alterations would be found as are found in Matthew's presentation of the Sermon on the Mount compared to Luke's. Certain illustrations have been used with different messages, including my infamous story of losing a tire on my lawnmower, which nearly ended with me colliding with a tree.

[1000] In fact, authors use literary devices in other genres of Scripture, including the historical narratives and prophecies of the Old Testament. If one were to look, I suspect you would find these devices used in all manner of literature.

semiformal controlled, informal controlled, and even the formal controlled methodologies of oral tradition transmission.[1001]

Additionally, Licona goes beyond paraphrasing and telescoping with his understanding of flexibility.[1002] In his book *The Resurrection of Jesus,* Licona suggests that Matthew added the resurrection of the saints in Matthew 27:52–53 as "special effects' with eschatological Jewish texts and thoughts in mind."[1003] I do not add this as a means to disparage Licona or disregard his scholarly work. Even though I do not always agree with his interpretations, I hold the highest respect for him as an individual, a scholar, and as a brother-in-Christ. However, numerous scholars have expressed concern over this take as it seems to suggest that the Evangelists falsified the material. Either the bodies of saints were raised after Jesus's crucifixion or not. And if Matthew reports that the saints raised from the dead and appeared to many others in Jerusalem after the time of Jesus's crucifixion and that did not happen (Matt. 27:52–53), then Matthew has introduced fallacious material to his Gospel narrative and presented it as a true historical event.

Yet if we accept that Matthew is reporting an early tradition that he heard from many of the eyewitnesses and wrote within a community of witnesses, then the event—regardless of how bizarre it may be—can be seen as representative of an early oral tradition related to the life of Jesus. Why should we question the character and integrity of the biblical writers, unless we have a solid reason to disregard their authenticity? It seems to me that we hold the Evangelists guilty until proven innocent instead of the other way around. Some may claim that the differences in the Gospels are sufficient of a reason to question the Gospel writers. However, if the Gospel writers are reporting early eyewitness testimonies from various strains, then we would not expect everything to align perfectly. Yet if this were the case, the door is increasingly opened to harmonization efforts as we work to unpack the events reported by the eyewitness testimonies.

Nonetheless, Licona's approach seems to introduce a fifth method to approach the oral traditions of Jesus—the formal uncontrolled method. Licona

---

[1001] Benjamin P. Laird, *Creating the Canon: Composition, Controversy, and the Authority of the New Testament* (Downers Grove, IL: IVP Academic, 2023), 41.

[1002] Telescoping is the shortening or contraction of concepts or events. Dr. Gary Yates, Professor of Old Testament at Liberty University, often likened telescoping to viewing two mountain peaks in the Blue Ridge Mountains. From a distance, the two peaks may look like they are next to each other. However, as one drives closer to the mountain peaks, the peaks would be shown to be several miles apart. In the same manner, prophets and historians alike may condense the events for ease of telling the story or to save space.

[1003] Licona, *The Resurrection of Jesus,* 552.

accepts that a formal group safeguarded the traditions and wrote them down in what we know to be the four Gospels. However, his arguments do not seem to place as much fixedness with the traditions of Jesus as do Bailey's informal controlled method, Gerhardsson's formal controlled method, and my blended semiformal controlled method. As earlier noted, Licona accepts that falsehoods could have been added for dramatic effect. Granted, the informal controlled, semiformal controlled, and even the formal controlled methods all allow for some flexibility with storytelling. However, the primary material does not change, and there is room for harmonization with a greater degree than the formal uncontrolled method allows.

To reiterate this point, this work is in no way trying to disparage Licona's work as a scholar and a person. Lord knows there has been way too much mudslinging in recent years. However, his take is merely added to show the overall apologetic landscape in recent years.

Therefore, we can say that there are at least five ways to navigate the transmission of oral traditions from the time of Jesus to today. The informal uncontrolled model of Rudolf Bultmann (the idea that no one was selected as the caretakers of the Jesus traditions and the traditions were told with little to no regard to the truth of what Jesus did or taught); the formal uncontrolled method of Michael Licona (the idea that the Evangelists served as the caretakers of the early Jesus traditions, but they freely used literary devices to include falsehoods for dramatic effect with some emphasis on historical fidelity); the informal controlled method of Kenneth Bailey (the idea that the Jesus traditions were preserved by communities rather than a select group, and they maintained fidelity with the historical events and voice of Jesus with no more than 15% flexibility); the formal controlled methodology of Birger Gerhardsson (the idea that the disciples followed the rabbinic traditions to memorize, document, and preserve the Jesus traditions with very little alterations); and my own semiformal controlled method (the idea that communities preserved numerous oral traditions but were safeguarded by the disciples chosen by Jesus and by fellow eyewitnesses, while permitting some flexibility with non-essential details). The chart below offers a visual of five views.

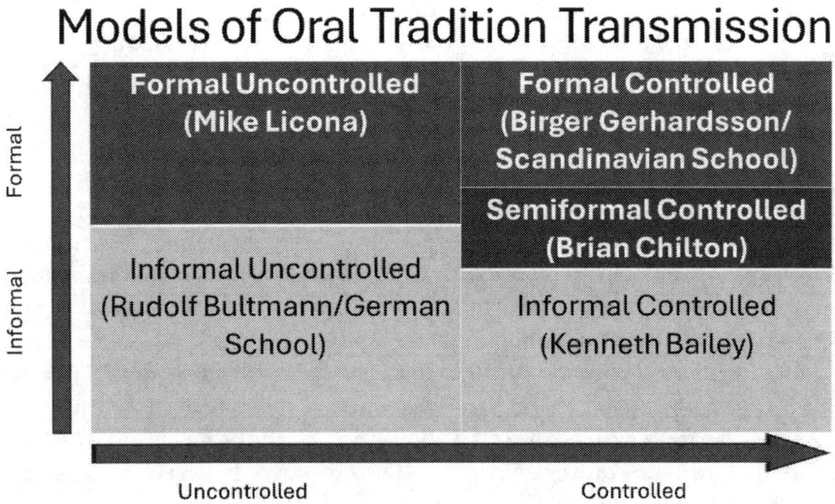

Second, what does this research say about the dating of the material in the Gospels? In full disclosure, this researcher believes there are good reasons for holding that the Synoptic Gospels were all penned before AD 64. However, many scholars, including those in the conservative evangelistic camp, date the Gospels post AD 70.[1004] Even if that should be the case, the Jesus traditions which are evidenced by their Semitic residue point to pre-Gospel traditions much as the creeds point to pre-Pauline material. Also, ancient Israelite Christians most likely took notes to help aid their memorization of larger bodies of information.[1005] Thus, one holds strong reasons to believe that the early Christians accurately preserved the earliest Jesus traditions because of their commitment to accuracy, their ability to remember volumes of information, and the use of written notes to help them precisely remember the core essentials of Jesus's teachings and deeds. Furthermore, this material

---

1004 Keener, *GMSRC,* 42.

1005 "The use of notebooks and the like seems to have been more usual in Palestine than in Babylon; opposition to the act of writing seems to have been weaker in the Palestinian colleges than in the Babylonian. Influence from the Hellenistic schools of rhetoric and philosophy was presumably stronger in *Eres Jisrael* than in Mesopotamia, and it is known that pupils in Hellenistic schools made good use of their skill in writing." Gerhardsson, *Memory and Manuscript,* 161–162. See also Shmuel Safrai, "Education and the Study of the Torah," in *The Jewish People in the First Century: Historical Geography, Political History, Social, Cultural, and Religious Life and Institutions,* S. Safrai, M. Stern, et. al., eds (Philadelphia, PA; Fortress, 1974), 966.

predates the material in the Gospels which makes the content much older than the finalized written product. The evidence of Semitic residue is one added clue to reveal the antiquity of the Jesus traditions.

Finally, how does this research impact how our views of biblical inerrancy? Some may find any kind of flexibility and fluidity in the preservation of materials to be challenging when it comes to biblical inerrancy. However, this need not be the case. Bailey observed that Middle Eastern cultures dramatically tell the stories they deem important..[1006] Scientists have noted that drawing in emotions and physical motions adds to the individual's ability to memorize material; the research of Helga Noice, professor emeritus of psychology, at the University of Illinois has shown that finding a "throughline" helps actors remember volumes of information for a play or script for a movie even years after first performing them..[1007]

Furthermore, many of the traits involved in this research—including reflecting on the meaning of what is being memorized, repetition, mnemonic devices, spatial thinking, and relaxation—are scientifically proven ways to ensure that information is retained..[1008] The crossover between the science of memory and the tactics employed by early Christian communities is uncanny. The data surrounding the memorization practices of ancient Jewish Christians and the modern science of memory adds to the credibility that the stories about Jesus and his teachings are indeed credible.

If we consider these testimonies to stem from early Jesus traditions as has been suggested in this work, then these testimonies represent the eyewitness testimonies of those who encountered and heard from the historical Jesus. Therefore, harmonization efforts are completely within reason and need not be viewed as stretching the text's meaning to elucidate a meaning beyond its intention—that is, unless those efforts force the testimony into a box that it was never meant to fit.

It seems, at least to this author, that many attempts to remove the more fanciful miraculous notions of Scripture stem from an inherent doubt of the interpreter. Is anything truly impossible for a God Who spoke the material universe into existence from immaterial light and sound? I would think not.

[1006] Bailey, "Informal Controlled Oral Tradition and the Synoptic Gospels," *Themelios* 20, 2: 6.

[1007] Annie Murphy Paul, "Learning to Remember: The Most Effective Memorization Techniques Draw on Physical and Emotional Engagement," *Time: Memory—How It Works & Science-Backed Ways to Improve It,* Special Edition, February 2022, 8–9.

[1008] Mandy Oaklander, "Remember This…Five Easy Tips to Improve Your Memory," *Time: Memory—How It Works & Science-Backed Ways to Improve It,* Special Edition, February 2022, 70.

These matters seem to come down to the strength of one's belief in God's ability to work in creation. Nevertheless, for the purposes of this study, one's confidence in biblical infallibility and inerrancy is strengthened by the merger of historical practices and scientific understanding of memory. But ultimately, biblical infallibility and inerrancy may come down to a person's theological mooring and faith in the Holy Spirit's ability to safeguard the revelation of God, regardless of which model is accepted.

Areas of Further Research

This research has unsurfaced additional areas that deserve further exploration. First, it would be interesting to gauge whether the remainder of the parables in Matthew score any higher than those in this research. Also, it would be fascinating to see if the parables in the other Synoptic Gospels score any higher or lower than those found in the Gospel of Matthew. These are undertakings that I hope to offer in future publications.

The second area of research is much in line with the first. How would the remainder of the Sermon on the Mount score in both the Gospel of Matthew and the Gospel of Luke? Perhaps more could be learned about these traditions when examining them in both Gospel texts. It would also be fascinating to examine the traditions found exclusively in Q as compared to the other independent sources—that is, M (information found exclusively in Matthew), Mark, L (information found exclusively in Luke), and John.

A third area of research needed is with the oral traditions found in the other Gospels. I would like to eventually research every Gospel, especially the Gospel of John, in their entirety to see whether there are further connections with the informal controlled model and if there are crossover areas that match the formal controlled model, thus indicating what I call the semiformal controlled method.

Finally, a pressing area of research that needs to be undertaken is one that I might place on a higher level than the others, and that concerns the resurrection of Jesus. Do the resurrection narratives find a home within the early oral traditions that we have discussed? From the Son of Man sayings, one would think that they would. Nonetheless, the resurrection Jesus traditions are of special interest. It is estimated that they would likely score very high on the tests that we established. But that remains to be seen.

Final Thoughts

I am more convinced than ever before that the Gospel of Matthew contains early Jesus traditions that predate the finalized written Gospel. Even if the Gospel of Matthew was written in AD 70 or even 80, the span of time is only 40–50 years from the time of Jesus. Given the memorization and transmission practices of the time, the early Jesus material can be dated at least as early as the creeds in the Pauline Epistles. Given the proclivity of ancient cultures to memorize and maintain large volumes of information, then it is no stretch to grant their ability to remember the messages and life of Jesus over 40 years, especially with the preservation occurring on a community scale and the high probability that early disciples employed the use of notebooks to help them remember. Much can be obtained from the transmission practices of Middle Eastern cultures. With a fairly high overall rating, it can be deduced that it is highly probable that the texts listed in green indeed contain Semitic residue pointing to early Jesus traditions. For those parables that did not score as high, one can credit that to the flexibility given in parabolic stories. Believers have every reason to have greater confidence that the sayings of Jesus preserved in the Gospels do indeed represent the authentic *ipsissima vox* of the historical Jesus.

Bibliography

Albright, William Foxwell, and C. S. Mann. *Matthew.* Anchor Bible. Garden City, NY: Doubleday, 1971.

Allen, David L. *Hebrews.* New American Commentary. Volume 35. Nashville, TN: B&H, 2010.

Augustine of Hippo. *City of God.* In *St. Augustine's City of God and Christian Doctrine*, A Select Library of the Nicene and Post-Nicene Fathers of the Christian Church. First Series. Volume Two. Edited by Philip Schaff. Translated by Marcus Dods. Buffalo, NY: Christian Literature Company, 1887.

Bailey, Kenneth E. "Informal Controlled Oral Tradition and the Synoptic Gospels." *Themelios* 20, 2 (1995): 4–11.

Bailey, Kenneth E. *Jesus Through Middle Eastern Eyes: Cultural Studies in the Gospels.* Downers Grove, IL: IVP Academic, 2008.

Barnett, Paul. *The Birth of Christianity: The First Twenty Years.* Grand Rapids, MI: Eerdmans, 2005.

Barry, John D., ed., et. al. *The Lexham Bible Dictionary.* Bellingham, WA: Lexham Press, 2016. Logos Bible Software.

Bauckham, Richard. *Jesus and the Eyewitnesses: The Gospels as Eyewitness Testimony.* Second Edition. Grand Rapids, MI: Eerdmans, 2017.

Bauckham, Richard. *Jesus and the God of Israel: God Crucified and Other Studies on the New Testament's Christology of Divine Identity.* Grand Rapids, MI: Eerdmans, 2009.

Bauckham, Richard. *The Christian World Around the New Testament.* Grand Rapids, MI: Baker Academic, 2017.

Betz, Otto. *What Do We Know About Jesus?* Philadelphia, PA; London, UK: Westminster, SCM, 1968.

Bird, Michael F. *The Gospel of the Lord: How the Early Church Wrote the Story of Jesus.* Grand Rapids, MI; Cambridge, UK: Eerdmans, 2014.

Black, Matthew. *An Aramaic Approach to the Gospels and Acts.* Third Edition. Eugene, OR: Wipf & Stock, 1967.

Blomberg, Craig L. *The Historical Reliability of the Gospels.* Second Edition. Nottingham, UK; Downers Grove, IL: Apollos; IVP Academic, 2007.

Blomberg, Craig L. *The Historical Reliability of the New Testament.* Nashville, TN: B&H Academic, 2016.

Blomberg, Craig. *Matthew.* The New American Commentary. Volume 22. Nashville: Broadman & Holman Publishers, 1992.

Bock, Darrell L., and Benjamin I. Simpson. *Jesus According to Scripture: Restoring the Portrait from the Gospels.* Second Edition. Grand Rapids, MI: Baker Academic, 2017.

Bockmuehl, Marcus, James Carleton Paget, eds. *Redemption and Resistance: The Messianic Hopes of Jews and Christians in Antiquity.* London, UK: T&T Clark, 2007.

Boring, M. Eugene. *Sayings of the Risen Jesus: Christian Prophecy in the Synoptic Tradition.* Society for New Testament Studies Monograph 46. Cambridge, UK: Cambridge University Press, 1982.

Brand, Chad, et al., eds. *Holman Illustrated Bible Dictionary.* Nashville, TN: Holman Bible Publishers, 2003.

Brown, Raymond E., Karl P. Donfried, and John Reumann, eds. *Peter in the New Testament.* New York, NY: Paramus, 1973.

Bruce, F. F. "The Book of Zechariah and the Passion Narratives." *Bulletin of the John Rylands Library* 43 (1961): 336–353.

Bultmann, Rudolf. *History of the Synoptic Tradition.* Translated by J. Marsh. Oxford, UK: Blackwell, 1963.

Bultmann, Rudolf. *Jesus and the Word.* New York, NY: Scribners, 1958.

Burney, C. F. *The Aramaic Origin of the Fourth Gospel.* Oxford, UK: Clarendon, 1922.

Burney, C. F. *The Poetry of Our Lord.* Oxford, UK: Clarendon, 1925.

Burridge, Richard. *What Are the Gospels? A Comparison with Greco-Roman Biography.* Grand Rapids, MI: Eerdmans, 2004.

Carson, D. A., et. al., eds. *New Bible Commentary: 21st Century Edition.* Fourth Edition. Leicester, England; Downers Grove, IL: Inter-Varsity Press, 1994.

Casey, Maurice. *Aramaic Sources of Mark's Gospel.* Cambridge, UK: Cambridge University Press, 1998.

Casey, Maurice. *Jesus of Nazareth: An Independent Historian's Account of His Life and Teaching.* London, UK: T&T Clark, 2010.

Casey, Maurice. *The Solution to the 'Son of Man' Problem.* New York, NY: T&T Clark International, 2009.

Charles, Robert Henry, ed and trans. *Pseudepigrapha of the Old Testament.* Volume 2. Oxford: Clarendon Press, 1913.

Chilton, Bruce. *Rabbi Jesus: The Jewish Life and Teachings that Inspired Christianity.* New York, NY: Doubleday, 2000.

Collins, John J. *The Apocalyptic Imagination: An Introduction to Jewish Apocalyptic Literature.* Third Edition. Grand Rapids, MI: Eerdmans, 2016.

Cullmann, Oscar. *The Christology of the New Testament.* Waco, TX: Baylor University Press, 1957, 2018.

Cullmann, Oscar. *The Earliest Christian Confessions.* Edited by Gary Habermas and Benjamin Charles Shaw. Translated by J. K. S. Reid. Eugene, OR: Wipf & Stock, 1949.

Cullmann, Oscar. *The State in the New Testament.* New York, NY: Charles Scribner's Sons, 1956.

Culpepper, R. Alan. *The Johannine School: An Evaluation of the Johannine-School Hypothesis Based on an Investigation of the Nature of Ancient Schools.* Society of Biblical Literature Dissertation Series 26. Missoula, MT: Scholars Press, 1975.

Davies, W. D., and Dale C. Allison. *A Critical and Exegetical Commentary on The Gospel According to Saint Matthew.* Edinburgh, UK: T&T Clark, 2001. Logos Bible Software.

Davies, W. D., and Dale C. Allison. *Matthew.* International Critical Commentary Series. Volume 2. Edinburgh, UK: T&T Clark, 1991. Logos Bible Software.

Davies, W. D. *Paul and Rabbinic Judaism: Some Rabbinic Elements in Pauline Theology.* Fourth Edition. Philadelphia, PA: Fortress, 1980.

Dodd, C. H. "The Fall of Jerusalem and the 'Abomination of Desolation.'" *Journal of Roman Studies,* 37 (1947): 47–54.

Dunn, James D. G. *Jesus Remembered.* Christianity in the Making. Volume One. Grand Rapids, MI: Eerdmans, 2003.

Dunn, James D. G. *The Oral Gospel Tradition.* Grand Rapids, MI; Cambridge, UK: Eerdmans, 2013.

Ehrman, Bart D. *Did Jesus Exist? The Historical Argument for Jesus of Nazareth.* New York, NY: HarperOne, 2012.

Elliott, Neal, and Mark Reasoner. *Documents and Images for the Study of Paul.* Minneapolis, MN: Fortress, 2011.

Evans, Craig A., Stanley E. Porter, eds. "Aramaic Language," *Dictionary of New Testament Background.* Downers Grove, IL: IVP, 2000.

Flusser, David. *Judaism and the Origins of Christianity.* Edited by Brad Young. Jerusalem, IL: Hebrew University Press, 1988.

France, R. T. *Matthew.* Tyndale New Testament Commentaries. Grand Rapids, MI; Leicester, UK: Eerdmans; IVP, 1985.

France, R. T., and David Wenham, eds. *Gospel Perspectives: Studies of History and Tradition in the Four Gospels.* Volume One. Eugene, OR: Wipf & Stock, 1981.

Freedman, David Noel, Allen C. Myers, and Astrid B. Beck, eds. *Eerdmans Dictionary of the Bible.* Grand Rapids, MI: W.B. Eerdmans, 2000.

Fruchtenbaum, Arnold G. *Yeshua: The Life of Messiah from a Messianic Jewish Perspective.* Volume 2. San Antonio, TX: Ariel, 2018.

Fruchtenbaum, Arnold G. *Yeshua: The Life of Messiah from a Messianic Jewish Perspective.* Volume 3. San Antonio, TX: Ariel, 2018.

Gabelein, Frank E., ed. *The Expositor's Bible Commentary: Matthew, Mark, Luke.* Volume 8. Grand Rapids, MI: Zondervan Publishing House, 1984.

Gerhardsson, Birger. *Memory and Manuscript: Oral Tradition and Written Transmission in Rabbinic Judaism and Early Christianity.* Grand Rapids, MI: Eerdmans, 1998.

Goldingay, John E. *Daniel.* Word Biblical Commentary. Volume 30. Edited by Bruce M. Metzger, David A. Hubbard, and Glenn W. Barker. Dallas, TX: Word, 1989.

Green, Gene L. *The Letters to the Thessalonians.* The Pillar New Testament Commentary. Grand Rapids, MI; Leicester, England: Eerdmans; Apollos, 2002.

Green, Joel B., Scot McKnight, and I. Howard Marshall, eds. *Dictionary of Jesus and the Gospels.* Downers Grove, IL: IVP, 1992.

Grillmeier, Aloys Grillmeier. *Christ in Christian Tradition,* Volume 1: From the Apostolic Age to Chalcedon (451). Translated by John Bowden. Atlanta, GA: John Knox, 1964).

Gundry, Robert H. *Matthew: A Commentary on His Literary and Theological Art.* Grand Rapids, MI: Eerdmans, 1982.

Habermas, Gary R. *The Historical Jesus: Ancient Evidences for the Life of Christ.* Joplin, MO: College Press, 1996.

Hagner, Donald A. *Matthew 1–13*. Word Biblical Commentary. Volume 33A. Dallas: Word, Incorporated, 1993.

Hansen, G. Walter. *The Letter to the Philippians.* Pillar New Testament Commentary. Grand Rapids, MI; Cambridge, UK: Eerdmans, 2009.

Hanson, K. C. *Jesus and the Message of the New Testament.* Fortress Classics in Biblical Studies. Minneapolis, MN: Fortress Press, 2002.

Harvey, A. E. *Jesus and the Constraints of History.* Philadelphia, PA: Westminster, 1982.

Hawthorne, Gerald F. *Philippians.* Word Biblical Commentary. Dallas, TX: Thomas Nelson, 1983.

Heiser, Michael S. *The Unseen Realm: Recovering the Supernatural Worldview of the Bible.* Bellingham, WA: Lexham, 2015.

Henry, Carl F. H., ed. *Revelation and the Bible: Contemporary Evangelical Thought.* Grand Rapids, MI: Baker, 1958.

Higger, M. *Masekhet Semachot.* Jerusalem, IL: Makor Foundation, 1970.

Hooker, Morna D. "The Solution to the 'Son of Man' Problem." *The Journal of Theological Studies* 60, 2 (2009): 639–643.

Horsley, Richard A., and Jonathan A. Draper, eds. *Whoever Hears You Hears Me: Prophets, Performance and Tradition in Q.* Harrisburg, PA: Trinity Press International, 1999.

Hunter, Archibald M. *The Message of the New Testament.* Philadelphia, PA: Westminster, 1944.

Hurtado, Larry W. *Lord Jesus Christ: Devotion to Jesus in Earliest Christianity.* Grand Rapids, MI: Eerdmans, 2003.

Hurtado, Larry W. *One God, One Lord: Early Christian Devotion and Ancient Jewish Monotheism.* Third Edition. London, UK: Bloomsbury, 2015.

Hyatt, James Philips. "The Dead Sea Discoveries, *Journal of Biblical Literature* 76 (1956): 1–12.

Jeremias, Joachim. *Jesus and the Message of the New Testament.* Minneapolis, MN: Fortress, 2002.

Jeremias, Joachim. *Jesus' Promise to the Nations.* London, UK: SCM, 1958.

Jeremias, Joachim. *New Testament Theology*. Translated by John Bowden. London: SCM, 1971.

Jeremias, Joachim. *The Parables of Jesus*. Second Edition. Upper Saddle River, NJ: Prentice Hall; SCM, 1972.

Jerome. *Commentary on Matthew 6:11*. In E. Klostermann, *Apocrypha II*. Berlin: KIT, 1929.

Johnson, Luke Timothy. *The Real Jesus: The Misguided Quest for the Historical Jesus and the Truth of the Traditional Gospels*. New York, NY: HarperOne, 1996.

Josephus, *The Works of Josephus*. Updated Edition. Translated by William Whiston. Peabody, MA: Hendrickson, 1987.

Keener, Craig S. *Christobiography: Memory, History, and the Reliability of the Gospels*. Grand Rapids, MI: Eerdmans, 2019.

Keener, Craig S. *IVP Bible Background Commentary: New Testament*. Downers Grove, IL: IVP Academic, 1993.

Keener, Craig S. "The Function of Johannine Pneumatology in the Context of Late First-Century Judaism." Ph.D. dissertation. Duke University Graduate School, Durham, NC, 1991.

Keener, Craig S. *The Gospel of Matthew: A Socio-Rhetorical Commentary*. Grand Rapids, MI; Cambridge, U.K.: Eerdmans, 2009.

Keener, Craig S. *The Historical Jesus of the Gospels*. Grand Rapids, MI: Eerdmans, 2009.

Kelber, Werner H. *The Oral and the Written Gospel*. Philadelphia, PA: Fortress, 1983.

Kittel, G. Kittel and G. Friedrich, eds. *Theological Dictionary of the New Testament*. Grand Rapids, MI: Eerdmans, 1964.

Kloppenborg Verbin, John S. *Excavating Q: The History and Setting of the Sayings Gospel*. Minneapolis, MN: Fortress, 2000.

Kohler, W. *Dogmengeschichte*. Volume One. Zurich, CH; Cambridge, UK: Cambridge University Press, 1951.

Kraeling, Carl H. *John the Baptist*. New York, NY: Charles Scribner's Sons, 1951.

Lachs, Samuel Tobias. *A Rabbinic Commentary on the New Testament*. Hoboken, NJ: KTAV, 1987.

Laird, Benjamin P. *Creating the Canon: Composition, Controversy, and the Authority of the New Testament.* Downers Grove, IL: IVP Academic, 2023.

Lewis, Naphtali. *Life in Egypt under Roman Rule.* Oxford, UK: Clarendon, 1983.

Licona, Michael R. *Jesus, Contradicted: Why the Gospels Tell the Same Story Differently.* Grand Rapids, MI: Zondervan Academic, 2024.

Licona, Michael R. *The Resurrection of Jesus: A New Historiographical Approach.* Downers Grove, IL; Nottingham, UK: IVP Academic; Apollos, 2010.

Licona, Michael R. *Why Are There Differences in the Gospels?: What We Can Learn from Ancient Biography.* Oxford, UK: Oxford University Press, 2017.

Lightfoot, Joseph Barber, and J. R. Harmer. *The Apostolic Fathers.* London, UK: Macmillan, 1891.

Lohmeyer, Ernst. *The Lord's Prayer.* London, UK: Collins, 1965.

Longenecker, Richard N. *New Wine into Fresh Wineskins: Contextualizing the Early Christian Confessions.* Peabody, MA: Hendrickson, 1999.

Mangum, Douglas, et. al., eds. *Lexham Theological Wordbook.* Lexham Bible Reference Series. Bellingham, WA: Lexham Press, 2014. Logos Bible Software.

Manson, T. W. *The Church's Ministry.* London, UK: Hodder and Stoughton, 1948.

Manson, T. W. *The Sayings of Jesus.* London, UK: SCM, 1979.

Meier, John P. *A Marginal Jew: Rethinking the Historical Jesus.* Volume Two. Anchor Yale Bible Reference Library. New York, NY: Doubleday, 1994.

McGrew, Lydia. *The Mirror or the Mask: Liberating the Gospels from Literary Devices.* Tampa, FL: DeWard, 2019.

McQuilkin, J. Robertson. *Understanding and Applying the Bible.* Chicago, IL: Moody Press, 1983.

Michaelis, Wilhelm. *Zur Engelchristologie im Urchristentum.* Berlin, DE: HMV, 1942.

Miller, Stephen R. Miller. *Daniel.* New American Commentary. Volume 18. Edited by E. Ray Clendenen. Nashville, TN: B&H, 1994.

Morris, Leon. *The Gospel According to Matthew.* Pillar New Testament Commentary. Grand Rapids, MI; Leicester, UK: Eerdmans; IVP, 1992.

Mowery, Robert L. "Son of God in Roman Imperial Titles and Matthew." *Biblica* 83 (2002): 100–110.

Myers, Allen C., Astrid B. Beck, and David Noel Freedman, eds. *Eerdmans Dictionary of the Bible.* Grand Rapids, MI: Eerdmans, 2000.

Neufield, Vernon H. *The Earliest Christian Confessions.* Leiden, NL: Brill, 1963.

Oaklander, Mandy. "Remember This…Five Easy Tips to Improve Your Memory." *Time: Memory—How It Works & Science-Backed Ways to Improve It.* Special Edition. February 2022.

O'Neill, J. C. *Messiah: Six Lectures on the Ministry of Jesus.* Cambridge, UK: Cochrane, 1980.

Paul, Annie Murphy. "Learning to Remember: The Most Effective Memorization Techniques Draw on Physical and Emotional Engagement." *Time: Memory—How It Works & Science-Backed Ways to Improve It.* Special Edition. February 2022.

Petuchowski, Michael, and Jakob Josef Brocke. *The Lord's Prayer and Jewish Liturgy.* London, UK: Burns and Oates, 1978.

Philo of Alexandria. In *Works of Philo.* Translated by Charles Duke Yonge. Peabody, MA: Hendrickson, 1993.

Polano, H., trans, *The Talmud.* San Diego, CA: Book Tree, 1876, 2003.

Polhill, John B. *Acts.* The New American Commentary. Volume 26. Nashville: Broadman & Holman Publishers, 1992.

Pseudo-Clementine Literature. In *Fathers of the Third and Fourth Centuries: The Twelve Patriarchs, Excerpts and Epistles, the Clementina, Apocrypha, Decretals, Memoirs of Edessa and Syriac Documents, Remains of the First Ages.* The Ante-Nicene Fathers. Volume Eight. Edited by Alexander Roberts, James Donaldson, and A. Cleveland Coxe. Translated by M. B. Riddle. Buffalo, NY: Christian Literature Company, 1886.

Quarles, Charles. "Sermon on the Mount." In *Holman Christian Standard Bible: Harmony of the Gospels.* Nashville, TN: Holman Bible Publishers, 2007.

Safrai, Shmuel, M. Stern, et. al., eds. *The Jewish People in the First Century: Historical Geography, Political History, Social, Cultural, and Religious Life and Institutions.* Philadelphia, PA; Fortress, 1974.

Sanders, E. P. *The Historical Figure of Jesus.* New York, NY: Penguin, 1993.

Sandy, D. Brent. *Plowshares & Pruning Hooks: Rethinking the Language of Biblical Prophecy and Apocalyptic.* Downers Grove, IL: IVP, 2002.

Schlesinger, Robert. "Greatest Speech Ever?" *USNews.com* (Sept. 20, 2013), https://www.usnews.com/opinion/blogs/robert-schlesinger/2013/09/20/greatest-speech-ever-jesus-christ-pericles-abraham-lincoln-or-bluto.

Shirock, Robert. "Whose Exorcists Are They? The References of οι υιοί ὑμων at Matthew 12.27/Luke 11:19." *Journal for the Study of the New Testament* 46 (1992): 14–51.

Smith, Gary. *Isaiah 40-66.* New American Commentary. Volume 15B. Nashville, TN: Broadman & Holman Publishers, 2009.

Stein, Robert H. *The Method and Message of Jesus' Teachings.* Revised Edition. Louisville, KY: Westminster John Knox, 1994.

Stone, Rabbi Abraham. "The World-to-Come." *The Jewish Press, Expounding the Torah* (May 2, 1986).

Stevenson, James, ed., *A New Eusebius.* London, UK: SPCK, 1957.

Stewart, Robert B., and Gary R. Habermas, eds. *Memories of Jesus: A Critical Appraisal of James D. G. Dunn's Jesus Remembered.* Nashville, TN: B&H Academic, 2010.

Taylor, Vincent. *The Formation of the Gospel Tradition.* Second Edition. London, UK: Macmillan & Company, 1935.

Twelftree, Graham H. *Jesus the Exorcist: A Contribution to the Study of the Historical Jesus.* Eugene, OR: Wipf & Stock, 2011.

Walker, William O. "The Lord's Prayer in Matthew and John." *New Testament Studies* 28 (1982): 237–256.

Walton, John H., and Craig S. Keener. *NIV Cultural Backgrounds Study Bible.* Grand Rapids, IL: Zondervan, 2016.

Wansbrough, Henry, ed. *Jesus and the Oral Gospel Tradition,* Journal for the Study of the New Testament Supplement Series 64. Sheffield, UK: Sheffield Academic, 1991.

Wenham, D. "The Structure of Matthew XIII." *NTS* 25 (1979): 517–518.

Wilcox, Max. *The Semitisms of Acts.* Oxford, UK: Oxford University Press, 1965.

Wilson, John Francis. *Caesarea Philippi: Banias, the Lost City of Pan.* New York, NY: I. B. Tauris, 2004.

Witherington, III, Ben. *The Christology of Jesus.* Minneapolis, MN: Fortress, 1990.

Wrede, William. *The Messianic Secret.* Translated by J. C. G. Greig. Cambridge, UK: James Clarke & Company, 1971.

Wright, N. T. *Jesus and the Victory of God.* Christian Origins and the Question of God. Volume 1. Minneapolis, MN: Fortress, 1996.

Wright, N. T. *The New Testament and the People of God.* Minneapolis, MN: Fortress, 1992.

Wright, N. T. *The Resurrection of the Son of God.* Christian Origins and the Question of God. Volume 3. Minneapolis, MN: Fortress, 2003.

Young, Brad H. *Jesus the Jewish Theologian.* Peabody, MA: Hendrickson, 1995.

Young, Brad H. *The Parables: Jewish Tradition and Christian Interpretation.* Grand Rapids, MI: Baker Academic, 1998.